THAT THEY MAY LIVE

Theological Reflections On The Quality of Life

ANNUAL PUBLICATION
OF
THE COLLEGE THEOLOGY SOCIETY

GEORGE DEVINE

alba house
A DIVISION OF THE SOCIETY OF ST. PAUL
STATEN ISLAND, NEW YORK 10314

142831

WITH ECCLESIASTICAL PERMISSION

Library of Congress Cataloging in Publication Data

College Theology Society.
    That they may live.

    Proceedings of the national convention of the
College Theology Society, held in St. Paul, Minn.,
Apr. 12-14, 1971.
    Includes bibliographical references.
    1. Theology—Addresses, essays, lectures.
I. Devine, George, 1941-   ed.   II.   Title.
BR50.C588   201'.1   72-3488
ISBN   0-8189-0243-4

ACKNOWLEDGMENTS

The editor of this volume wishes to thank all of those who have contributed to the successful publication of the College Theology Society's proceedings, based on its last annual Convention at St. Paul, Minnesota, on April 12-14, 1971. In particular, thanks to our President, Prof. James Wieland; our Vice-president, Sister Francis Regis Carton, S.S.N.D.; our Secretary, Sister M. Gertrude Anne Otis, C.S.C.; and our Treasurer, Brother Thomas F. Ryan, F.S.C. Also instrumental in the success of this volume was Brother C. Stephen Sullivan, F.S.C., who retired as Treasurer at the St. Paul Convention.

Thanks should also go to those who assisted the editor during and right after the presentation of the papers at St. Paul, particularly Sister Vera Chester, C.S.J.; Miss Liz Toth and Miss Teddi Tri. And the editor's burden has been lightened and his task made more enjoyable by numerous individuals who, in variegated ways, aided in myriad aspects of the project, including Sister Katherine T. Hargrove, R.S.C.J.; Mr. William J. Toohey, Mr. Peter R. Flynn, Mrs. Anthony Gran, Prof. Gerald Pire, Rev. James Doyle, C.S.C., and Rev. Michael Mullen, C.M. Valuable reactions to the book, at various stages of its formation, were received from the CTS Board of Directors.

Also, production of this book was facilitated by and through the firm of H. Reader and Co., New York City, and by the staff in the Department of Religious Studies at Seton Hall University, especially Mrs. Margaret Chiang, Miss Laura Waage, Mr. Michael E. Gubernat, and Mr. Joseph Gizinski. The physical appearance of the book is due to the fine work of Alba House, the publishing division of the Society of St. Paul.

Finally, the editor wishes to thank those who have been closest to him throughout this project: his wife Joanne and son George.

GEORGE DEVINE

CONTENTS

V RELIGIOUS STUDIES: TOWARD NEW QUALITY AND VITALITY

I

THE QUALITY OF LIFE

1 The Quality of Life: What Does It Mean?

DANIEL CALLAHAN

The meaning of "the quality of life" is elusive. It is in good company. Some of the most fundamental human concepts are no less elusive: love, peace, justice, honor, dignity, truth. We cannot get along without them; and yet we cannot readily define them either. Perhaps this is just as well. Yet an initial question must be faced. Is the concept of "the quality of life" useful and illuminating? That it is used all the time these days cannot be doubted. Many people, apparently, find it meaningful. Yet as Irving Howe has recently suggested, the notion of a "quality of life" may have "many trivial meanings, and no serious ones." That possibility always needs to be considered when phrases become too popular and on too many lips. The great attraction of vague ideas, to the media and to the public, is that they can be stuffed with any old content at all; they commit one to nothing. In this respect, suspicion is immediately aroused when one turns, in due scholarly fashion, to the dictionary for the definition of "quality." As usual, that is no help at all, for "quality" is therein defined as "a peculiar and essential character," or as "an inherent feature," or as "a degree of excellence," or a "social status," among other possible meanings. I didn't even bother looking up the word "life"; "quality" provides us with quite enough problems already.

My scholarly research thus completed, let me dip into the concept in a more reflective way, not attempting any precise definition but, instead, sampling it in much the way one might taste an unknown wine, which includes a bit of wary sniffing. I want to make two main points. The first, to continue my wine-tasting image, is that the concept of "the quality of life" is satis-

factory if offered as a very modest wine. It has its occasional
uses and will not, if sipped with prudence, make us ill. My second
point, however, is that "the quality of life" will prove a disaster
if offered as the finest product of the most renowned vineyard
in the best of all years, fit for those occasions when kings entertain
emperors, and when theologians, philosophers and ethicists want
an over-arching conceptual wine which will somehow bring an
illuminating glow to the essence of human life. On the contrary,
the very modest characteristics of the "quality of life" make it
ill-suited to banquets or high enlightenment.

Historically, other generations have been concerned with the
quality of life, even if they did not use the phrase. The biblical
observation that "man does not live by bread alone" is an expression of this concern; there ought to be more to human life than
sheer physical survival. Until recently, however, most human beings
could hope for little more than that. Only a tiny minority had the
chance to be educated, to build a culture, to develop their minds
and spirit. A great event of the twentieth century has been the
tremendous growth of this minority. In the West, it is already
a majority. To be sure, even in the West there are major pockets
of poverty, and poverty is still endemic in most of Asia, Africa
and Latin America. Millions of people are still forced to live
for bread alone. Even so, mankind as a whole now knows that
nature red of tooth and claw can be subdued. Life need no longer
be governed wholly by fate or inexorable powers beyond human
control. Human irrationality and mismanagement now appear
as far greater enemies than a once-hostile nature. We know that
many elements of a good life for human beings can be created.
The difficulty now is that of doing so, and it is human beings themselves who pose the greatest obstacle.

The present concentration upon the "quality of life" has
at least two major sources. One is the technological crisis. If
science and technology have provided the swords for the conquest
of nature, they have also shown that the swords are two-edged:
they can cut those who wield them as readily as they can cut
sickness, starvation and death. The control of nuclear energy has
brought with it nuclear weapons. The development of pesticides

has brought agricultural triumphs and ecological disasters. The creation of miracle drugs has lowered the death rate dramatically, and just as dramatically increased the population growth rate. Mankind has been prepared and eager to take advantage of technological progress. It has been totally unprepared to cope with the harmful side-effects of that same progress. Possibly this shows that nature is not so easily conquered after all. Or perhaps, more pointedly, it shows that man must learn to live with nature rather than attempt to conquer it. Either we teach ourselves to respect our environment or that environment will teach us—and we may not like its harsh pedagogical methods.

Another source of the concern with quality is a crisis of meaning and value, which finds its most acute expression in the alienation of the young. The children of affluence, they have found that quantity does not insure quality. They have all the material goods they need, but they do not have happiness. The technology their parents worked so hard to create appears to them more a source of disaster than of progress. Their parents' orientation to the future, expressed in an ethic of hard work, repression, saving and storing, seems to bring only futility. The promised salvation of an ascetic life style never appears; pleasure, play and pot seem more attractive. That so many adults are drawn to the youth culture, even as they attack it, suggests that the young have touched a sensitive nerve. If the young are not happy with the goals set forth for them by their parents, or the culture their parents have built, the latter harbor a sneaking suspicion that their children may be right. What is the point of life? How ought we to live? Those are the critical questions.

Most of the current discussion of the quality of life is an expression of this dual crisis: in the use of technology and in meaning and value. And they cannot readily be separated. The destruction of the environment, air and water pollution, and an excessive population growth can all be traced to technological causes. If it is the external impact which catches the eye—in massive junkyards and garbage heaps, in smog, in filthy rivers, in dying forests, in soaring population statistics—the internal impact is no less great, expressed in a drug culture, in feelings of emptiness and alienation, in a sense of hopelessness amidst plenty, in random violence and destruction.

It is easier to read the negative signs than to discern the positive. It is easier to say that we should not destroy our environment, misuse our technology, or overpopulate the earth, than it is to set forth what we should be doing. The worst mistake would be to repeat the past. In this case, that would be to think that a number of discrete counter-offensive steps could totally solve the problem— to assume that if we can only clean up the rivers, reduce the birthrate, or find different kinds of pesticides we will have insured a high quality of life. The equivalent logic of an earlier generation was to think that if we could only build better factories, improve our fertilizers, increase our transportation capacities, create superior utilities and utensils, the good life would then be insured. All of those things were done. We have a chicken in every pot and two cars in every garage. And where is the good life?

It is possible to distinguish three fallacies in most approaches to an understanding of "the quality of life."

1) *The technology fallacy.* This fallacy can take two forms: a) that technological progress insures a higher quality of life, and b) that the hazardous by-products of technological advance can be technologically overcome. That technological progress does not always insure a higher quality of life can be demonstrated in a visit to an urban slum, an auto graveyard or Lake Erie. That technology cannot solve all of the problems which technology creates may be a more debatable proposition; in most cases, it hasn't had a full opportunity to do so. Yet there is no special reason for optimism. Many of the changes wrought by technology affect more than the materialities of people's lives. They also affect their inner lives, their personal relationships, and the social structures of which they are a part. The problems raised in these areas are often not amenable to technological solutions. More often, nothing less than a change in values, a shift in life styles and new social arrangements will suffice. Technology, widely used, may be of some assistance in softening the blow of these transitions; rarely can it offer panaceas. That a machine has created a problem does not mean that another machine can solve it.

2) *The organization fallacy.* This fallacy takes the form of assuming there are no problems of modern life which cannot be solved by better organizational or management techniques. This is the fallacy of most totalitarian governments, which operate on the premise that right-thinking elites who act with total efficiency in totally rational ways can solve all economic, political, social and human problems. More mildly, it is the fallacy of over-zealous planners, even of a democratic sort, who see salvation in optimal forms of rational organization and planning. That it is a fallacy might be disputed by someone who argued that we have *not yet* found the perfect form of organization. But the burden of proof would be on him to show that we will.

3) *The freedom fallacy.* If it is contended that unfettered individual freedom will insure the highest quality of life then that would seem fallacious; at least there is no evidence to support such a sweeping assertion. Indeed, some of our present problems stem from too much freedom, e.g., the misuse of the environment, which has been left open to *laissez-faire* exploitation. Perfect freedom would be possible only in a world where there was no conflict between the desires of one person and those of another; such a world has yet to be seen. The old dilemma of individual vs. common good remains a dilemma, as fresh and pressing as ever. Freud's argument in *Civilization and Its Discontents,* that civilized life by its very nature requires some degree of individual repression, has yet to be confounded.

We are left with a paradox. Technology, organization and individual freedom do not guarantee a satisfactory quality of life. Yet without them we cannot have a high quality of life either. How might we resolve the paradox? It might be well at the outset to let the very vagueness of the phrase "the quality of life" tell us something. What it seems to be saying, in its variety of possible definitions, is that it should have no fixed meaning; that *it cannot have a fixed meaning.* If a commitment to individual liberty is taken seriously, then it is to be expected that different people will like, want and desire diverse satisfactions from life. Differences in genetic endowment, cultural background, personal histories and environmental setting all lead to differences in what people expect. At the minimum, we know human beings need some degree of psychological and physical security. They can't live with war or in slums and they can't get along without food, clothing and shelter. Beyond that we can say they need the possibility of self-realization and, with Freud, that they must be able to work and to love.

Instead of being specific about what "the quality of life" means, it might be more helpful to see it as a concept which encompasses a wide range of possibilities, with upper and lower limits. At the lower limits, it can be said that for life to have *any* "quality," it must move beyond the subsistence level. Thus any concept will have to take account of man's physical needs; that is the starting point. Slums, pollution, overpopulation and depersonalized bureaucracies can mean (and often do) that even the lower limits are not achieved; they can threaten survival, whether physically or psychologically. People will be forced to settle for less than they should have to. Passive, conditioned adults may put up with mediocrity—but the young are making clear that they will not. Yet when one speaks of the upper limits, human variation becomes important. What one person requires to achieve his personal potential may not be what another requires. Violinists need little equipment, peace and quiet for their practice, and large crowds for their audience if they are to make a career of their musical talent. Machinists need much equipment, will have to learn how to put up with noise and cannot, because of the danger, tolerate a crowd around their machine. Farmers need space; writers do not. Some people need little money for happiness; others seem to need very much. For some, the joy of Manhattan is the crowds, which make possible the kind of art, music and culture, the diversity of friends, not to be found in the sparsely populated regions of western Nebraska. For others, Manhattan is nothing but a threatening mob scene; the charm of a quick access to a forest far exceeds that of quick access to the Metropolitan Opera. There is no resolution to arguments of this kind. People differ, and there is no reason to want them all alike. That they are different, though, suggests a fundamental point about the quality of life. There must be room for diversity, for people to work out their own definitions of the quality of life—their life. The quality of life is threatened, at the upper limits, when some single-minded definition is imposed upon all, whether the imposition stems from environmental, political or cultural sources. It is threatened, at the lower limits, when the demand for survival overshadows all else. At the same time, it must be said that a culture which provides no definitions of quality—where every individual is forced to invent his own values —is probably a harmful culture also.

The most delicate point in any analysis of the quality of life comes when some hard choices must be made among available options. Pollution is a desperate problem, yet to introduce the tactics of a police state to keep the rivers clean and the forests green could be self-defeating; one misery would be exchanged for another. Excessive procreation endangers everyone, but an invasion of the bedroom or harsh sanctions against large families, which could harm the existing children, would be too high a price to pay. Some values are not open to trade-offs, and some kinds of freedom are undoubtedly among them. Some forms of human life would not be worth living, however clean the environment, however optimal the population size, however full the larder. This is only to say, and to stress, that many possibly quite effective cures could be worse than the diseases. Not all things can be done in the name of improving "the quality of life." That last remark brings me to my second major point. Whatever the minor and suggestive uses of the "quality of life" as one way of looking at the problem of life, it is miscast if thought of as potentially able to serve some transcendental role. Its inherent vagueness, I would argue, rules out that possibility from the outset; and its social vagueness—the variety of ways it is used in ordinary uplift dis-course—merely confirms the judgment. The worst possibility would be to see it set up as a new standard of ethical measurement, as a supreme test or norm for making fundamental moral judg-ments. Unfortunately, that is already beginning to happen in some places. In the remainder of this chapter I want to analyze one such instance, as a case in point of what can happen if the "quality of life" is allowed to carry too much weight.

My modal text is an unsigned editorial which appeared recently in *California Medicine* (Sept. 1970), the official journal of the California Medical Association. The title of the editorial is "A New Ethics for Medicine and Society." It opens with the following passage:

> The traditional Western ethic has always placed great emphasis on the intrinsic worth and equal value of every human life regardless of its stage or condition. This ethic has had the blessing of the Judeo-Christian heritage and has been the basis for most of our laws and much of our social policy. The reverence for each and every human life has also been a keystone of Western medicine and is the ethic which has caused physicians to try to preserve, protect, repair, prolong and enhance every human life which comes under their surveillance. This traditional ethic is still clearly dominant, but there is much to suggest that it is being eroded at its core and may eventually even be abandoned (p. 67).

The possibility that this ethic may be "eroded" and "abandoned," however, does not appall the author of the editorial. He goes on to say that "there are certain new facts and social realities which are becoming recognized, are widely discussed in Western society and seem certain to undermine and transform this traditional ethic" (ibid.). He then points to such realities and, most importantly, what he describes as "a quite new emphasis on something which is beginning to be called the quality of life, a something which becomes possible for the first time in human history because of scientific and technologic development" (ibid.). The upshot of this new emphasis is that:

> It will become necessary and acceptable to place relative rather than absolute values on such things as human lives, the use of scarce resources and the various elements which are to make up the quality of life or of living which is to be sought. . . . The criteria upon which these relative values are to be based will depend upon whatever concept of the quality of life or living is developed. This may be expected to reflect

the extent that quality of life is considered to be a function of personal fulfillment; of individual responsibility for the common welfare, the preservation of the environment, the betterment of the species; and of whether or not, or to what extent, these responsibilities are to be exercised on a compulsory or voluntary basis (p. 68).

I want to make three observations about this editorial, one short and two rather longer. The first is that, if such a new ethic is emerging, I, for one, will not approve of it and I would hope that the medical profession—to whom the editorial is directed—will not. The second is that, whether I like this new ethic or not, the editorial writer is probably correct in noting a trend, a new way of thinking about some of the demographic, medical and biological issues. Just why there should be a trend of this kind is not a great mystery. Where the product of medicine was once seen to be a more or less unmixed blessing, with diseases cured, lives extended, infant mortality reduced, we have now come into a period where the blessings of medicine are sometimes rather mixed. It is the success of medicine in reducing death rates and especially infant mortality rates which in great part accounts for the world population problem. By and large, birth rates have not dropped nearly so dramatically as death rates. Where it was once thought a great gain to see the average human life span extended, now we are beginning to live with some of the consequences— a very large number of elderly people, most gratefully and thankfully alive, but many living with little human dignity. Where disease once carried off many people who, because of one defect or another, could not hope to live anything approaching decent lives, we now have ways of curing or ameliorating the diseases; thus we probably have an increasing number of human beings with one or more defects, some genetically hazardous. That there should be suggestions of the need for a new ethic is, then, hardly surprising. Medicine has become very good at preserving life—indeed, almost too good. One is almost forced to ask about the kind and quality of life preserved.

For the physician this may mean, on an increasing number

of occasions, that he will be compelled to ask himself whether to keep striving, to the bitter end, to outwit death, using one miracle drug treatment after another, regardless of the future prospects of the patient for a decent human life. For society, it may mean decisions about how much money to put into finding new and better ways of keeping the elderly alive, or conquering hazardous genetic diseases, or trying to save the lives of those who would succumb from natural causes well before reaching three-score and ten years. It will almost certainly mean for society a decision against bringing into the world an excessive number of children, more than society or the environment can support. In short, one can well understand why the concept of the quality of life has come to the fore. I don't see anything necessarily wrong with the emergence of questions of this kind. The real question is: to what extent should we begin consciously taking into account the quality of life and of lives and, if we do so, who should do so? For it is quite possible that many decisions of who shall live and who shall die will come down to decisions where the quality of life is at least a consideration. Then we must ask how this consideration is to be handled.

My third comment on the editorial bears on these last issues. The thesis of the editorial is that the new ethic—stressing quality of life—is coming to replace the old—which stressed the intrinsic value, dignity and equality of all lives. Thus the editorial establishes a black and white dichotomy: either an ethic based on equal respect for all, or an ethic which discriminates among lives, on a relative scale. Some observations are in order:

First, it is a mistake to think that the traditional Western ethic has nothing to do with the concept of the quality of life. On the contrary, that ethic has been as much concerned with the kind and quality of human life as it has been about the value of life *per se*. On the contrary, it has seen—as its most penetrating and radical contribution—that there is a fundamental connection between the intrinsic worth and equal value of every individual life and the quality of both individual and social life. At the very least, it has said that if each and every life is not accorded full worth and equality, then the quality of life of the whole of society will be seriously endangered. It is also an ethic which, far from failing to recognize differences among lives—that some are weak and some are strong, that some are young and some are old, that some are intelligent and gifted and some are not—has made bold to say that, precisely because of these differences, a community must be brought into being. It is an ethic which has contended that the worth and equal value of every human life *is* intrinsic to those lives. The value of individual lives is not a gift of society, not something to be put on the balancing scales every time there is a new cultural, scientific or medical advance.

A major premise of the editorial is that "new facts and social realities" both can and should be allowed to undermine the traditional ethic. But this presumes that the old ethic was itself little more than the reflections of earlier generations on "facts and social realities." My contention is that it represented the good sense of many generations in seeking to find a foundation for human values which was not continually at the mercy of "new facts and social realities." For the most part, the high value accorded individual life flew directly in the face of facts and social realities; it sought to transcend and to criticize them. Our own times may be unprecedented in the rapidity with which new facts are discovered and social realities shifted. But the phenomenon itself is hardly new. The Jews both before and after the Christian era knew a thing or two about changing social realities—that has been their whole history. And Christians, at first persecuted and then triumphant, and then smashed by the Barbarians, have a word to say about the social realities also.

Second, it seems to me to be at the very least naive to think that the use of a criterion such as the "quality of life" will be of much help in deciding ethical issues, particularly those pertaining to who shall live and who shall die. People vary notoriously on what the quality of life encompasses, and what they personally would consider a decent quality of life. No concept is more subject to shifting tastes, to class, educational and economic differences. Whose notion of the "quality of life" will we count? And if facts and social realities continue to change as rapidly as at present, how will we fix a given point in time as providing the normative

standard of quality? Either we will end up letting one group decide
what counts as quality, or one group will seize for itself the right
to make that decision—most probably the latter. Moreover, one
need only think of some of the richer elements which go into
the current notion of "quality of life" to see some basic difficulties
arising if it is to be used to legitimate the relativizing of human lives.
For it is an important part of most serious notions of quality
that there be justice and political and social equality. It would be
an ironic outcome indeed, and a tragic one, if in the use of quality
as a standard we began depriving people of just those goods they
now seek: the right to be treated with dignity regardless of race,
class or color; the right to decent medical care, independent of their
personal ability to pay for that care; the right to an education and
to equality of opportunity; the right, if you will, not to be victim-
ized and dominated by "facts and social realities."

In the end, we are forced to ask whether human beings would
feel any great sense of the quality of life in a society which
announced to them that their lives were only a relative value and
that, dependent upon how society happened to interpret the quality
of life at any given moment, they would be allowed to live or to die.
I doubt that many of us would feel very secure in such a society;
and a sense of security at the hands of our fellows must surely
count as an ingredient in the quality of life.

Third, to put the previous comments in a positive way: I would
argue that it is central to the concept of the quality of life that
we maintain the traditional emphasis on the intrinsic worth and
equal value of every life. More than that, that we work to extend
that worth and value and make them real, not just hypocritical
slogans—which is what "facts and social realities" usually reduces
them to.

In the first place, I would say that our problem is not whether
we should choose between a new ethic and an old. If a choice
must be made, the old offers every advantage over the new—
for what in the end is "new," this generation's new ethic, or the
next generation's? Instead, the real prod is to find a way to refine
and develop the old ethic in a way that makes it a fine and precise
guide to our new problems. At the very least, this means finding

ways of making decisions which do fully recognize the quality and intrinsic worth of every life. It is fundamentally wrong, for example, for physicians to be forced by a shortage of renal dialysis machines to make choices about who is to live and who is to die. They should not have to make such decisions. A living tradition of the worth of each individual would lead society to provide enough machines and personnel trained to use them that such decisions would not have to be made. I think it wrong, too, that more people do not have family planning services available to them, so that the poor in particular have no real choice about whether to have another child or not. It seems fundamentally wrong to me that so many women are forced in our society to resort to abortion, whether legal or illegal, simply because they are too poor, too harried, too beleaguered, to continue their pregnancies. It seems wrong to me that we have created the kind of family structure where the old are separated off from the young and are, well before the end, sent off to the Happy Twilight Nursing Home—which is more midnight than twilight and rarely happy.

All of these points bear on the quality of life. But they all reveal its limitation as an ultimate or even penultimate criterion for judging how we are to respond to the problems of human life. I am tempted to say that, however occasionally pertinent the concept, any society which fastens on it is either sick or dead; it is probably already too late to do much about improving the quality. And any society where the quality of life begins to serve as a way of discriminating among lives—to the death, no less— is an abomination. Recollect that one of the dictionary definitions of quality was "social status." That was the one, whether he knew it or not, which the author of the editorial was using; given so much room for choice among definitions, we are told more than we want to know when someone manages to choose the worst one.

I began with the dictionary and I will end there. One of the definitions of "quality" there was "an inherent feature." That will do very nicely. For if we start thinking about what is "inherent," a notion rather far removed from what is of relative value, and far removed from the flux of changing facts and social realities, it might be possible for us to transcend the trivialities and downright dangers of that quality which bemuses the creators of this month's version of the "new ethic." We will, I suspect—having chatted about the "quality of life," and having enjoyed its modest bouquet and light body, but having rejected it as a wine fit for kings and philosophers—then move on to the more serious business of working out the inherent features of human life. And while I don't want to put theologians and philosophers out of work, my own intuition is that those inherent features are not really very mysterious or difficult at all. In an age of modern medicine, we may need fewer physicians of the body and soul inventing or blessing a new ethic, and many more midwives—the Socratic kind, who draw out from people what they already know.

Anthropocentricity: New Ways of Theologizing in an Evolutionary Context

Hugh McElwain

One of the most important contemporary issues, perhaps because most critical in our present ecological quandary, is the problem of "anthropocentrism." It seems to be a perspective of man *and* nature whose normal corollaries of domination or dominiondom of man *over* nature lead inevitably to man's judging all of reality self-centeredly and indeed selfishly. The correlative repercussions for environmental balance are obvious.

It is my contention that any such anthropocentrism or man-centered cosmology needs to be studied and rightly understood so that proper attitudes can be fostered for the acceptable and harmonious ordering of *all* the elements in our "eco-system," *including* man.[1] Specifically my hypothesis is built on the broad generalization that Western thought is characterized by a warped anthropocentrism, whether it is based on the origin of man by a direct creation of God (the traditional theological formula) or on the origin of man as an emergent in the evolutionary process, but indeed as its cutting-edge or lead-shoot. Thus whether one is operating out of the context of traditional theology wherein man's origin is unique (i.e., created directly by divine intervention) or out of an evolutionary perspective within which man is unique because he is the end-term and final (best) product of the process, one ends up in either context placing man at the center, the focal point of all reality. I would like to make some general observations

---

1. Cf. Frederick Elder, **Crisis in Eden** (New York: Abingdon, 1970), for the inclusionist-exclusionist discussion, pp. 21-80.

about the whole problem of the relationship between the *origin* of man and the *nature* of man and then to suggest a view of man that might furnish adequate theological basis of man's place *in* nature for good ecological perspective.

RELATIONSHIP BETWEEN THE "ORIGIN" OF MAN AND THE "NATURE" OF MAN

Under the general heading of the interrelationship between man's *origin* and his *nature,* I would like to suggest two further divisions for our purposes: (A) The Traditional Theological Understanding; (B) The Contemporary Evolutionary Perspective and its Correlative Theological Implications.

A. *Traditional Christian Doctrine and the Creation of Man*

The section in the traditional theological formulation dealing with the origin and nature of man was entitled "On God Creating and Elevating (*De Deo Creante et Elevante*)." Using this as our cue, it becomes helpful for us to separate out these two subheadings: (1) Creation of Man; (2) Elevation of Man.

1. Creation of Man

The questions which generally concerned the theologian elaborating a theology of man's creation were two, the *nature* of man and the *origin* of man.

a. *Nature of Man.*—Under this topic the theologian normally enunciated a definition of man as the composite of body and intellective soul so that the soul is truly the form of the body. A further elaboration was that the soul is a spiritual substance and, as such, immortal by its nature. Some general affirmation was made about the organism within which (or of which) the body was the form. In short, our traditional formulations about the nature of man concentrated on his "soul" or "spirit." In traditional language one probably could have gotten by with the affirmation, "I am my soul," in much the same way that currently we hear the existentialist principle, "I am my body." By the kind of approach traditional theology took to the question of the nature of man one could properly surmise that the understanding of the soul as a spiritual (and therefore separable from the body) substance and as immortal were the central philosophical and theological affirmations about man. It was thus quite a logical step to describe death as the separation of body *and* soul. That says much about the interrelatedness that devolves from such an anthropology or philosophy of man, so that to tamper with any element in the system is to jeopardize the whole structure. And thus, for example, if man is *not* "composed of body and soul" how does one face into the question of death? But let us move to the second point.

b. *The Origin of Man.*—Having elaborated the theology of man's nature, a traditional theological manual would then move to the question of human origins. This would involve two further questions: (i) The origin of individual men; and (ii) the origin of the human race.

(i) *The Origin of Individual (each and every) Man.*—The response to the question of each man's origin was direct and quite unequivocal, namely, God creates directly and immediately every human soul. The word "soul" or "spirit" should be underlined, since it was specifically asserted in the Encyclical *Humani generis* that one could hypothesize about the possible evolution of the body in the Providence of God to the point where it was suitable matter for the infusion of the soul by God. But it was beyond dispute that each person is directly created by God, since the soul is the very form of the body.

(ii) *The Origin of the Human Race.*—The question under discussion here is really about the beginning of the human community, i.e., whether the human race is from a single first couple (monogenism) or from some original group (polygenism, in the sense that every species emerges from a rather large group out of which the fittest finally survive).

Again, the question was confronted and answered in *Humani*

generis, wherein the response is somewhat controversial in its implications but clear in its affirmation. It is necessary, we are assured, to believe in monogenism (single first couple) because otherwise it would not be possible to explain the transmission of original sin throughout the human race. Again the rigid consistency of the traditional theological system becomes obvious. To undercut any single section is to create tremors throughout the total structure. This explains the difficult task of contemporary constructive theology. But that is matter for another time.

2. Elevation of Man

The second general section under the traditional theological treatise *De Deo Creante et Elevante* discussed the elevation of man to the supernatural state. It was generally assumed that the creation of man (the first couple) and his elevation to the supernatural state were simultaneous, so that indeed man never lived in the purely natural state. It is not possible here to get into this question in detail, although it is something of a critical question in any reformulation of the theological basis of Christian belief.[2] Suffice it to say that "supernatural" was generally defined in terms of "natural." Thus natural is that which is *due* or *essential* to man *qua* man (constitutionally, operationally, etc.). Supernatural then is that which is entirely *undue* to, or not necessary to, man as man. It is above any of his natural exigencies. Supernatural, therefore, corresponds to some gracious act of God on man's behalf, but only *theoretically* since man never existed in the purely natural state. Much has been written over the last fifty years about the question, from Rahner's "supernatural existential" backwards to Blondel's whole immanentist stance. Again this is an area for another chapter. Our concern has been the relationship between the *origin* of man and the *nature* of man in traditional Catholic theology. Let us move on to the challenge of contemporary understandings.

---

2. Cf. Eulalio Baltazar, **Teilhard and the Supernatural** (Baltimore: Helicon, 1966).

B. *The Origin of Man and his Nature in an*
   Evolutionary Perspective

If one begins a re-investigation of the entire traditional theological structure elaborated around the origin and nature of man
taking into account the fact of evolution, the central question quite
obviously becomes the Church's definitive declaration about the
direct creation of the soul by God. For indeed in evolutionist
language and thought man would have to emerge in the context
of evolution as all other species, unique as he may be in relationship to all the other emergents. From this obvious first and central
question, i.e., any unique creative act of God in man's origin, there
follow two equally explicit problems: first, the relationship between body and soul; and, secondly, the formulation of the question
of the relationship between *origin* and *nature* of man in new terms
and with significant differences.

1. Relationship Between Body and Soul

This issue occupies a central place in so much contemporary
theological dialogue. Whereas in traditional Christian philosophy,
and indeed in popular imagery, man was described in terms of
a *unity* between two distinguishable and separable substances,
body and soul, such language and imagery grates on the contemporary psychological and philosophical ear. This is not to affirm
that the tradition *intended* any dichotomy, but such division, and
indeed misunderstanding, did occur.

In contemporary thought from the point of view of the several
disciplines that key in on man (psychology, philosophy, biology,
etc.) it becomes impossible to talk in the language of earlier theological discourse and even less acceptable to subscribe to that
kind of clear imagery that accompanied the traditional concepts.
Whatever we might say about the definiteness of the Church's
teachings on the "direct creation of the soul by God," it cannot be
a description of man's origin, and that takes me to the second
related question.

2. Relationship Between the Origin of Man and the Nature of Man

This is the central point of the first part of the chapter. And it results from what I think was an ambiguity in the historical analysis between man's origin and his nature. Indeed, historically it seemed quite plausible when attempting to describe man as unique (i.e., when talking about his "nature") to talk about the direct concern of God in man's regard. In other words, to show the uniqueness of man (nature) traditional theology talked about the special creative act of God whereby man was brought into being (origin).

So the issue must be raised: Was theology *ever* concerned with the origin of man (except in some indirect fashion)? Or rather wasn't the central concern of theology all the while the nature of man, i.e., specifically *who* man is in his relationships and especially his relationship with God? However, since it appeared quite impossible to talk about the uniqueness of man, that is about his *nature,* without some kind of special intervention of God in his creation we received as part of our heritage the doctrine of the unique or special *origin* of man. This is not to say that historically the thesis about the direct creation of man was not believed as—at least in some sense—an explanation of man's real origin. But what I am saying is, even granting that fact, what our tradition really wished to get at was man's uniqueness, that is, his nature.

And in this sense I like to talk about new ways of theologizing which may relate one who is "doing theology" in a more realistic fashion to his tradition. The process is neither to simply repeat the doctrinal formulations of previous centuries nor is it to reject them as irrelevant, but rather to see most of them as answers to particular questions that represented serious concerns of the historical community. The task then of the contemporary theologian who is always within a tradition is to try to formulate as clearly as he can the questions to which dogmatic and/or doctrinal formulations are the answers.

Now in the case at hand, one has to ask "what is the question to which 'the direct creation of the soul by God' is the answer?"

Is it in other words an effort to describe *how* man came into being or *what* (who) man is? If we can affirm that the *real* question historically has been, What *is* man?, then we share the same question. And then it becomes a weighty challenge to create a constructive contemporary theological response to that question, as was the traditional response.

Thus, if we share the same question as has been central to the community of believers throughout history, that is, What *is* man? and if in an evolutionary framework we cannot answer the question by speaking of either the direct creation of man by God or man's being composed of body and soul, then the task of contemporary theology is to create a response that is not only consistent with the tradition, but that is adequate for our time and our place.

This, however, is not an easy task because there are a number of participating disciplines feeding into this response. If the question centers on the "origin" of man, the theologian has to keep his ear attuned to the findings of biology, anthropology, and to some extent the earth sciences (paleontology, geology, etc.). On the other hand, if the question focuses in on what the psychologist and the sociologist (and indeed all the humanities) are saying, in fact, the question sometimes appears to be: Does the theologian have anything to say?

Before the stark implications of this question, the theologian indeed has to think twice about making affirmations concerning man's origins. And so almost by necessity he is forced into pin-pointing the question of man's nature, which may have been the central question all along. And so it seems to me that an effective method of theologizing in the present circumstances of the "shifting sands of philosophical grounding" is to search out the questions that may have been historically focal so that answers to them became definitive declarations and to phrase the questions if possible so that we can in our day see if they are central also to us. If they are, then it becomes the task of theology to respond as creatively and constructively (if maybe with less definiteness) as did our tradition. This has been my perception of the task of theology.

ANTHROPOCENTRICITY AND THE ECOLOGICAL
CRISIS

After our investigation of the relationship between the "origin" of man and the nature of man, we begin to move more directly into the implications of that discussion for the ecological problem.

The first observation is that in either of the approaches discussed earlier, whether the *traditional* approach (which talked about the uniqueness of man as being attested to through God's special act on his behalf) or the *evolutionary* formulation (where man emerges as all other creatures, but somehow wrapping up in himself *all* of the development of *all* the cosmos over *all* the centuries), in either approach, I say, man emerges as or is posited as the central or focal point of reality. This is not to make an *a priori* negative evaluation of either approach in terms of their man-centered cosmologies. I do think it important, however, to reflect for a while on such anthropocentric cosmologies since they have some direct bearing on man's perception of himself and of *his* world. And it seems to me that there are three possible reactions to this man-centered posture: (A) Exaggerated Inclusionism or Materialism; (B) Exaggerated Exclusionism or Anthropomorphism; and (C) Moderate Anthropocentrism or Hominization (especially as that is elaborated by Teilhard de Chardin).[3]

A. *Exaggerated Inclusionism*

This point of view has been otherwise described by Philip Hefner as "materialism." It perceives man to be included *in* nature as all pre- and non-human elements. Therefore, man is seen to be just another species totally subservient to all of the

---

3. This section is a combination of language from Frederick Elder's **Crisis in Eden** and from a seminar on **Man and His Environment** given in the Chicago Cluster of Theological Schools. I acknowledge a special debt to my colleague Philip Hefner from whom I have borrowed much of this material.

laws (natural) of nature that govern every other cosmic reality. He is therefore not the governor (tiller in Teilhardian terms) but the governed. This is a somewhat stoic view of the cosmos and human reality. It has been described as seeing man's presence here as possibly fleeting, just like the match that is lit, glows briefly and then is spent. This may very well be the case of the human group. Nature determines human destiny (if one can distinguish of course between man *and* nature).

B. *Exaggerated Exclusionism*

This of course is quite the opposite kind of reaction to man-centered attitudes and sees man as the measure of all things and therefore can be called anthropomorphism in the sense that man makes and judges all things in his own image. It thus has all the overtones of domination, dominiondom, subduing the cosmos, etc. The consequences are a failure to come to grips realistically with the interrelatedness between man and nature and the kind of technological mania that has characterized Western man (for one who hails from the Ohio Valley, strip-mining is the perfect symbol of this attitude).

C. *Moderate Anthropocentrism*

The third reaction to the fact of man's centeredness in the cosmos is to try to steer a middle course between materialism or exaggerated inclusionism and anthropomorphism or exaggerated exclusionism, and this course is best described for me by the term *Hominisation,* especially as that is used by Teilhard in the following passage:

To the grand process of sublimation it is fitting to apply with all its force the word *hominisation.* Hominisation can be accepted in the first place as the individual and instantaneous leap from instinct to thought, but it is also, in a wider sense, the progressive phyletic spiritualization in human civilization of all the forces contained in the animal world.

Thus we are led—after having considered the element and pictured the species—to contemplate the earth in its totality.[4]

One has the image, therefore, of man emerging within the context of evolution bringing that whole context to a new level of perfection. This creates the sense of reciprocity wherein man brings all of reality to a higher plane (evolution become conscious of itself) on the one hand and man becomes at the same time nature's pupil regarding the overall direction of the process. Perhaps one might use the image of the globe before the appearance of plant life and afterwards to grasp the significance of hominization. From one point of view the cosmos is the matrix of life and growth and at the same time the planet is very different once life and growth appear and cover the globe. Thus it is with man. On the one hand he brings all the previous possibilities, tendencies, and potentialities to their fullness, and yet nature, i.e., the cosmos, is the matrix of his own development and progress.

The significant contribution (in Teilhardian terms) with the appearance of man is reflective consciousness, that is, thought. And so man for the first time in the history of cosmic development (as far as we know) asks the question of meaning. In his efforts to answer that question he is faced with the possibility of ignoring the cosmos as the matrix for human presence and that would lead to exaggerated exclusionism or to fail to realize his own uniqueness and distinct influence for success or failure in the cosmic enterprise and that would be exaggerated inclusionism.

CONCLUSION

What I want to say finally is that hominization as seen in the vision of Teilhard, as I understand it, is the ideal solution to both the issue of man's origin and of his nature. It says in-

---

4. Teilhard de Chardin, **The Phenomenon of Man** (New York: Harper, 1959), p. 180.

deed that man is unique, even though he has emerged in the context of evolution as have all other creatures. Yet at the same time, it affirms that man's place in nature is precisely that: his place *in* nature. It encourages the need for man to engage in the process of definition, not only of self-definition but in larger definition of the total evolutionary system. Yet while engaging in such definition, let man not forget that he is at once the latest creature and therefore highest in a true sense and yet the pupil who must learn by dialogue with cosmic reality his own destiny and purpose.

If we are going to talk about anthropocentricity therefore it will help immensely to understand it the way Teilhard speaks about hominization. And this would be my suggestion regarding an adequate theological base for good ecological practice.

3   Faith and Ecology

A Christian ethic of involvement in environmental change is, by itself, weak; value follows from meaning, and a Christian ethic must be based on a theological understanding. The need then is for a theology that integrates Christian faith and ecological involvement.[1] More exactly, the need is for an operational view of the relationship between God and the world, a view adequate to give meaning to contemporary Christian involvement in environmental improvement. Two common kinds of operational views of the God-world relationship must be rejected as inadequate. The romantic and quasi-pantheistic approach to the relationship between God and the world, a view that understands nature as simply mirroring God's attributes, is insufficiently dynamic to give meaning to Christian involvement in bettering the environment. It sees nature as somehow divine, but it stresses the sacredness of nature rather than man's responsibility to care for nature; and, in so doing, it belongs more to the eastern tradition of religions than to the Judaeo-Christian tradition.

Secondly, the approach to the relationship between God and the world that sees faith in God and involvement in the world

---

1. The intention behind this chapter is not to present a complete theology of ecology, but to provide some reflections on the biblical data concerning man's relation to his environment. Ian Barbour points out that a theology of ecology has three aspects: man's unity with nature, God's immanence in nature, and political responsibility for technology. See his concluding essay published in Ian G. Barbour, ed., **Earth Might Be Fair** (Englewood Cliffs, N. J.: Prentice-Hall, 1972). In this chapter, only man's relation to the world and God's immanence in the world are treated, but there is no intention of detracting from the need for an ethic of political responsibility for technology.

as somehow opposed and in tension cannot, by its very nature, provide a satisfactory framework for integrating faith in God and commitment to man's environment. This view of "God against the world" is what underlies the Two Kingdom doctrine of Augustine and of Martin Luther, and it is implicit in the medieval "*contemptus mundi*" literature. In this view, the world is seen as simply fallen and under God's judgment; it is a completely non-personalist view of the world. This is the understanding of the world that undergirds the nineteenth century attitude that nature is to be exploited.

What is needed is an operational view of the world that is rooted in Scripture and that meets contemporary needs. As opposed to the romantic view of the world, this view should take the world seriously as world, as close to God but not divine, as good but not sacred. As opposed to the exploitative view of the world, the world should be seen somehow in personalist terms, as made holy by the Incarnation; and so man's responsibility for taking charge of the world and the Christian value of his efforts to build the world should be made clear.

Such an operational view of the relationship between God and the world will be developed in a schismatic way here. Judaeo-Christian desacralization of the world will be studied in the first chapter of Genesis, the prologue to John's gospel will be looked at briefly, and the personalization of the world will be studied in the writings of St. Paul. From these investigations some theses will emerge.

THE TRANSCENDENCE OF GOD AND THE DESACRALIZATION OF THE WORLD

At the time of the formation of the New Testament, the Church understands itself as coming out of the salvation history of Israel, sees itself in terms of fulfilling the categories of the Old Testament. The Church understands the relationship between the Creator and his creation not only as a relationship in Christ, but also in terms of the Old Testament's theology of creation. Israel's theology of creation permeates the Old Testament, but it is found especially in Second Isaiah, in the Wisdom literature, and above all in Genesis 1:1-2:4.[2] The Genesis document is particularly important; it is a summary, in the form of a theologically polished creed, of Israel's theology of creation.

The prologue to the Old Testament is the theological creed of Genesis 1:1-2:4. This creed affirms that Yahweh, Israel's God, the God of election and salvation, the God of the exodus and the covenant, is Lord over all, gives all things their order, meaning, and value, and is faithful to what he creates.

Is this document a myth? Yes and no. Yes in the Bultmannian sense that it needs to be "demythologized." It deals with matters of ultimate concern to man, with matters of great existential import. The religious truth that the document contains is embedded in the historical and scientific notions of the period of formation of the document, and it is necessary to demythologize the document, to read the religious content through, prescinding from the historico-scientific matrix that is the vehicle of the religious truth. But in the ordinary academic sense of the word "myth," the sense in which the word is used in the discipline of the history of religions, Genesis 1:1-2:4 is clearly not a myth. It does have some common points with myths: it is a communal possession that originates in a distant past and it deals with ultimate questions. But it lacks the whole colorful tonality of a myth; its language is not at all the language of symbolic narrative. Furthermore, it is not a folk creation, as myths are, but a theological document. It lacks the naive and unreflective character of myth. And, far from personalizing cosmic forces as myths do, it depersonalizes them. The document is, in many ways, the antithesis of a myth; in fact, there are strong anti-myth elements in it. It is a doctrinal creed.

---

2. Old Testament theology of creation has been neglected in exegesis and as a basis for theology; see Walter Brueggeman, "The Triumphalist Tendency in Exegetical History," **Journal of the American Academy of Religion,** 38 (1970), pp. 373-375.

In keeping with the rest of the Priestly strata of tradition of which it is a part, Genesis 1:1-2:4 presents straight Priestly tradition doctrine, formally organized, austere, with no frills. Although it was surely not written all at one time, there is nothing present by chance. What is said is intended to hold true just as it stands. It is true that the narrative presents cosmological history as understood by the people of the time, but the main thrust of the text is theological. The religious truth that is declared is true for all times; in this sense, the document is an aetiology. It gives the permanent existential structures of reality; it tells *what is true* in the form of how it came to be.

The chief image used to show God's ineffable transcendence is the image of creation by God's word. For example, "God said 'let there be light,' and there was light." [3] The idea of creation by word preserves and points up the radical distinction between God and what he creates.[4] Creation is not an overflow or a necessary reflection of God's being; the only continuity between God and his creation is God's word. God's very word is creative. Thus creation is God's, for it is the product of his creative word.

But the main way in which Genesis 1:1-2:4 brings out Israel's belief in God's transcendence is by showing that creatures are in no way divine. God's transcendence is indicated by the desacralization of creatures. The idea is that only God is divine; there is no God but Yahweh. This is, for the most part, affirmed indirectly by showing that God is absolute Lord over all things because he has created them, and that the things he has created are simply what they are, creatures. Sun, moon and stars, then, which in many myths are living and somehow divine beings, are here desacralized. Genesis even denies the dependence of plant life on the sun and the moon; everything depends on the creative will and word of God. In reaction to the cultural atmosphere

---

3. Gen 1:3.

4. This idea runs all through the Old Testament, and is found especially in the Wisdom literature. See Eccl 42:15; Wis 9:1-3; Ps 33:6-9; and also Is 55:10-11.

around Israel, an atmosphere saturated with astrological beliefs, the stars too are stripped of all magic powers and divine connotations. The stars are not even creators of light but the mediators of a light that was there before they existed.

Creatures are not only radically distinct from God and belong to him but, also, they are good. "Good" here designates not so much a moral or aesthetic characteristic as the order, harmony, and purpose of the universe and of the elements that make it up. What God creates is good, has value, precisely because he creates it and sustains it in existence. Yet this goodness and value, although depending on God, is the creature's own. Creation is good because it is in covenant with Yahweh.[5] Yahweh's covenantal fidelity to what he creates is an extension of Israel's understanding of Yahweh as the God who is faithful to his covenant with Israel. And, like Israel in covenant, all creation and every creature is subordinate to Yahweh and has its role to fulfill. Again, Israel's dependence on God is not merely a status and a role; it is a God-given value. Yahweh has chosen Israel not because of any greatness or beauty or righteousness or obedience of Israel's but because of God's limitless love. This choice is a kind of creation, and is reflected back into the creation narrative. God, in creating, gives value to things in themselves; they are good.

When the text of Genesis 1:1-2:4 comes to the creation of man, the impressive introduction, "Let us make man," indicates a more personal and intimate creative activity on the part of

---

5. For other Old Testament texts that take up this theme, see particularly Ps 8, Ps 89, and Ps 136 with its beautiful refrain:

His wisdom made the heavens,
   his love is everlasting.
He set the earth on the waters,
   his love is everlasting.
He made the great lights,
   his love is everlasting.

See also Wis 11:21-27: "Yes, you love all that exists, you hold nothing of what you have made in abhorrence, for had you hated anything, you would not have formed it. And how, had you not willed it, could a thing persist, how be conserved if not called forth by you?"

God. The specialness of the creation of man is underlined by
the use of the word *bara* three times. Man, nevertheless, is put
simply in the rank of creatures; the stress remains on the transcendence of God. There is simply, on the one hand, creation (including man) and, on the other hand, God.

Unlike other creatures, man is created in the image and likeness of God. The use of two words that reinforce one another,
"image" and "likeness," emphasizes that man, the image, corresponds to the original, God. The notion of image, for a nation
that forbade images of God and reacted strongly to the idols
of its neighbors, is startling, and it is meant to be. God is not
only transcendent of man, but very near to him. "Image" here is
a parallel idea to that of "covenant"; both express God's close-
ness to man. Just as Yahweh commits himself in covenant to
Israel, and with covenant fidelity to all creation, here he commits
himself specially to the whole human race. Man has a special
relationship with God. God's transcendence is only one side of
the story; his nearness to man is the other. And yet, man is in
no way divine; man, too, is desacralized.

Man is, moreover, master of nature and responsible for it.
The passage concerning man as the master of plants and animals
is also present in many creation myths; in the creation myths, this
passage serves to introduce the fundamental precept, "You are to
take or to destroy nothing in nature except what is necessary for
your daily subsistence." This precept is significantly missing
in the Genesis document. Again, the entire tone and sense of the
text is anti-mythological. Man is master of the plants and animals
because he is in the image of a transcendent and all-powerful God,
the Lord of all things, man and plants and animals included. So,
then, not only is nature desacralized, but also man's relation to
nature. In creation myths, nature belongs to God or to the gods;
man is part of nature, and may take and use only what is necessary, for it is not really his. In the Genesis document, however,
although nature belongs to God, God has made man in his image
and given him dominion over nature.

What is most important about man's resemblance to God is
man's function in the world, his dominion over the rest of nature.

It is not man who is related to God through nature, but nature that is related to God through man. Nature, having been desacralized, is nonetheless related to God; it receives the dignity of being under God's sovereignty through being under man's sovereignty. Man is responsible to God for the world, and the rest of the world is related to God through man. Nature is now completely desacralized. Nature has been shown to be radically distinct from God, and man has been distinguished from nature. In this way, the view of reality that is presented here is a complete departure from the mythical view of reality. The world has no magical power to save man or to destroy him; the power belongs to God. A fearful and awe-filled attitude toward the world has been replaced by a matter-of-factness about the world, and magic has been replaced by prayer. Thus man is freed from nature, and nature itself is freed for man's use. Both man and nature are desacralized and freed for progress. This matter-of-factness about both man and nature is the precondition for the development of science, for technology, and for social, political, and economic progress. No progress is possible except to the extent that man can face the world without intimidation. This is not to say that man is free to exploit man or nature; his task is to take care of and to build the world, exercising the dominion given him by God.

Not only are man and nature desacralized in the Genesis document but also, in the desacralization of marriage, the proto-type and most basic of human institutions, all human institutions are desacralized. "Male and female he created them." [6] The import of the statement might be missed unless it is realized that the declaration dispels a widespread world of myth and the deification of sexuality and also a world of cynicism and false asceticism and fear of sex. Sexuality and marriage, like God's other creatures, are here desacralized. Sexuality and marriage are taken out of the purely religious sphere and set squarely in the area of the human. From a sociological point of view, of course, there was

---

6. Gen 1:27.

little or no difference between marriage in Israel and marriage in the neighboring nations. The difference is in the meaning of marriage in the light of faith in Yahweh and in the light of the prevalent mediterranean myths and religions. In Canaan particularly, where Israel had settled, worship of fertility gods was dominant; sexuality and procreation were seen as deeply mysterious and belonging to the divine sphere. The fertility gods were deities of the forces of nature and of the cycle of fertility in both the human and the natural world. Both male and female, their intercourse was regarded as the prototype of everything that happened on earth.[7] They were worshipped in order to assure the fertility of both lands and wives. Life and generation at all levels depended on these gods and the worship of them in ritual orgies. Some of this fertility-god worship had made inroads in Israel; the text, then, is reacting against a mythological and "sacred" view of sexuality, fertility, and marriage.

It is true that both for Israel and the surrounding nations, sexuality and marriage and all that they involve was God's gift. What is different about Israel is this: not that sexuality and marriage have less value as divine gifts, but that, in Israel's understanding, God is not restricted to nature or to nature's cycles of fertility. Sexuality and its institutionalization, marriage, are brought directly into the sphere of Yahweh, the sovereign God of the covenant and of universal history. That is, sexuality and marriage are removed from the sphere of the fertility cults and are transferred into the sphere of Yahweh's lordship. Marriage, now desacralized, acquires a deeply religious significance; it is a good gift of creation; it comes from God. Marriage is made holy by the fact of creation itself.

Before leaving the Genesis creation document, it is important to note the significance of the genealogy of chapter five of Genesis. Chapter five was originally continuous with the creation document; eventually, the second creation document, chapters two and three, along with chapter four, all of this from the Yahwist stream

---

7. E. Schillebeeckx, Marriage, Human Reality and Saving Mystery (New York: Sheed & Ward, 1965), pp. 12-15.

of tradition, was inserted between 2:4 and chapter five. In the genealogy of chapter five, the desacralization process is again at work. The genealogy connotes a sense of human universality and of kinship with other humans. Once again, man is not defined by his relationship with nature but by his relationship with God. Again, this is an unmythical view of reality. Israel has no tribal totems by which, through identification with different animals, man is related through nature to God. Man is related directly to God and through other men to God through kinship. Moreover, history itself is desacralized; time is secular. The cyclical view of time gives way to a linear sense of history and of progress. But the progress of history is not a new myth substituted for old myths. Yahweh is the Lord of history. History, for Israel, is made up primarily of the series of events that mark Yahweh's dealings with his people and with all men; these points, connected, form the line of history. Further, the mythical view of reality in which the cyclism of time functions to help man face the terrors of history gives way to a linear concept of history, a history which is open-ended toward the future, a history of which God is the lord. It is a history that is eschatological and that holds no terrors for man because God is in charge of it.

THE TRANSCENDENCE AND IMMANENCE OF GOD

The prologue to St. John's gospel is, like Genesis 1:1-2:4, a theological document and a creed. Whatever its origin, even if it was previously a liturgical hymn or something else, it stands in the gospel as straight theology and as an affirmation of faith. It is a solemn document and, again like the Genesis creation creed, it is carefully structured both as to its literary form and as to the development of its content. The structure of the prologue is that of a chiasm. The first eleven verses lead to the central verse, verse 12, and the remaining verses are parallel, but in reverse order, to the first eleven verses. The theme of verses one through eleven is that God's creative Word has become flesh and dwelt

among us. The first phrase of the prologue, "In the beginning,"
is a direct reference to the first phrase of the creed of chapter one
of Genesis. The author of the prologue is deliberately identifying
the Word, who is God and who is with God, with the word by
which God created all things in the beginning. This creative
Word of God, the prologue continues, has entered into the world
that came to be through him; the Word has become flesh and
dwelt among us.[8] That is to say, the ineffable and transcendent
God has taken flesh and become part of creation, immanent in
the world. The prologue uses the very image, the word, that Genesis, chapter one, uses to affirm God's transcendence; but here the
image of the word, without losing its previous connotation, is used
to express God's immanence, in Christ, in the world. God is present
in Christ, and "we saw his glory, . . . full of grace and truth." [9]
"Glory" is the sign of God's presence, and "grace and truth"
recall the traditional Old Testament attributes of God, his merci-
ful love and his fidelity. In Christ, God has entered his creation;
he is immanent in the world.

THE IMMANENCE OF CHRIST AND THE
PERSONALIZATION OF THE WORLD

In the Old Testament, God's absolute transcendence is affirmed and the world is seen as desacralized. This desacralization
of nature and of man's institutions is a necessary prerequisite
to technology and to political and social progress; but, by itself,
desacralization tends to impersonalization. "When nature is desacralized, the tendency is also to depersonalize it." [10] This ten-

---

8. This is a reference to Ex 25:8, to Ez 37:26-27, and to similar texts;
just as God dwelt with his people during the exodus, so now, in a much
fuller way, he has come to dwell with his people.

9. Jn 1:14.

10. James Logan, "The Secularization of Nature," **Christians and the
Good Earth,** Faith-Man-Nature Papers, Number 1 (Alexandria, 1968)

dency is overcome in the New Testament. In the theologies of John
and Paul, the affirmation of God's transcendence and of the
strictly non-divine or secular quality of the world remains. But
now God is also seen as immanent in the world in Christ, and the
world is seen in personalist terms. This personalization of the
world through its being rooted in Christ is brought out especially
in the writings of St. Paul.[11]

There is general agreement among theologians that Paul affirms an organic relationship between the risen Christ and the
Church: the Church is the body of Christ. There has been less
theological writing concerning another affirmation of Paul's, that
of the organic relationship between the risen Christ and the cosmos.
Paul's theology of the relationship between God and the world
sees all of creation as grounded in Christ and as centered on him.
For Paul, all that exists comes from God.[12] But everything comes
from God *in Christ*. "There is one God, the Father, from whom
all things come and for whom we exist. And there is one lord,
Jesus Christ, through whom all things come and through whom
we exist." [13] Paul's teaching on the relation of the world to Christ
is presented in the first three chapters of the letter to the Ephesians.
God has "let us know the mystery of his purpose, the hidden plan
he so kindly made in Christ from the beginning to act upon when
the times had run their course to the end: that he would bring

---

p. 104. The whole article, pp. 101-127, is excellent. In the present paper,
I have followed Logan's general thesis that the world, desacralized in
contemporary man's attitude toward it, needs to be seen in personal
as well as in secular terms. For a similar approach to the relationship
between faith and ecology, see Robert H. Platman, "Theology and
Ecology: A Problem for Religious Education," **Religious Education,** 66
(1971), pp. 14-23.

11. It is brought out especially in Paul's so-called "cosmic" texts,
which will be considered here. For a different approach to Paul's thought,
one that understands Paul's theology as limiting man's relationship with
the world, see Alfred von Rohr Sauer, "Man as Steward of Creation,"
St. Louis University Magazine, Special Supplement, Fall, 1970, pp. 43-48.

12. Rm 11:33-36.

13. 1 Cor 8:6.

everything together under Christ as head, everything in the heavens and everything on earth." [14]

Furthermore, God has made Christ "the ruler of everything, the head of the Church—which is his body, the fullness of him who fills the whole creation."[15] Centered on Christ from the beginning, God's plan for the world has not yet been completely worked out; God's plan will be fulfilled when all things are finally brought together under Christ. The Church has a central place in this plan. It is through the Church that God's plan is revealed; and, although Christ's active presence fills the whole universe, it is in the Church that he is most fully present.

The same teaching is found in the letter to the Colossians, 1:13 to 2:15. Christ is the head of his body, the Church; and Christ is the head of the cosmos which is also his body.[16] The Church, then, has a certain character and has a central place in the cosmos. Paul also expresses the idea that the cosmos is related to Christ by the concept of *pleroma,* or perfection or plenitude. "God wanted all perfection (*pleroma*) to be found in him and all things to be reconciled through him and for him."[17] The sense here of *pleroma* is that Christ fills the universe with God's creative presence. All things are created in Christ, are reconciled in him, and find their fulfillment in him in whom is the fullness (*pleroma*) of all that exists. Everything is seen as somehow suspended from the risen Christ, and all things find their meaning and value and even their existence in Christ.[18] It is not yet, however, that all things are truly reconciled in Christ. That reconciliation has been accomplished in principle by Christ's death on the cross, but the actual working out of that reconciliation takes place in history.

---

14. Eph 1:9-10.

15. Eph 1:22-23.

16. Col 2:10: "In his body lives the fulness of divinity"; see Heinrich Schlier, "The Pauline Body-Concept," in **The Church,** ed. at Canisianum (New York: Kenedy, 1963), pp. 44-58.

17. Col 1:19.

18. See Christopher F. Mooney, **Teilhard de Chardin and the Mystery of Christ** (New York: Sheed & Ward, 1966), pp. 88-99; see also the works cited by Mooney.

To the theology of Ephesians and Colossians, the hymn of Philippians 2:6-11 adds the idea that it is through Christ's incarnation and death that he descended into the world so that, having risen, he could take the world to himself. For Christ to be lord of the cosmos, of the whole process of the universe, he had to become part of that process, and this meant the incarnation. Living out the incarnation necessarily implied death, and even death on the cross. Christ, in the self-emptying of his incarnation and his death, descended into the heart of the universe so as, in his resurrection, to become its lord. To become the central and focal element of the process of the universe, Christ had first to become an element of that process. It is the risen Christ who holds the world together, and to be risen he had to die, and to die he had to be born. It is through his incarnation and death that Christ descended completely into the heart of the world to become, in his risen life, the heart of the world. Since Christ has entered not only mankind but the world, it is the whole world that is the object of God's saving love. This is the doctrine that Romans 8:18-25 adds to the writings of Paul that have already been considered. All of creation shares in God's plan. The universe itself is not simply an instrument of man's salvation; it is itself, somehow, object of salvation.[19] The world is related to Christ through man in such a way that the world itself is an object of resurrection, of ultimate transformation. We can conclude from this text that, because Christ is, through man, the hope of the final redemption of the world, he is the guarantee to man of the meaningfulness of the world and of what man builds in this world.

FOUR THESES

From these brief studies of the desacralization of nature and of human institutions and of the personalization of the world

---

19. Stanislaus Lyonnet, "The Redemption of the Universe," **The Church,** ed. at Canisianum, Innsbruck, (New York: Kenedy, 1963), pp. 136-156.

in the risen Christ there emerge four theses that are important
for the question of Christian involvement in environmental change.

Thesis one: *The Christian attitude toward the world is secular.*
The Christian understands nature and human institutions in their
secular reality. He sees natural resources as good but in no way
divine; there are no sacred taboos on man's using the goods of the
earth. Nature is not to be exploited, but it is to be worked with,
to be used. There is no Christian mystique of nature. Nature,
in the Christian perspective, is not looked at romantically, nor
with reverential awe, but with responsible pragmatism. The Christian understands human institutions—political, social, military,
economic, and educational institutions—in a matter of fact way
and even in a pragmatic way. Institutions are not necessarily to be
attacked and torn down, but they are to be reformed and made
effectively useful for man. Furthermore, human institutions are
not to be revered with the reverence reserved for God. The Christian repudiates the divinization of the political that was typical of
Nazi Germany and that is typical of today's communist and fascist
regimes. He repudiates the divinization of the economic that was
typical of nineteenth century capitalism. He repudiates the divinization of the physical and the social sciences. The Christian affirms
and respects nature as nature, and human institutions as human
institutions. He affirms the world as world.

Thesis two: *The Christian attitude toward the world is personalist.* The Christian sees the world as Christic, as centered on
the risen Christ. The Christ to whom the Christian is committed
is the risen Christ who is the future focal point of the convergence
of all human history and progress. It is not so much Christ who
is coming a second time as it is the world that is moving gradually
in history toward the risen Christ who awaits it and who is now
actively drawing it to himself. The world and its history and
its progress are the Lord's; he holds the world together, and it is
his creative love that is the most profound dynamism of history's
movement. Christ is not only the world's goal, but he is, by his
universal influence, immanent in the world. The world, in its
natural resources and in its human institutions, is personalized
in Christ because it is rooted in him, held together by him, headed

toward him. Because the entire world is grounded in Christ and centered on him, the Christian can have faith in the world and faith in Christ. Commitment to Christ and commitment to the betterment of man's environment are not opposed but, rather, synthesized.

Thesis three: *There is a Christian imperative to better man's environment.* In Genesis 1:1-2:4, man is given a mandate to care for the world; man has dominion over the world that is for man and that is related to God through man. This Old Testament mandate to man to take responsibility for the world takes on new significance in the New Testament. Man's responsibility, then, is to participate in the progressive reconciliation of all things in Christ. An essential part of man's participation in this process of reconciliation is his task of building the world, of taking responsibility for the improvement of the human environment. The Christian has a greater responsibility toward environmental betterment than has the unbeliever; for the Christian knows by faith the goal toward which he is building and the religious value of his work.

Thesis four: *Christian involvement in environmental change is properly Christian only when it is motivated and sustained by personal relationship with the risen Christ.* The world can be seen in personal terms only to the extent that the Christian understands the world within the framework of his own personal relationship with the risen Christ. To be truly personal, this relationship with Christ must be conscious, loving, and constant; it must, in other words, be a prayerful relationship. The faith that enables the Christian to understand the world as centered on Christ and as moving toward him is a faith that goes far beyond simple intellectual assent to Christian teaching. It is a faith that is a personal and loving adherence to Christ; and it is a faith that finds its sustenance and its highpoint in prayer. Prayer and responsibility to improve man's environment are two distinct aspects of the Christian's mission in the world; but although they are distinct, they cannot be separated.

II

LIFE IN BELIEF AND ACTION

4   Toward An Environmental Ethic

MERLE LONGWOOD

Kenneth Boulding, the maverick economist who suggests that the GNP should be regarded as a cost rather than a product, since it assumes that economic activity is a throughput, "a linear process from the mine to the garbage dump,"[1] provides me with a good justification for my own concern for the environment. He writes:

> I am something of an ecologist at heart, mainly because I am really a preacher, and we know that all ecologists are really preachers under the skin. They are great viewers with alarm. Is there any more single-minded, simple pleasure than viewing with alarm? At times it is even better than sex.[2]

Being neither middle-aged nor celibate, I do not want to go *that* far, but it may well be the preacher under the skin in me that makes me an ecologist at heart. If so, I am in good company, for even Stewart Udall, whose present title is Visiting Professor (Adjunct) of Environmental Humanism at the Yale School of Forestry, has taken to calling himself an "environmental evangelist" since he left the ranks of government. Taking a cue from Boulding, I propose to view the deterioration of our environment with alarm.

The seventies, we are told by all the media, will be the Decade of Ecology. The national television networks, establishment publications like *Fortune, Life* and *Time,* and left-of-center publications like *Ramparts, The Progressive, Motive, Saturday Review* and

---

1. Kenneth E. Boulding, "Fun and Games with the Gross National Product—The Role of Misleading Indicators in Social Policy," **The Environmental Crisis**, ed. Harold W. Helfrich, Jr., p. 162.
2. **Ibid.,** 160.

Earth-Times have all joined the crusade to save the environment. "Ecology" has become a fashionable word, and it is being bandied about until people are growing tired of it before they understand what it means—the science of the organism in relation to its whole environment, in relation to other organisms of different species, and to those of its own kind[3]—and under the banner of "ecology" liberals and conservatives, farmers and urbanites, prim suburban housewives and shaggy-haired "eco-freaks" have fallen into step.[4] "Everyone wants to save the environment but no one knows quite what to do."[5] One can hardly pick up a newspaper today without reading at least one story on the environment. People who read these stories are increasingly sympathetic in their reactions.[6] Environmental concerns are no longer the private preserve of the elite who have been long-time members of the Sierra Club, the Audubon Society or the Wilderness Society; the same bell tolls for us all.

Our air, especially in 212 metropolitan areas in which two-thirds of our nation's population lives, is becoming more and more polluted with filthy particles, aerosols, sulphur dioxide, and a whole host of other potentially dangerous gases.[7] We know that sulphur dioxide corrodes brick, stone, metal bridges, car bodies

---

3. This is the definition proposed by a long-time ecologist, Frank Fraser Darling, in his **Wilderness and Plenty** (Boston: Houghton, Mifflin Company, 1970), p. 7.

4. There are, of course, some anti-war activists and some blacks who see the whole matter as an attempt to distract attention from the more crucial issues with which they are more immediately concerned.

5. Frank M. Potter, Jr., "Everyone Wants to Save the Environment But No One Knows Quite What to Do," **Center Magazine**, Vol. 3, No. 2 (March, 1970).

6. Local news stories in Minnesota, however, suggest that people are much more willing to have controls placed on pollutants that relate to someone else's activities than on their own, which they do not see as a serious hazard to the environment.

7. A good primer on air and water pollution is Gerald Leinwand's **Air and Water Pollution** (New York: Washington Square Press, 1969). A good popular treatment of the issues related to air pollution is Donald E. Carr's **Breath of Life** (New York: W. W. Norton & Co., Inc., 1965).

and women's nylons; we are not yet sure what it does to human lungs, but there is increasing evidence that the incidence of chronic respiratory disease rises as the level of sulphur dioxide in the air rises.[8] Experiments have established that benzpyrene, found in urban air, can produce cancer in rodents and dogs.[9] Our milk and fish and hundreds of other foodstuffs are contaminated with DDT and organochlorine pesticide residues. Rachael Carson's popular book, *The Silent Spring,*[10] followed by more erudite scientific accounts of the pesticide story found in Robert Rudd's *Pesticides and the Living Landscape*[11] and Kenneth Mellanby's *Pesticides and Pollution,*[12] has warned us about the insidious chemical warfare we are carrying on against ourselves and our descendants in our effort to stamp out bugs. Our water resources are on a permanent decline thoughout the nation. Though the earth has a bountiful, intricate water system which will never run dry, the usable, reachable, potable water is in increasingly shorter supply. Lake Erie, for example, is fast becoming a huge septic tank. Once a fisherman's delight, it has virtually no fish left.[13] A report by a committee of the National Academy of Sciences estimated that within about twenty years the wastes from industrialized urban centers are expected to overwhelm the biological life in most of the nation's waterways.[14] Our continent-long strips of asphalt

---

8. See Virginia Brodine, "A Special Burden," **Environment,** Vol. 13, No. 2 (March 1971), 22-24, 29-33.

9. **Ibid.,** 33.

10. Rachael Carson, **The Silent Spring** (Boston: Houghton, Mifflin Co., 1962).

11. Robert Rudd, **Pesticides and the Living Landscape** (Madison: University of Wisconsin Press, 1964).

12. Kenneth Mellanby, **Pesticides and Pollution** (London: Fontana Books, 1970).

13. Donald E. Carr's **Death of the Sweet Waters** (New York: W. W. Norton & Co., Inc., 1966) is a good popular treatment of the various facets of water supply and water pollution. Peter Schrag describes the deterioration of Lake Erie in "Life on a Dying Lake," **Saturday Review,** 52 (September 20, 1969), 19-21.

14. Barry Commoner, **Science and Survival** (New York: The Viking Press, 1967), p. 12.

and concrete, with their omnipresent billboards and neon jungles, cover more and more of the nation's earth[15] and pare away the community neighborhoods and remaining wilderness areas.[16] Our blighted and decaying cities have their own perverse ecology, each problem interrelated with others, with stop-gap "solutions" merely shifting the crisis from one area to another.[17] Throughout the land, the refuse of industries' planned obsolescence[18] piles up. Each year we discard seven million automobiles, one hundred million tires, twenty million tons of paper, forty-eight billion cans and twenty-six billion bottles and jars[19]—many of the cans in the form of non-rustable aluminum and the bottles and jars of indestructible plastic. We produce seven pounds of solid waste per capita per day. The sobering remark of the former mayor of Detroit may be true, when he said that we may be remembered as the generation which went to the moon while standing knee-deep in garbage.

My primary task, however, is not to serve as a publicist of the "environmental crisis"; as important as that role is in moving people to action, there are others who can play that role better

---

15. Jesse Unruh, Speaker of the House of Representatives in a state where this problem is especially severe, California, writes: "About 60 percent of all land in fully developed urban areas is handed over, lock, stock, and barrel, to the automobile ... the result is that our cities are overrun by acres of concrete and choked by traffic and life-destroying smog" ("The Highway Lobby," **Earth Day—A Beginning** [New York: Bantam Books, 1970], p. 169).

16. The last chapter of Lewis Munford's **The Highway and the City** (New York: Harcourt, Brace & World, Inc., 1963) is a devastating critique of the United States' "ill conceived and preposterously unbalanced" transportation policy, which is oriented so strongly toward highway programs. See also A. Q. Mowbray's **The Road to Ruin: A Critical View of the Federal Highway Program** (Philadelphia: J. B. Lippincott Co., 1969).

17. At least one large city mayor, John V. Lindsay of New York, shows real sensitivity to the ecological perspective in viewing the problems of urban life. See his article "The Plight of the Cities," **The Progressive**, Vol. 34, No. 4, 29-31.

18. Vance Packard exposes the "planned obsolescence" of American industries in **The Waste Makers** (New York: David McKay Co., Inc., 1960).

19. Richard M. Fagley, "Earth Day and After," **Christian Century**, Vol. 87 (April 15, 1970), 441.

than I. Rather, I shall limit myself to a discussion of those aspects of the "environmental crisis" that can be most clearly illuminated by one whose competence is academic reflection from the perspective of Christian ethics.

Man and Nature

In a widely quoted article, "The Historical Roots of Our Ecologic Crisis,"[20] Lynn White, Jr., an historian of medieval technology, argues that modern technology is, in important respects, a Western phenomenon supported by religious beliefs in the Judeo-Christian tradition, which emphasize man's transcendence of and mastery over nature. In contrast to the creation stories in the mythology of Greco-Roman antiquity, White avers that the Judeo-Christian accounts of creation reflect a highly anthropocentric religion, emphasizing the uniqueness and superiority of man, who has a special calling to dominate nature and to exploit it for human purposes. Because it has nurtured this exploitative attitude toward nature, Christianity bears a huge burden of the guilt for the fact that during the past one hundred-fifty years science and technology have combined to give mankind powers which, from the ecological perspective, have spun out of control. White contends that the only way to solve the ecologic crisis we are now facing is to "reject the Christian axiom that nature has no reason for existence save to serve man."[21]

Those familiar with the multitudinous debates on the "Weber thesis"[22] might well suggest the kinds of arguments that could be raised against White's thesis, which is similar in significant respects to Weber's thesis on the "Protestant ethic." In fact, White's is probably more susceptible to the kind of criticism that has been

---

20. Lynn White, Jr., "The Historical Roots of Our Ecologic Crisis," **Science**, Vol. 155, No. 3767 (March 10, 1967), 1203-1207.

21. **Ibid.**, 1207.

22. For a sample of the debates, see Robert W. Green, ed. **Protestantism and Capitalism: The Weber Thesis and Its Critics** (Boston: D. C. Heath and Co., 1959).

leveled at Weber's thesis, since White is not nearly so careful as Weber to make clear the limitations of the methodology he is employing to explain a complex cultural phenomenon. One can accept White's statement that "human ecology is deeply conditioned by beliefs about our nature and destiny—that is, by religion,"[23] without reducing the cultural influences conditioning human behavior toward the environment to one.[24]

Even if we limit our discussion to the role of ideas in understanding the relationships of culture to the environment, the historic juxtaposition of "man against nature" may well depend much more on modern thought and on more secular ideas expressed by men like Francis Bacon, René Descartes and Gottfried Wilhelm von Leibniz than on religious doctrines derived from Genesis. In an extremely important and comprehensive historical study of the relation between nature and culture in western thought, Clarence J. Glacken demonstrates that it was during the period from the end of the fifteenth until the end of the seventeenth century that the ideas of man as controller of nature began to crystallize along more modern lines. It was in the thought of that period, and not in the commands of God in Genesis, Glacken argues, that there began "a unique formulation of Western thought, marking it off from the other great traditions, such as the Indian and the Chinese, which also are concerned with the relationship of man to nature."[25]

Nevertheless, we cannot deny that there has been a strong tendency in the history of Christian thought to pit "man against nature" and to assert "man's mastery over nature," and it is not difficult to find biblical support for this. The creation account in Genesis 1 is striking. In verses 20-28 a distinction is made

---

23. White, "The Historical Roots of Our Ecologic Crisis," 1205.

24. Lewis W. Moncrief, an anthropologist, strongly criticizes White's thesis for its reductionistic tendencies in "The Cultural Basis for Our Environmental Crisis," Science, Vol. 170 (October 30, 1970), 508-512.

25. Clarence J. Glacken, Traces on the Rhodian Shore, Nature and Culture in Western Thought from Ancient Times to the End of the Eighteenth Century (University of California Press: Berkeley and Los Angeles, 1967), p. 494.

between the acts of God in relation to all of life except man, and the acts of God in relation to man. In the first case, all life is to increase and to multiply; in the second case, man is not only to increase and to multiply but to "fill the earth and subdue it; and have dominion over the fish of the sea and over the birds of the air and over every living thing that moves upon the earth" (v. 28).[26] The theme occurs again after the flood when God blesses Noah and his three sons and tells them to be fruitful and to multiply, to fill the earth, that they are to have dominion over all living things (Gen. 9:3). There is, of course, a second creation account in Genesis.[27] Here instead of being given dominion over the earth, man is given the task of naming things (Gen. 2:20). In this account, "The Lord took the man and put him in the Garden of Eden to till and keep it" (Gen. 2:15). The language of the myth suggests that nature is a garden, and man is to be a gardener or caretaker, not a farmer exploiting nature for economic profit.

The first creation account has undoubtedly been more influential in the history of men's interpretation of their relationship to the earth than the second. Though in their original context the verses in Genesis 1 probably expressed the idea of man set in the midst of creation as a steward, responsible for all that happens to the earth,[28] the interpretation of the Christians who most strongly influenced cultural attitudes toward the environment has not been

---

26. Concerning this verse, Gerhard von Rad writes: "The expressions for the exercise of dominion are remarkably strong: rādā, "tread," "trample" (e.g., the wine press) . . ." (**Genesis: A Commentary,** trans. John H. Marks [Philadelphia: The Westminster Press, 1961], p. 58).

27. The first creation story, Genesis 1:1-2:4a is part of the "P" tradition, and is actually not as old as the second story, Genesis 2:4b-3:24, which is part of the "J" tradition.

28. G. Ernest Wright and Reginald H. Fuller maintain that this passage indicates that man is unique and in the center of the universe, and that he is set apart from all other life forms because God has willed such a role for him. He is "the climax of God's work, set here as a steward, responsible to his Creator for all he does with the world over which he is given dominion" (**The Book of the Acts of God** [Garden City: Anchor Books], 1960, p. 49).

that. A kind of manichean hostility toward nature has been deeply imbued in much of Christian piety in the West. For example, Roderick Nash, in an important though perhaps one-sided study, *Wilderness and the American Mind*,[29] points out how the Puritans inherited a half-conscious bias against the realm of nature, and that they used texts such as Genesis 1:28 to justify their "tradition of repugnance" for nature in the wild. In fact, they tended to regard the "hideous and desolate wilderness" of America as though it were filled with conscious malevolence toward them. The wilderness was the domain of moral wickedness, an extension of the Evil One, the Enemy who opposed the spread of the Kingdom of God. The wilderness favored spontaneity, and therefore sin.

Observers, especially non-Western observers,[30] frequently cite the Genesis passages in criticizing Western civilization and its preoccupation with man and his struggle against nature. Their analysis along with the analysis by Professor White is, I believe, in error because the matter is much more complex. The anthropocentric view of man versus nature has been the predominant concept in the Western tradition, reinforced oftentimes by themes in the Judeo-Christian tradition, but there is also a contrary view in the Western tradition which sees man and nature much more harmoniously, in terms of a sense of unity, an encompassing natural order within which man exists. Historically, we could point to Duns Scotus, Joannes Scotus Erigena, Francis of Assisi, Wordsworth, Goethe, Thoreau, Gerard Manley Hopkins, and the nineteenth and twentieth century naturalists, who all insisted that nature is a sensible order within which man exists; some went so far as to say that nature was a manifestation of the divine demanding deference and reverence. Furthermore, Glacken argues convincingly that modern ecologic theory owes its origin to the design argument in which a wise Creator was inferred from the

---

29. Roderick Nash, **Wilderness and the American Mind** (New Haven: Yale University Press, 1967).

30. See, for example, Daisetz Suzuki, "The Role of Nature in Zen Buddhism, **Eranos-Jahrbuch 1953**, Vol. 22 (Zurich: Rhein-Verlag, 1954), pp. 291-321.

arrangement and harmony of the world where everything is inter-related, and no living thing is useless but shows evidence of purpose.[31] Therefore, though the major theme has been anthropocentric, a minor theme has been biocentric. The major theme speaks of man above and against nature; the minor theme speaks of man in and with nature. There is much theological work to do if we are to reverse the order of the major and minor themes and undo the theological justifications still present in much of contemporary theology[32] which support the destruction of ecosystems, high and low.

The traditional dichotomies of the world of man and the world of nature—man above nature, man against nature, man's control over nature, progress as a divorcement from nature—are outmoded in their usefulness and should be replaced.[33] At the present time, the idea of an ecosystem seems to be a much more illuminating construct for understanding the organization of nature and man's relationship to it. An ecosystem, simply stated, is

a functioning, interacting system composed of one or more organisms and their effective environment, both physical and biological. All ecosystems are open systems. Ecosystems may be stable or unstable. The stable system is in a steady state. The entropy in an unstable system is more likely to increase than decrease. There is a tendency toward diversity in natural ecosystems. There is a tendency toward uniformity

---

31. Glacken, **Traces on the Rhodian Shore**, p. 423.

32. H. Paul Santmire has shown the paucity of Karl Barth's theology of nature in "Creation and Nature: A Study of the Doctrine of Nature with Special Attention to Karl Barth's Doctrine of Creation" (unpublished Th.D. thesis, Harvard University, 1966). He finds support for charging Barth, as well as Bultmann and the so-called "secular theologians" like Harvey Cox, with being guilty of practicing and encouraging an attitude of "compulsive manipulation" toward nature in **Brother Earth** (New York: Thomas Nelson, Inc., 1970), chap. 3.

33. A very helpful essay, making precisely this point, is Clarence Glacken's "Man Against Nature: An Outmoded Concept," **The Environmental Crisis**, ed. Harold W. Helfrich, pp. 127-142.

in artificial ecosystems or those strongly influenced by man.[34]

Stable ecosystems are complex, diverse, and interdependent; unstable ecosystems are simple, uniform, and independent. The ecosystem concept helps us perceive and understand world population growth, the effects of technology, conservation, pollution and wildlife protection. Though we popularly view our human civilization as an increasingly complex one, from the ecological point of view it is enormously and dangerously oversimplifying the natural environment. One-crop farming, urbanization, chemical control of insects are all examples of reducing natural diversity and natural stability.

The anthropocentric view of man versus nature has wreaked its havoc. But perhaps a word of caution needs to be added to guard against the current misanthropic tendencies of many ecologists and their fellow-travelling environmentalists. The uniqueness of the role of man as initiator, and not merely as passive agent, must be understood and affirmed. We need not be reductionistic and submerge the distinction between human and other life forms as it has developed in varying cultural traditions, so there must necessarily remain a central preoccupation with man. In the words of an ecologist,

> What society needs is an ecological humanism: the humanist
> must counteract the misanthropic tendencies of ecologists, and
> the ecologists must make clear to the humanist that human
> life is an integral part of a beautiful system with definable
> limits. If these limits are exceeded, no matter how humanistic
> the intent may be, the consequences can be dehumanizing.[35]

---

34. F. R. Fosberg, "The Preservation of Man's Environment," **Proceedings of the Ninth Pacific Science Congress, 1957**, Vol. 20 (1958), 160, quoted by Ian L. McHarg in "The Place of Nature in the City of Man," **The Annals of the American Academy of Political and Social Science**, Vol. 352 (March, 1964), 5-6.

35. **Peter A. Jordan**, "An Ecologist Responds," **A New Ethic for a New Earth**, ed. Glenn C. Stone (New York: Friendship Press, 1971), p. 93.

The concern for seriously wrestling with the question of what is normatively human must not be dismissed by misanthropic, ecological slogans.

Much of what we have been discussing pertains as much to theology proper as to theological ethics, and it is encouraging to see several recent attempts to develop an "ecological theology."[36] These creative theologians are trying to answer affirmatively the question poignantly put by Joseph Sittler at the third assembly of the World Council of Churches: "Is it possible to fashion a theology catholic enough to affirm redemption's force enfolding nature, as we have affirmed redemption's force enfolding history?"[37] But Christian ethics also has a stake in this enterprise. The convictions about man and nature delineated in theology are a major ingredient in a Christian ethic. The way in which man is understood in relation to God, fellow men, and nature—to add a fourth dimension to H. Richard Niebuhr's interpretative faith triangle to make it a tetrahedron—affects man's disposition toward the world, which belongs to God. The Christian man's disposition toward the world is governed by his acknowledgment of God as the good, the ultimate source of value. As a servant of God, he is to tend and care for the world—with all of its intricate ecosystems— which is God's and not man's. A theological understanding of man which takes ecology seriously also affects the ways in which men think about their purposes and actions in the world. Men are related to one another and to nature in a manner fitting to God's

---

36. Though the term may seem a little too "camp" to some of the authors, there has been a number of sustained treatments of nature from a theological perspective. Among these, a few stand out as noteworthy: Conrad Bonifazi, **Theology of Things: A Study of Man in His Physical Environment** (Philadelphia: J. B. Lippincott Co., 1967); Frederick Elder, **Crisis in Eden: A Religious Study of Man and His Environment** (New York: Abingdon Press, 1970); H. Paul Santmire, **Brother Earth: Nature, God and Ecology in Time of Crisis** (New York: Thomas Nelson, Inc., 1970).

37. Joseph Sittler, "Called to Unity," an address delivered at the World Council of Churches, New Delhi, 1961 (Philadelphia: Muhlenberg Press, 1962).

creation and redemption, both of which encompass the universe as well as man.[38]

An Ethical Framework

Traditionally, ethicists have delineated criteria either as goals or ends to be sought in action, or as laws or governing rules telling us what we ought or ought not to do. Philosophers call the first type of criteria teleological and the second type of criteria deontological. The primary ethical concept in the first is "the good"; the primary ethical concept in the second is "the right." Although some ethicists hew rather closely to one general pattern or the other, many ethicists move freely between them. H. Richard Niebuhr, for example, developed an ethics of "responsibility" as a broader framework within which both the "right" and the "good" might be placed, because he was unhappy with the limitations of the two traditional patterns of ethical reflection. The primary ethical concept of "responsibility" ethics is the "fitting." The idea of "responsibility" emphasizes interaction; men are seen as "responsive beings, who in all [their] actions answer to action upon [them] in accordance with [their] interpretation of such action."[39] Niebuhr elaborates four elements in his theory of moral responsibility, but for the purposes of our discussion two of these elements stand out as important. The first important element of responsibility is accountability.[40] The idea of responsibility as accounta-

---

38. A standard presentation of this cosmic way of viewing God's creative and redemptive activity is Allan D. Galloway's **The Cosmic Christ** (London: Nisbet and Co., 1951).

39. H. Richard Niebuhr, **The Responsible Self** (New York: Harper & Row, 1963), p. 57.

40. My development on the idea of "accountability" moves in a slightly different direction, though not necessarily in an opposing direction, from that proposed by Niebuhr. Basically, I stress the juridical model more than he wanted to do in his discussion of responsibility. I am especially indebted to two authors for clues to the direction taken here. The first is Julian N. Hartt, who in an essay, "Faith and the Informed Use of Natural

bility suggests a forensic setting and relationship. To be responsible is to be required or to be able to answer to charges. Whether in the external forum of law or the internal forum of conscience, one can be judged as to the extent of credit or guilt one is due as a result of one's actions. To be responsible means to accept the obligations one has by virtue of his commitments, his role in society, his power and authority to act in specific situations.

Responsibility as accountability suggests that one must answer for something. We can distinguish two ways in which answering for something can be construed. First, one answers for something by accepting the consequences and punishment for one's actions: "You will answer for this!" In the environmental crisis, man will be held accountable for his nefarious crimes against the ecosystems, for his brutal raping of the environment. The one who acknowledges responsibility bears the burden of his own culpability but also answers for the crimes of others. He will answer, in some sense, not only for his own sins against the biosphere but for the sins of his forefathers as well. Secondly, one "answers for" by speaking on behalf of someone: "Who will answer for him?" Parents answer for their children who are baptized as infants. Consumer organizations attempt to speak for the interests of the unorganized consumer public. The assumption is that those who are "answered for" cannot effectively speak for themselves. This is obviously the case when we think of the members of the biosphere who cannot represent their own interests before the bar of justice. But they do not deserve the death sentence, just because we human beings value our own convenience, appearance or love of killing (which some call sport) more than the lives of these relatively defenseless creatures. As Julian Hartt has put it: "God said to Man in the beginning: 'Over all of this you shall have dominion.'

Resources," **A New Ethic for a New Earth**, ed. Glenn C. Stone, (New York: Friendship Press, 1971), made some suggestive comments concerning "responsibility." A second author to whom I am indebted is H. L. A. Hart, who works out very carefully the various aspects of "responsibility" in the legal framework in his essays in **Punishment and Responsibility** (Oxford: Clarendon Press, 1968).

God did not say: 'For all of this you shall be the executioner.' "[41]

The second element of responsibility that is pertinent to our topic is social solidarity. This idea might best be understood by comparing it with the view of the relationship between man and community that is found in classical liberalism, the ideology which has had a profound influence on American political culture and for which John Locke is an eloquent spokesman. Locke views man as "absolute lord of his own person and possessions . . . and subject to nobody." The reason men join together in the "social compact" is the "mutual *Preservation* of their Lives, Liberties and Estates," the three basic goods which he sums up in one general term, "Property."[42] He thinks of the individual as essentially able to fulfill his life on his own. The chief end of community, specifically of government, is to help one preserve his property, something he is unable to do by himself. Ultimately, the purposes, as well as the limits, of governmental action are determined by the one end or value which must be established or secured: the free and unhampered development of the individual. Thoroughly consistent with this view is the attitude of those today who argue that their land is their own to do with as they please and that what they do is strictly their own affair. In basic disagreement with this way of understanding the relationship between the individual and society, the idea of "social solidarity" emphasizes that man is fundamentally, by nature, a social being. That is not simply to say that he is gregarious, that he enjoys the company of his fellows, although this is true of man, as it is also of baboons and honeybees. Rather, man is social in the sense that his true being, his essence, necessitates involvement in a human community. Aristotle, in the opening pages of the *Politics,* says that man is

---

41. Julian N. Hartt, "Faith and the Informed Use of Natural Resources," p. 79.

42. John Locke, **The Second Treatise of Government: An Essay Concerning the True Original Extent and End of Government,** Chap. VI, par. 57; Chap. IX, par. 123, in **Two Treatises of Government** (A Critical Edition), ed. with an introd. and apparatus criticus by Peter Laslett (Cambridge: The University Press, 1950), pp. 323-24, 368.

by nature a being intended to live in a political community. Those men who, by choice, live outside such a community are, he says, either lower or higher than other men—that is, either animals or angels.[43] The human personality, in its development, structure, and continued functioning, is bound up with the social group or groups of which it is a significant member. The influence of the community upon the individual is primarily positive, formative, and supportive. The idea of social solidarity, especially when viewed within the Christian faith, does not conceive of man as able to fulfill his life on his own. He is created for others, and only in sharing in the life of the community can his own life be fulfilled.

If we take "social solidarity" seriously, we become aware that we cannot maintain a *laissez - faire* attitude toward private property. We become aware of the artificiality of private property boundaries —even of city, state, national and continental boundaries. We are all bound together in a vast network of interconnected systems of life. The pollution emerging from one manufacturing plant becomes the common pollution of the city, which becomes the common pollution of all cities, which becomes the common pollution of the earth, as the gaseous effluents being poured into the air shed mix together. All men share one environment, and we must begin to treat the earth as a total system of air, water and land.

The idea of "social solidarity" suggests that all relationships exist in a continuity through time and across the space boundaries of human communities. While particular actions take place in particular moments, these actions have a continuity with actions of the past and have effects that shape the future. Present actions are part of a whole pattern that looks forward as well as backward. While one is not bound by all past actions—in a kind of historical determinism which prevents meaningful decision—and cannot anticipate all the future consequences of one's actions, one must understand that actions are responsible when they are conscientiously related to a continuing community of beings.

---

43. Aristotle, **Politics**, 1253a.

This provides us with significant insight when we reflect upon our relation to the environment. We have inherited our trusteeship for the present environment—the air shed, the river systems, the oceans, the forests, the wild-life—from past generations, and we will transmit the trust to future generations. We have been great exploiters, but poor trustees. We and our forefathers have said, in effect, in the words of the British scientific journalist, Lord Ritchie-Calder:

> To hell with posterity! After all, what have the unborn ever done for us? Nothing. Did they, with sweat and misery, make the Industrial Revolution possible? Did they go down in the carboniferous forests of millions of years ago to bring up coal to make wealth and see nine-tenths of the carbon belched out as chimney soot? Did they drive the plows that broke the plains to release the dust that the buffalo had trampled and fertilized for centuries? Did they have to broil in steel plants to make the machines and see the pickling acids pour into the sweet waters of rivers and lakes? Did they have to labor to cut down tall timbers to make homesteads and provide newsprint for the Sunday comics and the celluloid for Hollywood spectaculars, leaving the hills naked to the eroding rains and winds? Did they have the ingenuity to drill down into the Paleozoic seas to bring up the oil to feed the internal-combustion engines so that their exhausts could create smog? Did they have the guts to man rigs out at sea so that boreholes could probe for oil in the offshore fissures of the San Andreas Fault? Did they endure the agony and the odium of the atom bomb and spray the biosphere with radioactive fallout? All that the people yet unborn have done is to wait and let us make the mistakes. To hell with posterity! That, too, can be arranged.[44]

Responsibility suggests that it is up to us to reverse this attitude, to reassign priorities so that the inheritance we leave to pos-

---

44. Lord Ritchie-Calder, "Polluting the Environment," **Center Magazine,** Vol. 2, No. 3 (May 1969), 7.

terity might be at least as good as that which we have ourselves received.

An additional dimension needs to be added to the idea of social solidarity to make it relate to the concerns we have been addressing. Thus far our comments concerning social solidarity have focused primarily upon the human community, and we have tended to look at the environment in a utilitarian manner, that is in terms of the "resources" it provides for the community of man. But if we are to take seriously the need for reordering our understanding of the relationship between man and nature, as I suggested earlier, it would be quite inappropriate to stop there. We need to think of nature as having a value and a significance and a *raison d'etre* which is at least in part independent of the value and significance and *raison d'etre* of man. We need an ethic that includes all the members of the biosphere, and not only man. In this vein, in a book which was written more than twenty years ago and which has become classic in the conservation-ecological movement, *A Sand County Almanac,* Aldo Leopold penned some prophetic words calling for the development of a "land ethic" and an "ecologic conscience." He wrote:

> The extension of ethics, so far studied only by philosophers, is actually a process in ecological evolution. Its sequences may be described in ecological as well as in philosophical terms. An ethic, ecologically, is a limitation on freedom of action in the struggle for existence. An ethic, philosophically, is a differentiation of social from anti-social conduct. . . . The thing has its origin in the tendency of interdependent individuals or groups to evolve modes of cooperation. The ecologist calls these symbioses. Politics and economics are advanced symbioses in which original free-for-all competition has been replaced, in part, by cooperative mechanisms with an ethical content. . . . There is as yet no ethic dealing with man's relation to land and to animals and plants which grow upon it. . . . The extension of ethics to this third element in human environment is, if I read the evidence correctly, an evolutionary possibility and an ecological necessity. . . . All ethics so far

evolved rest upon a single premise: that the individual is a member of a community of interdependent parts. His instincts prompt him to compete for his place in community, but his ethics prompt him also to cooperate (perhaps in order that there may be a place to compete for). The land ethic simply enlarges the boundaries to include soils, waters, plants, and animals, or collectively, the land.[45]

The ethic which Leopold was calling for might well be delineated in terms of a reinterpreted version of the "common good," a concept which has a long history in the tradition which most of you know much more intimately than I; but the notion of a "common good" has not seeped very deeply into popular American consciousness, in which the notion of private "interests," or at best an aggregative "public interest," has predominated. The distinction between the notions of "good" and "interest" is an important one and requires elaboration.

There is room only for a cursory review of the meaning of the concept of the "common good" in the tradition which has articulated it most fully. It obviously traces back at least to Aristotle, who used the analogy of a living organism when he wrote about the *polis*. Just as the function of a human organism cannot be conceived as merely the sum of the functions of the heart, liver, limbs, brains, etc., so the function of the *polis* cannot be conceived as merely the sum of its parts, in Aristotle's view. The organism is a whole of which the heart, liver, limbs, etc. are parts; and without all the parts the whole organism cannot perform its function—or perform it so well. But the function performed by the whole is a function of the whole alone, and it can never be simply resolved into its physiological components. Thus when Aristotle insists that man exists ultimately for the sake of the good life, he is referring to the good life of each man and the good life of the *polis,* which he regards as one and the same.[46]

---

45. Aldo Leopold, **A Sand County Almanac** (New York: Oxford University Press, 1966), pp. 217-219.

46. Aristotle, **Nicomachean Ethics**, 1097a13-1098a20.

In Aristotle's theory there is an exact correspondence between the *polis* and the "good" for man, which he calls *eudaimonia* or "well being." [47] The *polis* is the term or end of all human communities; and it is the organized expression of the unity which does or ought to govern all human activities in all their diversity. Likewise, the "good" for man, *eudaimonia* or "well being," is the term or end of all human action, and it is implicit as the term or end of every human action. This exact correspondence helps us understand why Aristotle views the final end of human life, the "good" for man, as being one and the same whether we are considering one man or the *polis*.

Without going into the modifications of this conception of the "common good" which were made by St. Thomas and later Roman Catholic theorists—we can see the usefulness of this general conception of man as inter-related in a larger whole, whose "well being" is intrinsically tied to the "well being" of the whole community. In developing an environmental ethic, however, we must go beyond Aristotle, and talk not merely of the "common good" of the community of men, but of the "common good" of the total biotic community. [48] The basic principle of Leopold's ecologic conscience is applicable here: "A thing is right when it tends to preserve the integrity, stability, and beauty of the biotic community. It is wrong when it tends otherwise." [49] The "good" for man is

---

47. I am following W. D. Ross here, in translating **eudaimonia** not as "happiness," which seems to have reference to emotions or feelings, but as "well being," which is more non-committal and refers to a kind of activity—as Aristotle insisted was the case with **eudaimonia** (**Aristotle** [Cleveland: Meridan Books, 1962], p. 186).

48. I have not provided a full treatment of Aristotle's theology of nature here, but one can find in the **Politics** the suggestion that nature exists for man. Plants are intended for the use of animals; animals, we can infer, exist for man. He writes: "Now if Nature makes nothing incomplete, and nothing in vain, the inference must be that she has made all animals for man" (**Politics**, 1256a18-30, 1256b10-25). The conception of the relationship between man and nature here is clearly anthropocentric.

49. Quoted by Thomas Merton in "The Wild Places," **The Ecological Conscience,** ed. Robert Disch (Englewood Cliffs: Prentice-Hall, Inc., 1970), p. 43.

intrinsically tied to the "good" of the biotic community, and the "good" of that community is that which is conducive to its "health" as a dynamic yet balanced ecosystem.

This general interpretation of the ends of man, which emphasizes the inter-dependence between men, and between men and the other members of the biosphere, is in notable contrast to the "liberal" view of man, to which we have previously alluded. While those in the Aristotelian tradition refer to the ends men seek as "goods," those in the "liberal" tradition refer to the ends men seek as "interests." Although the concept of "interest," in various forms, is now a commonplace in political discourse, it is a relatively recent innovation. It has considerably different connotations from the "common good," which we have just discussed. The term "interest" carries individualistic and subjective connotations which, at least until very recent interpretations of ethical theory, have seldom been associated with the concept of "good." Indeed, it was not until the satisfaction of subjective, individual interests came to be regarded as the primary objective of politics, during the rise of modern utilitarianism in the seventeenth and eighteenth centuries, that "interest" could replace "good" as the primary justificatory concept related to the collective ends in political life.[50] Individual interest came to be conceived as "desires" of which the individual is aware and of which he is the best judge,[51] in contrast to the notion of "good" which suggests that which would promote or entail the healthy functioning or well-being of a person, group or community.

---

50. S. S. Wolin provides an extensive analysis of the transition of thought referred to here in his book, **Politics and Vision** (Boston: Little, Brown & Co., 1960). Another good treatment of this same issue is provided by Richard E. Flathman in **The Public Interest** (New York: John Wiley & Sons, Inc., 1966), esp. chap. 2.

51. Jeremy Bentham, for example, insisted upon "interest" as the standard for evaluating public policy. Concerning the "public interest," Bentham writes: "The interest of the community then is, what?—the sum of the several members who compose it" (A Fragment on Government and Principles of Morals and Legislation [Oxford: Basil Blackwell, 1948], p. 126).

The distinction between "interest" and "good" is thus partially one of difference between a "subjective" and an "objective" determination of what ends are to be valued; "interest" has a more subjective connotation than "good."[52] Another way to differentiate "interest" from "good" is, following Brian Barry, to distinguish "want-regarding" principles, "which take wants as given," from "ideal-regarding" principles, "which rank the satisfaction of some wants higher than the satisfaction of others even if the preferences of the person whose wants are in question are different."[53] According to Barry, ideal-regarding principles are the contradictories of want-regarding principles. This is a helpful way to distinguish "interest" concepts from "good" concepts, but I do not follow Barry in his undue deprecation of ideal-regarding principles as so "idiosyncratic, fluctuating and vague" that it is scarcely correct to speak of them as "principles" at all.[54] We need ideal-regarding principles, such as the "common good," because the reordering of governmental policies, urban and educational planning, consumptive habits, individual life styles and basic cultural attitudes, in such a way as to take into account the ecological facts of life, cannot be accomplished by merely allowing men to express their "wants" or "interests" in the pluralistic, political market place. Unless one assumes, à la Adam Smith, the existence of a benevolent "invisible hand"—the existence of which could be called into serious question by the present state of our environmental crisis—

---

52. For a discussion of the distinction between "subjective" and "objective" determinations of the social good, see Alan Gewirth, "Political Justice," Social Justice, ed. Richard B. Brandt (Englewood Cliffs: Prentice-Hall, Inc., 1962), pp. 158, 162. Gewirth, however, does not relate these two connotations to "interest" and "good," as I have done. He prefers to refer to both connotations as aspects of "good." In arguing as I have above, I am well aware that there are many ethical theorists who would define the "good" as the object of desire, thus making it subjectively determined. However, I think G. E. Moore's "open question" argument in Principia Ethica (Cambridge: The University Press, 1966), p. 43, is persuasive in refuting those who would define the good in this manner.

53. Brian Barry, Political Argument (London: Routledge & Kegan Paul, 1965), p. 287.

54. Ibid., 95.

one cannot avoid the task of formulating ethical principles to help interpret and direct our actions in political life.

A notion of the "common good" which takes ecology seriously is an important, perhaps *the* most important, element in the development of an environmental ethic. We should not be misanthropic, but we must be aware that there is finally only one ecology—not a human ecology on the one hand and a subhuman ecology on the other. Ecology allows us to see the complex mosaic of the world from the human vantage point without being fanatically man-centered, remaining pre-Copernician, insisting that the cosmos revolves around us. The environment is a complex, subtly balanced system, and it is this integrated whole which maintains and guarantees the quality of human life concomitant with the quality of life in the whole biotic community. And it is this environment which is being subjected to such diverse and potent attacks, which if left unchecked may prove fatal to the complex fabric of the biosphere. It is this environment which we must include within our refurbished doctrine of the "common good" as we develop an environmental ethic. May this be our hope, our commitment and our pledge as we courageously venture into the future.

5 The Ethics of Belief: Methodological Implications

JOHN J. MAWHINNEY

The problem of religious doubt and unbelief is a foremost problem for the consciousness of many today. Van A. Harvey recently stressed a fascinating aspect of this problem: many today experience it not so much as an intellectual problem as a moral one. Religious belief is seen as a temptation to one's moral integrity, as an act of intellectual dishonesty, and so, for some, "religious doubt becomes a matter of conscience."[1] Though Harvey does not say this, we might add that this is perhaps true for any kind of belief—religious, so-called quasi-religious or otherwise. An increasing number fear that to believe is to run the risk of being co-opted, of being used and thus of endangering one's personal integrity. To paraphrase Harvey in a slightly different context: The pathos of modern man does not lie primarily in his realization that his craving for certainty can never be satisfied, but rather "in his awareness of the falsifying influence belief frequently exercises on critical judgment, so that he is most distrustful of just those answers he would most like to believe."[2] In brief, an awareness of a desire to believe often presents us with a serious moral problem: is it honest to do so?

Harvey believes that the moral element in religious doubt became especially evident in the nineteenth century when the new

---

1. Van A. Harvey, "Reflections on the Teaching of Religion in America," *Journal of the American Academy of Religion*, 38 (1970), 18.

2. Van A. Harvey, **The Historian and the Believer: The Morality of Historical Knowledge and Christian Belief** (New York: Macmillan, 1966), p. 103. In the context Harvey is concerned with the impact of the new ideal of historical knowledge on the modern mind.

ideal of historical judgment precipitated a confrontation between biblical criticism and traditional belief. Though this confrontation involved issues of epistemology, metaphysics and methodology as well as other elements, Harvey thinks that it can be best understood if it is seen as a "conflict between two kinds of sensibilities, two moralities of judgment, and the ways in which these moralities are compounded with beliefs about the world in general and the past in particular."[3] In *The Historian and the Believer* he explores this hypothesis for the light which it may throw on the contemporary discussion of the so-called problem of faith and history. He holds that the stance and ideal of critical judgment to which the historian is committed is an expression of a certain morality of knowledge which has most profound revolutionary implications for religious belief in general and Christian belief in particular.[4]

What is this new ideal of knowledge and of historical judgment? Harvey's answer to this question is a reformulation of the view of Ernest Troeltsch. The new ideal of critical historical inquiry rests on three interrelated principles.[5]

First, no historical judgment can claim more than a greater or lesser degree of probability. Consequently, it is always subject to revision and incapable of supporting any claim of absolute truth. Harvey sees this principle as offering a profound challenge to traditional Christian faith: "If the theologian believes on faith that certain events occurred, the historian regards all historical claims as having only a greater or lesser degree of probability, and he regards the attachment of faith to these claims as a corruption of historical judgment."[6]

Secondly, these judgments of probability can be made only if we assume that the experience of men in the past was basically analogous and comparable to our own present experience. Without some principle of analogy we could not hope to understand the

---

3. "Reflections on the Teaching of Religion in America," loc. cit.
4. **The Historian and the Believer**, op. cit., pp. xiii-xiv, 68 and 103-104.
5. **Ibid.**, pp. 14-15.
6. **Ibid.**, p. 5.

past at all. This principle rules out any claim which would regard a religious event or truth as unique, final or absolute. As Harvey puts it: "If the theologian believes that the events upon which Christendom rests are unique, the historian assumes that those events, like all events, are analogous to those in the present and that it is only on this assumption that statements about them can be assessed at all."[7]

Thirdly, and closely related to the first two principles, the phenomena of human life are so interrelated and interdependent that a radical change at one point cannot occur without effecting changes throughout the space-time continuum. In other words, not only are all events historically conditioned, but also no event can be isolated from other events in space and time. All events can be explained and understood only in terms of their antecedents and consequences. The theologian may believe that the Scriptures, origins, dogmas and practices of Christianity, and even Christian faith itself, have a divine or supernatural origin. The historian, however, must regard such explanations as a hindrance to true understanding. He must assume that they are intelligible only in terms of their historical context and that they are subject to the same principles of interpretation and criticism as are other ideas and social institutions.[8] But though the conclusions of the new ideal of historical inquiry present a serious challenge to traditional Christian faith, they are not the most serious issue involved. The really crucial issue lies in the method itself, in its ideal of judgment and of knowledge and in the assumptions on which it rests. The method implies a new morality of critical judgment and of knowledge. This morality is incompatible with the traditional Christian ethics of belief. Harvey distinguishes some interrelated aspects of this new moral ideal.[9]

---

7. **Ibid.**

8. **Ibid.** Here one thinks of the work of E. Durkheim, M. Weber, E. Troeltsch, and more recently, P. Berger, Thos. Luckmann and Robt. Bellah among others. The discipline of the sociology of knowledge, in particular, raises serious issues for traditional interpretations of Christian Faith.

9. **Ibid.**, p. 38.

First, the modern critical ideal insists that man has a right, free of any authority, to think for himself. The intellectual autonomy of the scholar and the will-to-truth take precedence over obedience to authority and the will-to-believe. Accordingly, the past, including all its beliefs and values, has no authority apart from what critical inquiry can confer upon it. This stress on man's autonomy, however, cannot be regarded as a form of subjectivism, nor does it presume a naive confidence in man's actually achieved rationality, for other aspects of the new morality of knowledge stress that man has the responsibility to exercise sound and balanced judgment and to communicate his "conclusions to others in such a way that these conclusions can be assessed" by competent persons.[10]

Finally, the new ideal of critical judgment requires that the historian use the same canon for making judgments about the past as he uses for making judgments about the present. In making judgments about the present the historian presupposes his present, critically interpreted experience, and so he makes use of the best knowledge and methods of investigation available to his time even though he realizes that subsequent generations may question their adequacy. The new method of critical inquiry, however, insists that the historian, irrespective of any faith claims or inherited beliefs, *must* use this same present, critically interpreted experience also in making judgments about the past.[11] The *must* of this last sentence is important because it is at this point that the new morality of knowledge or ethic of assent clashes with the moral ideal and ethic of belief which has long characterized Christian faith in the West. Faith and belief, instead of being virtues, are now sins, while doubt, once a sin, has become a virtue. The dictum of the old morality was that faith seeks understanding, or, as Pascal put it, the heart has reasons which reason itself cannot know. However, the new ethic of assent demands that faith seek not understanding but conformity to the methodological procedures and knowledge of the present intellectual community. It requires

---

10. **Ibid.**, p. 43.
11. **Ibid.**, p. 99.

that the reasons of the heart be subjected to severe critical scrutiny. Thus it identifies integrity, moral as well as intellectual, not with loyalty to one's inherited faith, but with loyalty to the thought structures and critical standards of the present.[12] (Of course, these thought structures and critical standards of the present must not be regarded as beyond scrutiny. Like the standards of the past, they, too, must be constantly criticized, re-evaluated and revised.) In brief, the new ethic of assent questions the honesty and sincerity of the old morality. It fears that the old morality corrodes the delicate machinery of sound historical judgment because it lets the desire to believe convert assertions with a very low degree of probability into statements of high probability.[13]

Yet these elements by themselves can hardly account for the moral and intellectual revolution that today challenges traditional Christian faith. Historical thinking and the moral ideal of knowledge it implies produced revolutionary consequences for Christian faith only after the new critical ideal had become "informed by the new way of looking at the world created by the sciences."[14] The so-called common-sense and taken-for-granted view of the world of modern man results from the absorption into our natural habits of thought two elements: first, the new ideal of critical judgment; and secondly, the new world-picture of the sciences. Accordingly, when a conflict occurs today between faith and reason, our tendency is to resolve it not only in terms of a new morality of judgment but also in terms of a new way of understanding ourselves and the world.[15] Traditional Christian faith, then, is doubly periled: its ethics of assent has been reversed; its way of understanding man, the world and thus God has been replaced.

---

12. **Ibid.**, p. 103.

13. **Ibid.**, pp. 104, 119 and 123-124.

14. **Ibid.**, p. 68.

15. The point here is not that present knowledge or the current world-view can be simply equated with the world picture derived from the sciences, for this is certainly not the case. Even for scholars the current world-view includes many truisms, generalizations, value-judg-

This brings us to the so-called problem of faith and history. The issue here is not whether Christian faith is immune to all historical criticism, for Harvey takes for granted that it is not so immune. The issue is whether Christian faith is tied to certain specific historical assertions which are less than fully justified; or more positively, how we might understand the significance of the event of Jesus of Nazareth for the Christian "without so stating it that one necessarily collides with the morality of historical knowledge."[16]

Harvey finds his answer to this question in what he terms "the perspectival image or memory-impression of Jesus." What he means by this expression can best be grasped by distinguishing it from three other possible levels of meaning of "Jesus of Nazareth" and by pointing out the relationship of these four levels of meaning to one another.[17] (1) The actual Jesus, or Jesus as he really was: this refers to Jesus as he was in the past when he lived on earth. Since no historical personage can ever be fully recovered or described, *a fortiori*, Jesus, about whom so little information is known, can never be recovered as he actually was. (2) The historical Jesus: this term describes Jesus insofar as he is actually recoverable through the data which is discoverable by modern historical methodology. (3) The perspectival image or memory-impression of Jesus: this term designates Jesus as he was actually remembered by those who knew him, and so, refers to the way he impressed those who came into contact with him. This impression was, of course, highly selective and even subjective, but it is not necessarily less true just because it was not obtained through methods of modern historical research; "otherwise we would have to discard most of the memory-impressions of our

---

ments and so forth which are certainly not derived simply from the sciences. Harvey's point is that the way modern men look at the world and themselves as well as their ideal of critical judgment is by-and-large the reverse of what it was traditionally in the West. Cf. Harvey, **ibid.**, pp. 73-89, **passim.**

16. **Ibid.**, pp. 265-266.
17. **Ibid.**, pp. 266-268.

families and friends." (4) The Biblical Christ: this refers to the transformation of the memory-impression "under the influence of the theological interpretation of the actual Jesus by the Christian community."[18]

How does the perspectival image or memory-impression of Jesus of Nazareth help us to understand the significance of his event without our colliding with the morality of historical knowledge? Harvey argues that though the memory-impression reflects an interpretation, this interpretation is in close contact with an authentic historical tradition, and its historical accuracy can be tested in accordance with accepted, modern historical methodology.[19] The distinction between the memory-impression and the Biblical Christ suggests, first, the possibility of the historian comparing the two images, whereas a failure to distinguish among various images would obscure this possibility. Secondly, it suggests the arbitrariness of assuming that the historian cannot get behind an interpreted picture. Thirdly, those who have handed down the memory-impression may thereby have unintentionally (unconsciously) provided data which the historian can sort out and even use to test the historical accuracy of the memory-impression itself. The new questers (Fuchs, Ebeling, Käsemann, Bornkamm, etc.) have shown that much more historical data can be obtained from the memory-impressions of Jesus in the New Testament than many had once thought.[20] Therefore, it is possible for the Christian to accept in faith a certain understanding of the significance of the event of Jesus of Nazareth without colliding with the modern ethic of assent or the new morality of knowledge. The Christian does not need to fear historical criticism nor does he have to accept specific historical propositions that are not fully justified.

---

18. Ibid., p. 267. Harvey would have done well if he had also distinguished a fifth level of meaning: the post-Biblical Christ or the Christ of the tradition, referring to further transformations of the memory-impression under the impact of post-biblical theological interpretations and popular religious devotional activity.

19. Ibid., p. 276.

20. Cf. ibid., pp. 251-252 and 277-281.

What is the relationship between this memory-impression of Jesus and Christian faith? Harvey holds that Christian faith "does not depend on getting behind the Biblical picture of Christ" nor does it have any clear connection with "any particular set of historical beliefs." Faith is "trust and commitment." As such, it is concerned "with one's confidence in God" and "with one's surrender of his attempts to establish his own righteousness and his acceptance of his life and creation as a gift and a responsibility." Some may link their faith-awareness with specific historical beliefs, but this is not necessary. The Johannine Christ has always been a powerful medium of grace even though it is judged today to have only a slight resemblance to the historical Jesus. Likewise, throughout the centuries the faith of many Christians has been tied to stories and theological doctrines which we today judge to be false or mythological. Yet these stories and doctrines have often been extraordinarily forceful and even the chief vehicles for passing on the genuine faith of the Church. Thus certain kinds of historically false stories and mythological doctrines can mediate faith as well as genuine history can.[21]

But while granting this point, Harvey still argues "that the call to faith may be made far more powerful for modern men if interpreted in terms of the memory-image of Jesus."[22] He distinguishes two kinds of belief, each with its corresponding kind of certitude.[23] First, there is the belief about a contingent fact remote from our own experience, namely, that the actual Jesus was as the perspectival image depicts him. Depending on the data and warrants that support it, this belief may or may not possess a high degree of certitude, but "it can never have the immediacy of an event that impinges on my own life." Secondly, there is the belief that the perspectival image illumines our present experience and "our relationships to that upon which we are absolutely dependent." This second belief is concerned with the revelatory value of the perspectival image, that is, "with the adequacy of this

21. Ibid., pp. 280-281.
22. Ibid., p. 281.
23. Ibid., pp. 281-282.

image for interpreting the structure and character of reality itself."
No contingent event of the past can guarantee the revelatory value
of this image, for there is no intrinsic connection between this
second belief and an objective, external historical event *"unless
faith is already presupposed."* Such a belief must have its ground
in one's present experience. Appeal to a past event can have
importance here only in that it may provide a symbol or image
"to which we can return again and again and use in our present
relationships with others [*sic*]."[24]

Accordingly, though there may be a relationship between the
perspectival image and the historical Jesus, faith finds its object
and certitude not in this relationship but in the viability of the
image for interpreting reality as a whole. For Harvey, then, the
significance of Jesus Christ consists in his being "the key image
in a parable which the Christian uses to interpret the more inclusive reality with which all men are confronted and of which
they try to make some sense."[25] This image or symbol is "a function
of the weight and valence attached to this or that experience and
the way in which these, in turn, influence the symbols and categories
men use to relate themselves to other experiences in the light
of certain interests."[26] The "existential" certitude of the believer
lies not in a historical verification of the correlation between this
symbol and the actual Jesus, but "in the brute givenness of these
experiences although, if he is not a 'blind' believer, he will seek
to compare these experiences with those of other men and to test
his interpretation in all the ways that seem possible."[27]

As we noted above, Harvey believes that for most Christians
today the most powerful interpretation of the Jesus of Nazareth
symbol would be in terms of the memory-image of Jesus. Yet,
the Jesus of Nazareth symbol could be interpreted in any way that
"illumines our experience and our relationship to that upon which

---

24. **Ibid.,** p. 283.
25. **Ibid.**
26. **Ibid.,** p. 284.
27. **Ibid.,** p. 285.

we are absolutely dependent."[28] But however this symbol may be interpreted, it is never just a timeless truth. A symbol is always rooted in history because we understand the present only as it is revealed in the past, and this means in terms of past events. Harvey calls such events paradigmatic events—that is, events which "are believed to focus some insight into the nature of reality insofar as it bears on the human quest for liberation and fulfilment"[29] or which constitute "a central focus of illumination that provides the basis for interpreting life as a whole."[30]

Harvey concludes by arguing for the need "to appreciate the implications of the historicity of human existence for theology itself."[31] He suggests that his position might be called "a radical historical confessionalism" in that it

> tries to take with utmost seriousness both the Protestant principle of justification by faith and the historical character of human existence, of which the morality of historical knowledge is but a formalized constitutive part. *The Christian community cannot disavow its own historical past,* a past that constitutes the Christ event as the decisive one for its self-understanding. Consequently, it has no other vocation than to represent the proclamation about Jesus again and again. On the other hand, the significance of Jesus lies precisely in the relevance of his image for understanding that final reality which confronts men in all events. *Christians turn to Jesus* not in order to rehabilitate any exclusive claim that a defensive Christianity wishes to make but because it understands that human beings only seem to decide concerning the truth about life in general when they are confronted by a life in particular. The Christian community confesses that this has happened to it and that this can happen again to those who would attend

---

28. **Ibid.,** p. 282.

29. **Ibid.,** p. 258.

30. William A. Christian, **Meaning and Truth in Religion** (Princeton: Princeton U. Press, 1964); cited by Harvey, loc. cit.

31. Harvey, **ibid.,** pp. 286-287.

to this image. This is its *historical* destiny. It is most faithful to that destiny and the image of *him who initiated it* when it simply accepts and rejoices in that destiny and ceases to claim for this *historical reality* an exclusiveness that, when claimed, surrenders the very truth to which it witnesses. [emphasis added][32]

This concluding paragraph of Harvey's book raises for me some questions about the nature of the theological enterprise itself—questions which I believe Harvey, in his concern with the problem of the morality of knowledge, should have confronted explicitly even though he did not need to make them a central concern.

On the one hand, Harvey admits, indeed, "stresses" that the existential certitude of the believer lies in the viability of the symbol for illuminating the character and structures of reality itself and not in any correlation between the image and what it is supposed to represent.[33] He points out that throughout the centuries the faith of Christians has often been mediated through stories, doctrines and images which we today consider false, mythological or unhistorical. Yet, on the other hand, Harvey emphasizes the importance of history for Christian faith.[34] He points out that the Christian community "cannot disavow its own historical past— a past that constitutes the Christ event as the decisive one for its self-understanding." He tells us that "Christians turn to Jesus" as the one who initiated their historical destiny because "human beings only seem to decide concerning the truth about life in general when they are confronted by a life in particular." Harvey is surely referring here to something more than just the history of the Church's self-understanding and faith, for otherwise he would be dissolving Jesus into a creation of the community of believers. Nor does he mean merely that after Easter Jesus was given titles and designations which he did not previously have.

---

32. **Ibid.,** pp. 288-289.
33. Cf. **ibid.,** p. 285.
34. **Ibid.,** p. 288.

It is clear that for Harvey the convictions stirred up by the Biblical story are responses to beliefs about certain facts. The very fact that Harvey even wrote this book testifies to this point.

How might these two juxtaposed points about Christian faith precipitate for the Christian a conflict with the new morality of knowledge? From one point of view it could be maintained that they do not precipitate such a conflict. We could argue, as Harvey does, that the real power of the Christian symbols lies precisely in their functional role and not just in the fact that something happened.[35] The task of the Christian theologian would then be to elucidate what this functional role is without precipitating a conflict with the new morality of knowledge. Using Robert N. Bellah's term I would say that this was an interpretation of Christianity along the lines of a symbolic realism in contrast to the more traditional interpretations of Christianity in terms of historical realism.[36] Eugene Fontinell's *Toward A Reconstruction of Religion* is another good recent example of interpreting Christianity along the lines of symbolic realism.[37] From this point of view Harvey has presented a good case to show how the Christian can assent to certain historical propositions without "corrupting the balance of judgment which is the *sine qua non* of critical historical work."[38] Certainly some Christians today (how many is another issue) would find the call to faith more powerful if it were interpreted in terms of the memory-image of Jesus of Nazareth. Harvey's effort, then, to accomplish the task he sets for himself is a good one.

But Harvey accomplishes this task by working as a *Christian* theologian. He takes the various Christian symbols which the community has inherited from the past and tries to clarify them and see how these symbols might illumine the historical and

---

35. Cf. **ibid.,** pp. 251-252.

36. Robert N. Bellah, "Christianity and Symbolic Realism," **Journal for the Scientific Study of Religion,** 9 (1970), 89-96; reprinted in his **Beyond Belief: Essays on Religion in a Post-Traditional World** (New York: Harper & Row, 1970), pp. 246-257.

37. (Garden City: Doubleday, 1970).

38. Harvey, **op. cit.,** p. 33.

present character of reality insofar as it bears on the human quest for liberation and fulfillment. Now there is no logical reason why a theologian cannot delimit his task in this way, but there is a twofold danger.

First, if a theologian delimits his task to clarifying, developing and reconstructing the symbols of some religious tradition, he can easily blind himself to the possibility that this tradition is no longer a vital force in the world he lives in, that the religion and culture to which these symbols give expression are dying or are already dead. Certainly, many cultures, civilizations, religious traditions and institutions which had once been vital forces in the world have died and disappeared—or at least they have been so sublimated or transformed by the confluence of other cultures and civilizations that they have ceased to exist as factors distinguishable in their own right. We need only to recall the religions of many primitive peoples or the great civilizations of the Babylonians, Assyrians, Aztecs and, in many ways, even the Greeks and Romans.

In the judgment of many today what we know as the Western world is in a state of collapse and has, in fact, been collapsing for several centuries. They would compare our present turmoil both to the desperate effort of the dying to resist extinction as well as to the labor pains of a mother struggling to give birth. They would see a convergence of a number of social, technological, cultural and religious forces, both old and new. Out of this convergence there would emerge a new culture and civilization with its own social and religious symbols. Though this new order would be conditioned by, and thus have some continuity with, the old order, it would at the same time be something genuinely novel and distinct.

A theologian who wishes to do his theology within the confines of a particular tradition must be willing to face the challenge of the new morality of knowledge and the position of those who hold for the collapse of the so-called Western world. In my judgment the two writers whom I mentioned earlier, Eugene Fontinell and Robert N. Bellah, have faced up to this challenge with re-

markable success. I confine my remarks here to the work of
Fontinell.

Fontinell is convinced that though the Western world and its
religion are in a state of collapse, a new and better form of human
relations can be best achieved by transforming those relations
in which and by which one now exists.[39] He uses the term convergence to describe what he is proposing.[40] Convergence "rejects
any unity through superficial syncretism, mechanical synthesis or
lowest-common-denominator ecumenism and affirms a unity which
will be the fruit of a positive growing-together." It not only "demands fidelity to the deepest values and ideals of one's community
or tradition" but also requires the fullest possible communication
with, and openness to, the values and ideals of other communities
and traditions. It demands the willingness to let one's own tradition
as well as those of others be radically transformed, if necessary,
even beyond recognition. It is likely that in this process much will
be lost. Yet there is also the hope that what was truly worthwhile
in these faith-communities and faith-traditions will not only survive
but even be enriched through mutual transactions and cross-
fertilization. Fontinell even admits to the possibility that, though
it does not appear likely at the moment, in the distant future the
doctrines, institutions and symbols that now belong to Christianity
could disappear. But even in this eventuality, according to Fontinell,
it could still retain the name Christian "insofar as it had grown
out of and was a continuing development of that existential relationship designated 'faith in God' " which had defined it in the past.[41]

I stated that there was a twofold danger when a theologian tries
to confine himself to theologizing within a single religious tradition.
Let us now assume that the culture of the Christian West is not
dying, though perhaps it is being radically reshaped. Let us
assume also that though its symbols will need to be reformulated
and renewed, they will still remain quite valid and relevant for
future generations. In this second case the theologian working

---

39. **Op. cit.**, p. 245.
40. **Ibid.**, p. 246.
41. **Ibid.**, pp. 247-248.

within a single religious tradition runs the risk of tacitly assuming that he can understand it by concentrating on it almost exclusively. But, as Claude Welch has recently stressed, we can significantly understand and develop a religious tradition only through a cross-cultural approach.[42] A cross-cultural approach does not mean a mere juxtaposition of the different religious traditions and phenomena. Mere juxtaposition would at best generate only that superficial breath of knowledge that is so serviceable for our cocktail party conversations. It certainly does not help to enrich our understanding of either our own religious tradition or those of others.

Welch mentions three theories or approaches which promote this kind of superficiality.[43] Unfortunately, these three approaches are all too common in American educational institutions whether they be church-related, state-related or private. First, there is the zoo-theory. The department assumes that its approach is cross-cultural because it can exhibit a variety of religious species to its students: the Protestant minister, the Roman Catholic priest, the Jewish rabbi and, if especially advantaged, the far eastern holy man. This theory is closely related to the second approach, the "insider theory" or "confessional principle." This second theory assumes that only one who has a faith-commitment to a religious tradition can truly understand it. Finally, there is the approach of the ecumenical institute where a number of persons with serious faith-commitments to particular religious traditions come together in the hope of arriving at a better understanding of each other. The danger I see in this last approach is that too often when the "chips are down," one will let his faith-commitment, usually subconsciously, tip the balance in his weighing of the arguments.

The only sufficient justification for a cross-cultural approach

---

42. "Identity Crisis in the Study of Religion? A First Report from the ACLS Study," **Journal of the American Academy of Religion**, 39 (1971), 3-18. The remainder of my essay is heavily indebted to this article. However, since I have used his ideas for my own purposes, my essay may not be regarded as necessarily giving a faithful account of Welch's views.

43. **Ibid.,** 8.

to religious studies is the special light which this method can throw on the issues under investigation. For example, the comparative study of the Dead Sea scrolls, the Nag Hammadi texts and the Jewish and Christian scriptures has thrown considerable light on how religious texts function in a community. Likewise, the study of revitalization movements in a number of quite diverse cultures has contributed significantly to our understanding of innovation, renewal and reform in many religious traditions.[44]

Moreover, we must remember that the symbols, beliefs and ritual practices of all religions are hybred. This point has been quite well established and is generally accepted in regards to the sacred writings of the Jews and even for the New Testament of the Christians. However, it does not seem that by and large Christian theologians are ready to come to full terms with the issues which cultural cross-fertilization raises for the dogmas, beliefs and institutions of Christianity. When one considers the possible extent to which religious ideas, beliefs and institutions are culturally and historically conditioned, he inevitably is faced with the question of their uniqueness and transcendent origin. These kinds of issues tend to relativize religion and make it appear as a humanly or socially constructed product. The theologian who theologizes primarily within the confines of his own religious tradition may not find himself forced to face these kinds of questions with the same urgency as is the scholar who stresses the cross-cultural approach.

The new morality of knowledge does not allow anything to remain sacrosanct and unquestionable. It requires that we be willing to question all our commitments, values and beliefs. Thus a Roman Catholic Christian would have to be willing to question any and every dogma—the divinity of Christ, eternal life, the infallibility, indefectibility and perpetuity of the Church and the existence of God. It does not follow of course that because something must be questionable, it will be proved by and large wrong—

---

44. For example, see Anthony F. C. Wallace, "Revitalization Movement," American Anthropologist, 58 (1956), 264-279.

but the risk must be faced if one is to avoid a conflict with the new ethic of assent.

Therefore, though I would hold for the legitimacy of a theologian choosing to work within the confines of a particular religious tradition, I would also stress the need for him to be in open communication with those who pursue the study of religion from a broad cross-cultural (and I should add, cross-disciplinary) approach. For this reason I have reservations about institutes and departments structured largely along the lines of Jewish studies, or Buddhist studies or Christian studies.[45] These institutes can provide a useful service as places where one might come, usually on a short-term basis, for intensive study in one religious tradition. But to devote practically all one's time and interest to a single religious tradition could lead to a superficial understanding even of that one tradition. Thus I would side with Max Müller when he writes: "if one knows one religion, he knows none." These institutes could also be academically justifiable as transitional arrangements for a contingently present situation. In this case they would be striving to broaden the understanding and outlook of some group. Thus, for example, an institute of Roman Catholic studies could have the useful purpose of helping their membership through a present identity crisis. So also an institute of Judaic or Buddhist studies may be a necessary but hopefully temporary corrective to the almost exclusive structuring of religious studies along Christian perspectives.

In conclusion, the theologian who wishes to theologize within the confines of his own religious tradition may do so, but this choice does not relieve him of his ethical obligation to be familiar with the content of the best available knowledge of his time and with its best available methods of investigation. He is still morally responsible for seeing that he does not isolate himself from the challenge which present, critically interpreted experience presents.

---

45. On this point confer Victor Preller in **The Study of Religion in Colleges and Universities** (edited by Paul Ramsey and John F. Wilson, Princeton: Princeton U. Press, 1970), p. 145; cited by Welch, **op. cit.**, 12.

Likewise, departments of religious studies and theology have a parallel responsibility to take precautions that they structure themselves in such a way as to encourage cross-cultural fertilization in their professors and students rather than isolationism.

6 Roman Catholic Social Ethics: Past, Present and Future

CHARLES E. CURRAN

This discussion of Roman Catholic social ethics will consider only the important statements of the hierarchical magisterium during the past century. Obviously there are other aspects to Roman Catholic social ethics, but these papal and conciliar statements dominate the theological reflection and the pastoral life of the Church in this area of social ethics. In the future a changed understanding of ecclesiology and the magisterial function in the Church will reduce the importance attached to similar statements of the hierarchical magisterium. The comparatively sparse theological literature generated by Pope Paul's encyclical *Populorum progressio* published in 1967 appears to indicate a future trend.[1] Our purpose is to point out some changes and developments that have occurred in the methodological approach to social ethics as found in these documents and to indicate possible areas of development and problems for the future.

EMPHASIS ON CONTINUITY

Unfortunately there have been comparatively few critical studies of the development of the papal social teachings.[2] Most of the

---

1. The indices to theological literature illustrate this fact. For the lack of courses on the papal encyclicals in Catholic colleges, see Benjamin L. Masse, S. J., "On Campus the Encyclicals are Out," **America**, CXXI (July 5, 1969), 5.

2. The best of these commentaries include: J. Y. Calvez, S. J., and J. Perrin, S.J., **L'Eglise et société économique: l'enseignement social des Papes de Leon XIII à Pie XII, 1878-1958** (2d ed.; Paris: Aubier, 1959);

Catholic commentaries on these documents have tended to explain the papal teaching and indicate some applications in different circumstances. Often the commentaries of the papal documents paralleled the biblical commentaries by concentrating on an exegesis of the papal text to determine its precise meaning. Many commentaries employed a rather apologetic approach which did not enter into critical dialogue with the papal teaching. Likewise, an evaluation of the social encyclicals generally skipped over the historical *sitz im leben* which is so necessary for a truly critical appraisal.[3] Catholic commentaries on the papal encyclicals also stressed the continuity in the doctrine of the various popes so that the papal teaching appeared as a number of immutable principles which were applied to new situations as they arose.

The popes themselves took great pains to stress continuity with their predecessors even though in reality there were many examples of discontinuity and change from one pope to the next. Pius XI in *Quadragesimo anno,* for example, defines his scope as recalling the benefits derived from *Rerum novarum* of Leo XIII, defending the teaching of Leo and passing judgment on the contemporary economic and social scene.[4] John XXIII in *Mater et magistra*

English translation: **The Church and Social Justice** (Chicago: Henry Regnery Co., 1961); John F. Cronin, S. S., **Social Principles and Economic Life** (Milwaukee: Bruce, 1959); Oswald von Nell-Breuning, **Die soziale enzyklika; erläuterungen zum weltrundschreiben papst Pius XI** (Köln: Katholische tat-verlag, 1932); English translation: **Reorganization of Social Economy: The Social Encyclical Developed and Explained** (Milwaukee: Bruce, 1936). All three of these commentators have published articles and other books dealing with the later papal documents and other aspects of the social question.

3. Richard L. Camp, **The Papal Ideology of Social Reform: A Study in Historical Development** (Leiden: E. J. Brill, 1969), pp. vii-viii.

4. Pope Pius XI, **Quadragesimo anno**, n. 15. Unless otherwise noted, the translations and paragraph numbers for the encyclicals of Pius XI are taken from: **The Church and the Reconstruction of the Modern World: The Social Encyclicals of Pope Pius XI,** ed. Terrence P. McLaughlin, C.S.B. (Garden City, N. Y.: Doubleday Image Books, 1957); **Acta Apostolicae Sedis,** XXIII (1931), 181.

follows the same generic format in his encyclical. Pope John wrote *Mater et magistra* "not merely to commemorate appropriately the Encyclical Letter of Leo XIII, but also, in the light of changed conditions, both to confirm and explain more fully what our predecessors taught, and to set forth the Church's teaching regarding the new and serious problems of our day."[5]

One of the obvious areas of development in the papal social teachings concerns private property. Leo XIII staunchly defended the right to private property but in terms of the needs of the individual person. Leo also did mention but not emphasize the social aspect of property.[6] Later papal teaching underscores the social aspect of property all the while recalling that Leo also mentioned this aspect in *Rerum novarum*. Pius XI begins his consideration of private property by asserting: "First, then, let it be considered as certain and established that neither Leo nor those theologians who have taught under the authority and guidance of the Church have ever denied or questioned the twofold character of ownership, usually individual or social according as it regards either separate persons or the common good."[7] On the question of the just distribution of capital or property, Pius argues for the "wise words of Our Predecessor" insisting that the earth serves the common interests of all.[8]

John XXIII begins his discussion of the social function of property with words that have almost become a caricature: "Our Predecessors have always taught that in the right of private prop-

---

5. Pope John XXIII, **Mater et magistra**, n. 50. Unless otherwise noted, the translation and paragraph numbers of this encyclical are taken from **Mater et magistra**, tr. William J. Gibbons (New York: Paulist Press, 1961); A.A.S., LIII (1961), 413.

6. Pope Leo XIII, **Rerum novarum**, nn. 4-31. Unless otherwise noted, the translation and paragraph numbers of the encyclicals of Leo XIII are taken from: **The Church Speaks to the Modern World: The Social Teachings of Leo XIII**, ed. Etienne Gilson (Garden City, N. Y.: Doubleday Image Books, 1954); **Acta Sanctae Sedis**, XXIII (1890-91), 643-655.

7. **Quadragesimo anno**, n. 45; A.A.S, XXIII (1931), 191-192.

8. **Ibid.**, n. 56; A.A.S., XXIII (1931), 196.

erty there is rooted a social responsibility."[9] John then cites
Leo XIII to prove his point. *The Pastoral Constitution on the
Church in the Modern World* (*Gaudium et spes*) asserts the
common purpose of created things and bases this assertion not
on the Scriptures or the Fathers but rather on Pius XII and John
XXIII.[10] Paul VI in *Populorum progressio* envisions the universal
purpose of the goods of creation as a cornerstone of his theology
of development which he proves not by quotations from earlier
statements of the hierarchical magisterium but rather from citing
Scripture and from developing a theology of the goods of creation.[11]
Even Paul's discussion of private property in the following paragraph is anchored in quotations from the Scripture and St. Augustine with no mention made of the teaching of his predecessors.[12]
Thus the style of the hierarchical magisterium especially before
Paul VI indicates the intention of the authors to stress the continuity in the papal teaching.

But there are even more subtle indications of the magisterial
preference for continuity with past teachings and a reluctance
to give any semblance of discontinuity with the predecessors of
happy memory. Pius XI, for example, in *Quadragesimo anno* calls
for a very thorough reconstruction of the social order; whereas
Leo XIII forty years earlier did not envision the need for such
a radical restructuring. John XXIII obviously abandoned Pius'
plan for such a reconstruction and expressed a much more positive

---

9. *Mater et magistra*, n. 119; A.A.S., LIII (1961), 430.

10. *Pastoral Constitution on the Church in the Modern World*, n. 69,
footnote 221. Unless otherwise noted, the translation and paragraph
numbers of the documents of the Second Vatican Council are taken from:
The Documents of Vatican II, ed. Walter M. Abbott, S.J., translation ed.,
Joseph Gallagher (New York: Guild Press, 1966); A.A.S., LVIII (1966),
1090-1091. The original Latin text also has the same paragraph numbering
as the English translation.

11. *Populorum progressio*, n. 22. Unless otherwise noted, translations
and paragraph numbers are from the Paulist Press booklet: *On the Development of Peoples*; A.A.S., LIX (1967), 268. The original Latin text also has
the same paragraph numbering as the English translation.

12. *Ibid.*, n. 23; A.A.S., LIX (1967), 269.

attitude to the existing structures of political, social and economic life. However, the popes never mention such existing differences.

Richard L. Camp in his study of papal teaching on social matters points out that Pius XI neatly covered one of the weaknesses in Leo's exposition of the defense of private property.[13] One should note that Leo's defense of private property did not really meet the major objections which were directed not against the small property holdings of working men but rather against the great accumulation of wealth and property among a few people in the midst of much economic need and want. Leo's failure to justify private property by any other title than labor was also an obvious source of embarrassment in the discussion with socialists. Pius XI deftly fills in the lacuna in such a way as to give the impression that he is merely quoting Leo. "That ownership is originally acquired both by occupancy of a thing not owned and /or by labor, or, as it is said, by specification, the tradition of all ages as well as the teaching of our predecessor Leo clearly testifies."[14] No precise citation is given to Leo apparently because Leo did not explicitly mention this other title to property.

THE THEOLOGICAL QUESTION INVOLVING NATURAL LAW

Undoubtedly the most important change in the teaching of the hierarchical magisterium in social ethics concerns the shift away from a strict natural law approach and methodology. Even in the last decade the social teachings of John XXIII invoked natural law as the basic methodological approach to social questions. John XXIII begins *Mater et magistra* by summarizing papal teaching on the social question from the time of Leo XIII, who in *Rerum novarum* "proclaimed a social message based on the requirements of human nature itself and conforming to the precepts of the Gospel and reason."[15] John then summarizes Pius XI's

---

13. Camp, p. 66.

14. Quadragesimo anno, n. 52; A.A.S., XXIII (1931), 194.

15. Mater et magistra, n. 15; A.A.S., LIII (1961), 405.

social teaching insisting on its "natural law character."[16] *Mater et magistra* then quotes from Pius XII's Pentecost message of June 1, 1941 which based the social order on the "unchangeable order which God our Creator and Redeemer has fixed both in the natural law and revelation."[17]

The Pastoral Constitution on the Church in the Modern World, the longest document produced by Vatican II, which deals precisely with the questions of the economic, political, social and cultural order, employs the term natural law only three times in the entire document and then only in the second part of the Constitution, and studiously avoids any implication that natural law furnishes the methodological foundation upon which the entire document is based. *Populorum progressio* uses the term natural law only once and then in a citation taken from Leo XIII.[18] Obviously the framers of these documents made a conscious and concerted effort to avoid the term *natural law* which indicates an unwillingness to accept the natural law methodology which had been associated with the older teaching of the hierarchical magisterium on social matters.

The natural law is a very ambiguous term and includes many different aspects. Basically one should clearly distinguish the philosophical and the theological aspects of natural law. The philosophical question concerns the precise understanding of nature and the way in which the theory develops moral norms in the light of its understanding of nature. From a philosophical viewpoint there have been many different understandings of natural law precisely because there are many different understandings of nature. I shall prescind from the philosophical aspect of the question even though there are undoubtedly philosophical reasons behind the changing use in the documents of the hierarchical magisterium.

From a theological perspective natural law has been the general

---

16. **Ibid.,** n. 30; **A.A.S.,** LIII (1961), 408.
17. **Ibid.,** n. 42; **A.A.S.,** LIII (1961), 410.
18. **Pastoral Constitution on the Church in the Modern World,** nn. 74, 79, 89; **A.A.S.,** LVIII (1966), 1096, 1102, 1111. The Latin text uses the word **lex** in n. 74 and n. 89, while n. 79 employs the word **ius**.

answer of Roman Catholic theology to the questions: is there a source of ethical wisdom and knowledge for the Christian which exists apart from the explicit revelation of God in Christ in the Scriptures? Does the Christian share ethical wisdom with all mankind because of the common humanity they share? What is the relationship between the wisdom the Christian shares with all men and the specifically Christian moral wisdom, between the natural and the supernatural? Recently the question has been posed in terms of pure agapism versus mixed agapism; i.e., does Christian ethics rest solely on the distinctively Christian aspect here assumed to be *agape* or is Christian ethical wisdom combined with an ethical knowledge which exists outside the pale of explicit Christianity? This section will discuss the question of natural law from such a theological perspective.

The papal social encyclicals in line with the Roman Catholic theological tradition firmly admit the existence of an ethical wisdom and knowledge which the Christian shares with all mankind. Perhaps the most explicit affirmation of natural law as the primary basis of the papal social teaching and the best illustration of its applications in social morality are found in *Pacem in terris*. (One can only surmise that at a time when Catholics were beginning to question natural law in other areas, the Pope made a concerted effort to indicate that natural law was the basis for the widely acclaimed social teaching of the Church and also took the pains to describe his understanding of natural law). The introductory paragraphs of *Pacem in terris,* after extolling the work of creation, assert: "But the Creator of the world has imprinted in man's heart an order which his conscience reveals to him and enjoins him to obey: They show the work of the law written in their hearts. Their conscience bears witness to them."[19] By these laws men are most admirably taught how to conduct their mutual dealings, how to structure relationships between the individual and the state,

---

19. Pope John XXIII, **Pacem in terris**, n. 5. Unless otherwise noted, the translation and paragraph numbers of this encyclical are taken from: **Pacem in Terris**, ed. William J. Gibbons (New York: Paulist Press, 1963); A.A.S., LV (1963), 258.

how states should deal with each other, how men and political communities should be related to the world community. These four types of order and relationships serve as the structural foundation for the four basic chapters of the encyclical.[20]

Perhaps in no other papal teaching is there such an explicit affirmation of the natural law as the primary basis for the social teaching of the Church. Generally speaking the papal social encyclicals mention two different sources of knowledge and wisdom for the Church's social teaching—revelation and natural law. These two sources of wisdom in the gnoseological order correspond to the ontological order of nature and supernature. Commentaries on the papal social teaching underscore the methodological role of these two sources. "We see that the Popes have customarily juxtaposed the two sources of the social doctrine of the Church; revelation and natural law."[21] Near the beginning of his first chapter, Guerry asserts that the concepts which make up the social teaching of the Church are drawn from revelation and the natural law.[22] One could point out frequent references in the encyclicals themselves to this twofold source of ethical wisdom—gospel and reason, divine revelation and natural law, supernatural and natural.

I personally agree with the recognition that all men because they share the same humanity also share a common ethical wisdom and knowledge which has been described in various theological terms such as natural law or common ground morality. For various theological reasons some Protestant theological approaches in the past have denied such a valid source of ethical wisdom for the Christian, either because a reliance on the Scriptures excluded all other possible sources of knowledge, or because sin affected or even destroyed the structures of creation, or because they were

20. **Ibid.**, n. 7; **A.A.S.**, LV (1963), 259.
21. Calvez and Perrin, p. 40.
22. Emile Guerry, **The Social Doctrine of the Catholic Church** (New York: Alba House, 1961), pp. 15-19.

unwilling to accept any natural theology or coalition ethics involving the Christian and the human.[23]

CRITIQUE OF THE PRE-VATICAN II APPROACH

The primary fault with the methodological approach of the papal encyclicals before Vatican II was the way in which reason or natural law was related to the whole ethical perspective. Either natural law and revelation or gospel were juxtaposed as Calvez describes the general approach, or else the natural law served as the foundational starting point for the entire structure then added on top. Such a concept of the natural viewed in isolation from the reality of sin, redemption and resurrection destiny failed to see the complexity of human reality in the proper Christian perspective and did not properly relate the area of the natural to the realities of sin and grace. The natural law or the area of the natural remains integral in itself and is not really affected or transformed by the supernatural which is merely added on top of an already constituted natural order. Thus in the gnoseological order natural law and revelation remain two different sources retaining their own autonomy and identity corresponding to the same type of distinction between nature and supernature.

In such a theory the transforming power of grace or redemption does not really affect the understructure of the natural; or, in the famous terminology of H. Richard Niebuhr, Christ is not seen as transforming culture.[24] A view of grace or Christian eschatology as transforming nature and culture furnishes a more dynamic foundation for Christian ethics. The eschatological fullness stands as a constant critique of all existing structures and institutions,

---

23. John C. Bennett, "Issues for the Ecumenical Dialogue," in **Christian Social Ethics in a Changing World,** ed. John C. Bennett (New York: Association Press, 1966), pp. 377-378.

24. H. Richard Niebuhr, **Christ and Culture** (New York: Harper Torchback, 1956).

thus asserting in a positive fashion the need for continual change and improvement. An ethic which sees the natural as unaffected by the transforming power of the eschaton tends to be more conservative and to view existing structures as reflections of the immutable, eternal law of God. Obviously there are also philosophical presuppositions in the approach of the papal encyclicals which would reinforce this more conservative view of a somewhat static order reflecting the eternal and immutable order in the mind of God.

In fairness to the papal social teaching the popes did not hesitate to see and criticize the inadequacies of the existing social order in the light of the ideal of natural law and natural justice. Some Popes, especially Pius XI, called for a seemingly thorough reconstruction of the social order.[25] However, the theological foundations of the natural law theory were somewhat inadequate especially in the area of social change which was manifested in some of the papal teachings. There was always the danger of identifying a particular order or structure as the immutable order of God when in reality it was only an historically and culturally conditioned attempt to respond as well as possible to the needs of a particular period and very often manifested the desires of the dominant power group in the society rather than the eternal order of God.

The response of the nineteenth century popes to the question of freedom in all its political, cultural and religious ramifications shows an undue preference for the forms of the past and an inability to come to grips with the problem of change. There was a tendency, for example, to see the union of Church and state as the ideal social order reflecting the eternal order of God, when in reality it was only a time conditioned reality. I for one would admit many of the problems with the concept of liberty proposed in the nineteenth century (Karl Marx was a severe critic of this individualistic liberty especially when applied to the economic area), but the solution to the problem was not to turn back

---

25. Camp, pp. 38-40.

to an older historical form as if this were the representation of the eternal plan of God.[26] Even Pius XI's severe critique of existing structures seemed to indicate that the older solution as found in the guilds was necessary in our own times.[27] Perhaps there was wisdom in his suggestion, but there still remains the danger of identifying the eternal plan of God with a particular historical order, and usually in the case of Catholic theology an order which existed in a previous historical period. An understanding of the transforming aspect of grace and the eschaton would avoid the danger of canonizing any historical order as an expression of the eternal order willed by God.

Catholic natural law teaching in general and the papal social encyclicals in particular also failed to give enough importance to the reality of human sinfulness. Obviously, no Christian theology can ignore the reality of sin. The papal social encyclicals do frequently mention sin and its effects, but sin and its power do not possess the significance they should have. *Pacem in terris* well illustrates the failure of papal social teaching to give enough importance to the reality of sin. Even the very title of the encyclical implies that peace is a possibility here on earth, but a more sober reflection reminds us that sin and its effects will always be with us until the end of time and the consummation outside history.

A person reading the introductory paragraphs of *Pacem in terris* today realizes the romantic and utopian view which finds in the heart of man an order and the laws by which men know how to regulate their lives. Our own contemporary experience reminds us of another important factor—the disorder which exists in the hearts of men because of which men do not know how to live in order and peace with one another, because of which tensions between individuals and the government have become escalated, because of which individual nations remain suspicious of one another and unwilling to give up their own power of autonomy to any supranational body. One could very easily take the four

---

26. Étienne Borne, "Le problème majeur du Syllabus: verité et liberté," **Recherches et Débats**, L (1965), 26-42.

27. Calvez and Perrin, pp. 415-427; Camp, pp. 125-128.

main parts of *Pacem in terris* and, beginning from the sin and disorder existing in man's heart, show the opposite tendency to that
which is alone emphasized in the papal document. One could
argue that *Pacem in terris* merely proposed an ideal based on
reason, but a more realistic vision of peace and the world order
calls for a greater realization of the existence of sin and its disruptive effects in human existence.

Catholic theology is vulnerable to the charge that it does not
give enough importance to the reality of sin precisely because the
area of the natural is not integrated into the full Christian perspective. In general Catholic theology, perhaps in an overly defensive posture to safeguard its valuable assertion that creation is
good, did not give enough importance to the reality of sin. Even
reconstructions of the notion of the natural such as proposed by
Josef Fuchs do not seem to give enough importance to the role
of sin or of grace for that matter.[28] Fuchs, in responding to Protestant critiques, points out that Catholic theology does not mean
by nature that which corresponds merely to creation. Nature is that
which is essential to man and present in all the different possible
states of salvation; whereas Protestant theology sees nature in terms
of creation and then argues that creation is affected by sin.[29] Fuchs'
approach is obviously better than some other explanations which
do seem to equate nature with creation; but even he must admit
there is still a connection between creation and nature, even the
more abstract concept of nature which he sees as present in all
the states of man. Fuchs speaks of an essential human nature which
then is modified in its application to the different aspects of the
history of salvation. Thus the natural remains the primary concept
which is affected in different ways by grace or sin but really not
internally affected or transformed.

In some forms of Catholic theology with an even less adequate
understanding of nature as grounded in the work of creation
to which supernature is added, there remains the greater danger

---

28. Josef Fuchs, S. J., **Natural Law: A Theological Investigation**
(New York: Sheed & Ward, 1965).

29. **Ibid.**, pp. 42-52.

of not giving enough importance to the reality of sin. Sin can be easily and mistakenly viewed as the loss of the supernatural aspect which is merely added on to the natural order, but sin does not intrinsically affect the natural order. In one school of Catholic theology man after the fall is related to man in the state of pure nature as *nudatus ad nudum*.[30] There was a somewhat better aspect of Catholic theology in this matter, but unfortunately it was not always systematically applied throughout the area of theology. In theory Catholic theology held that man after sin was *vulneratus in naturalibus* (wounded in those things pertaining to nature), and also that grace was morally necessary for a man to observe even the substance of the natural law for a long time.[31] But too often in practice sin was viewed as the loss of the supernatural while the order of the natural remained intact.

Sin obviously has an effect on many existing social structures and institutions. Very often the papal social encyclicals leave the reader with the impression that reason alone is the only element in establishing the proper social order and reason alone is sufficient to bring about the necessary changes in this order. A failure to recognize the reality of sin plus an overly idealistic or rationalistic understanding of reality combine to give a somewhat inadequate view of the social order and of effecting social change. The existing social order is never the product of pure reason but results also from the power struggles existing within the society itself. Minorities are discriminated against in many societies precisely because of the power and thus even the tyranny of the majority who control the power and thus greatly influence the social structures. Likewise the struggles and the tensions within society are greater than a theory based solely on reason can account for. Sin obviously becomes incarnate in society in the struggles between rich and poor, developed nations and developing countries, capital and labor. An older papal teaching does not seem to take this reality

---

30. Iosephus F. Sagües, S. I., **Sacrae Theologiae Summa** (Madrid: Biblioteca de Autores Cristianos, 1955), II, pp. 988-998.
31. Severinus Gonzalez, S. I., **Sacrae Theologiae Summae** (3d ed.; Madrid: Biblioteca de Autores Christianos, 1956), III, pp. 521-542.

seriously enough. On the other hand, the existence of sin in the world will mean that perfect justice is never attainable in this world no matter how hard man will strive to find it. The Christian vocation to struggle against the reality of sin serves as another motive for the Christian to engage in the struggle to strive for a more just social order and not merely to accept the present structures as the immutable order of God.

DEVELOPMENTS OF VATICAN II AND AFTERWARD

The Pastoral Constitution on the Church in the Modern World marks a decisive turning point in the understanding of natural law and tries to integrate the natural law more fully into the whole schema of salvation history. Both in explicit words and in theory the document generally avoids understanding the natural as a relatively autonomous order unaffected by sin and grace. The first three chapters of Part One of the Constitution illustrate the newer methodological approach which tries to integrate the reality of the natural or the order of creation into the total Christian perspective. Chapter One on man begins with the fact of creation because of which man is made in the image of God. A second paragraph asserts the reality of sin and the resulting fact that man experiences within himself a dramatic struggle between good and evil. After a discussion of many other aspects the chapter ends with a paragraph on Christ as the new and perfect man. Thus creation, sin and redemption together explain the meaning of man for the Christian. The same general structure also governs the following two chapters on human community and human action.

An important idea that appeared in the draft drawn up at Ariccia in 1965 is the notion of the truly or the fully human.[32]

---

32. This fact has been documented and explained by William J. Bergen, S. J., in his doctoral dissertation, "The Evolution of The Pastoral Constitution on the Church in the Modern World: A Study in Moral Methodology," which will shortly be completed at the Catholic University of America. I am grateful to Father Bergen for documenting the ideas summarized in this paragraph.

This term had appeared in the earlier drafts but refers to nothing more than what would correspond to the natural as distinguished from the supernatural. The draft proposed at Ariccia definitely tried to overcome the false separation between the natural and the supernatural order. In this draft Christ assumes a more important place than in the earlier drafts, and Christ appears especially as the perfect man, the fulfillment of the human.[33] For example, in the close of the third chapter the draft maintains that the history of humanity tends toward Christ who is the focal point of the desires of history and civilization.[34] The Spirit not only arouses a desire for the age to come, but He animates, purifies, strengthens those noble longings by which the human family strives to make its life more human and to render the whole earth submissive to this goal.[35] The references added at Ariccia referring to the more human and the truly human must be interpreted in terms of this newer understanding of Christ as the perfect man and the Spirit working now in the hearts of man to develop his love which is the basic law of human perfection and brings the earth towards its goal. The terms *truly human* and *fully human* thus seem to be concepts that overcome the previous dichotomy between the natural and the supernatural in earlier statements of the papal magisterium. One should note that such concepts do not have a primary and foundational place in the final document, although it seems to me that many of the framers of the final draft did see this as a very fundamental concept.

Gaudium et spes definitely avoids the term *natural law*. The pivotal paragraph introducing the second part of the Constitution with its consideration of five different practical areas employs a new phrase to describe its theological methodology. "To a con-

---

33. "De Christo, Homine Perfecto" is the title of the final section of Chapter One of Part One of the Ariccia draft (Ariccia draft, Part I., Chap. I, n. 20).

34. Ariccia draft, Part I, Chap. III, nn. 45-46. This does not appear as such in the final version of **Gaudium et spes**.

35. Ariccia draft, Part I, Chap. I, n. 20; Part I, Chap. IV, n. 49; Part II, Chap. V, n. 91. These references are substantially incorporated into the final version of **Gaudium et spes**.

sideration of these in the light of the gospel and of human experience, the Council would now direct the attention of all."[36] Obviously there are many reasons of a more philosophical nature involved in the shift from natural law to human experience. However, it would be wrong to see no importance from a theological perspective in this change. In such a perspective human experience does not mean the same thing as natural law. There is not a dichotomy between gospel and human experience as there was between gospel and natural law. Human experience is not restricted merely to the supernatural. Chapter One in its discussion of sin remarks that what divine revelation makes known to us about the existence of sin "agrees with experience." Examining his heart man finds that he has inclinations to evil and is engulfed by evils which do not come from the good Creator.[37] Human experience is not impervious to the reality of grace, for the Constitution speaks of all men of good will in whose heart grace works in an unseen way. The ultimate vocation of all men is in fact one and divine.[38] Thus human experience does not correspond to the natural order as distinguished from the supernatural, for grace and sin are not foreign to human experience even apart from the gospel as such.

Extrinsic evidence also supports the thesis that *Gaudium et spes* makes a decided shift away from the theological understanding of natural law and the natural as pertaining to natural theology and totally unaffected by the reality of redemption. Canon Charles Moeller, presently the sub-Secretary of the Vatican Congregation for the Doctrine of the Faith and one of the drafters of the Pastoral Constitution, made this precise point in a speech he gave as an official Catholic observer to the meeting on Church and Society sponsored by the World Council of Churches in Geneva in the summer of 1966. Moeller explained that the terms *nature* and

---

36. **Pastoral Constitution on the Church in the Modern World**, n. 46; A.A.S., LVIII (1966), 1066.

37. **Ibid.**, n. 13; A.A.S., LVIII (1966), 1034-1035.

38. **Ibid.**, n. 22; A.A.S., LVIII (1966), 1043.

supernature were not employed in the document because of ecumenical reasons. The Orthodox use the term nature to describe what Catholics call supernature; whereas in Protestant theology there are difficulties connected with a concept of a natural theology of human nature because such a concept cannot be found in the Scriptures.[39]

The Encyclical *Populorum progressio* issued by Pope Paul VI in March 1967 again avoids the nature-supernature, natural law-gospel dichotomies and continues along the lines proposed in *Gaudium et spes*. The central and foundational idea of the encyclical is development. The first part of the encyclical treats man's complete development, while the second part treats the development of the human race in a spirit of solidarity. Paul describes human life as the vocation of every man to fulfill himself. This self-fulfillment is obligatory for man who as a spiritual being should direct himself to God. "By reason of this union with Christ the source of life, man attains to new fulfillment of himself, to a transcendent humanism which gives him his greatest possible perfection. This is the highest good of personal development."[40] In a technical age Pope Paul realizes that it is necessary to search for "a new humanism which will enable modern man to find himself anew by embracing the higher values of love and friendship, of prayer and contemplation"[41] In one important paragraph the encyclical proposes a united ideal of what true development means. More human conditions of life "clearly imply passage from want to the possession of necessities, overcoming social evils, increase of knowledge and acquisition of culture.... Then comes the acknowledgement by man of supreme values and of God their source and finality. Finally and above all, is faith, a gift of God accepted by man's will, and united in the charity of Christ, who

---

39. Msgr. Charles Moeller, "Conference sur L'Eglise dans le monde d'aujourd'hui," La Documentation Catholique, LXIII (1965), 1500.

40. Populorum progressio, n. 16: A.A.S., LIX (1967), 265.

41. Ibid., n. 20; A.A.S., LIX (1967), 267.

calls us all to share as sons in the life of the living God, the Father of all men."[42]

This new methodological approach does not deny the basic affirmation of the goodness of creation and the continuity between creation and redemption. However, the area of the natural no longer appears as merely extrinsically juxtaposed to the supernatural but rather creation is constantly affected by the drag of sin and the pull of grace.

CRITIQUE OF THE NEW APPROACH

The newer approach proposed originally in *Gaudium et spes* still creates some theological problems. *The Constitution on the Church in the Modern World* does not really follow in practice the methodology proposed in the important introduction to the consideration of practical problems in the second part of the Constitution. Especially, the problems considered in the last three chapters of Part Two (economic life, political life, peace among nations) do not receive a methodological discussion in the light of the gospel and human experience. Rather the approach is one based primarily on the dignity of the human person which is an extension of the older natural law approach. These chapters contain frequent references to past papal teaching but comparatively few references to a broader history of salvation approach. Thus these three important chapters do not really implement the newer methodological approach proposed in theory at the beginning of Part Two. Canon Moeller admits this diversity between the two parts of *Gaudium et spes* and explains it in terms of a dialectic between biblical anthropology and the understanding of the human person. This dialectic or antinomy attempts to bring together in a vital tension the biblical and the human or the eschatological

---

42. **Ibid.**, n. 21; **A.A.S.**, LIX (1967), 267-268. Also see Antonio Messineo, S. I., "L'Umanismo plenario e lo sviluppo integrale dei popoli," **La Civiltà Cattolica**, Part I, CXIX (1968), 213-226; Jean-Yves Calvez, S. J., "Populorum progressio," **Projet**, XV (1967), 515-530.

and the incarnational approach.[43] I cannot agree with Moeller's explanation which appears to be too apologetic. It seems to me that the first part of the document does try to maintain this tension within itself by constantly developing the principal chapters in a history of salvation approach which integrates creation, sin and redemption. The Introduction for Part Two, understood in the light of Part One, should now apply this particular methodological approach to the particular problems under discussion. The tension resulting from such an approach is precisely what is missing in the last three chapters of Part Two, since the approach is based almost solely on the dignity of the human person as known from reason. There is an obvious explanation of this lack of consistency. The chapters of Part Two were at one time intended only to be appendices to the real constitution. Later it was decided to incorporate them into the text, but in a true sense they were just juxtaposed with a text which from the fifth draft spelled out in theory a different methodological approach.[44]

The Pastoral Constitution did try to integrate the natural into the total Christian perspective so that it was no longer seen as a relatively autonomous area not affected by sin and redemption. However, in the process it seems that other important aspects did not receive enough attention. In integrating the "natural" into the "supernatural," the document and other Catholic writing tend to forget about the finiteness and limitations of the creaturely which will always be present despite the basic goodness of creation. Secondly, the reality of sin, which was even somewhat neglected in the older approach, did not receive enough attention. This fault in the newer approach resulted in a too optimistic and even naive

---

43. La Documentation Catholique, LXIII (1965), 1505.

44. Mark G. McGrath, C.S.C., "Note storiche sulla Costituzione," in La Chiesa nel mondo di oggi, ed. Guilherme Baraúna, O.F.M. (Florence: Vallechi, 1966), pp. 141-156; Charles Moeller, "History of the Constitution," in Commentary on the Documents of Vatican II, Vol. V: Pastoral Constitution on the Church in the Modern World, ed. Herbert Vorgrimler (New York: Herder & Herder, 1969), pp. 1-76.

view of the world. Thirdly, the eschatological element was too easily collapsed.

With emphasis on Christ the perfect man, for example, in the last paragraph of Chapter One, the eschaton somehow becomes collapsed with too great a stress on realized eschatology.[45] Perhaps the whole reality of Christ should have been discussed after creation and sin and then followed by the other considerations with a closing paragraph considering the eschatological future both in terms of its continuity and its essential discontinuity with the present. In this way the structure of the first three chapters of Part One would present a more realistic understanding of the Christian's view of man, community and human action. The aspect of future eschatology is missing almost totally from the closing paragraph of the discussion on human community in Chapter Two.[46] Chapter Three does devote its last paragraph almost exclusively to the future and its different relationships to the present and this presents a more adequate theological understanding of our pilgrim existence than the first two chapters.

Precisely the first two criticisms mentioned above were also directed by many Council fathers at the draft drawn up at Ariccia.[47] These interventions at the fourth session of the Council objected to a tendency to forget the distinction between the order of nature and the order of grace and to an undue optimism arising from a lack of the sense of sin. There is no doubt that the framers wanted to overcome the rigid division of two orders, the natural and the supernatural, and two vocations which had characterized much of earlier Catholic teaching especially on a more popular level. I believe that these objections to the text of Ariccia were pointing out important defects in that draft and also in the final document itself. The solution is not to reinstate a rigid division

45. **Pastoral Constitution on the Church in the Modern World**, n. 22; **A.A.S.**, LVIII (1966), 1042-1044.

46. **Ibid.**, n. 32; **A.A.S.**, LVIII (1966), p. 1051.

47. Philippe Delhaye, "Histoire des textes de la Constitution Pastorale," in **L'Église dans le monde de ce temps**, ed. Yves Congar, O.P. (Paris: Éditions du Cerf, 1967), I, pp. 267-273.

between the two orders but rather to realize the existence of the creaturely, with its goodness and also its limitations, which is affected by the reality of sin, but gradually trying to be transformed in the times in between the comings of Jesus who will bring to completion the work he has begun, a perfection or completion or fullness which always lies outside history.

The three criticisms of *Gaudium et spes* also have validity in assessing some of the theological literature commenting on this document. For example, a paper by Joseph Gremillion at the Notre Dame symposium on Vatican II in 1966 merits the same criticisms despite some perceptive comments about the changing approach of *Gaudium et spes*.[48] The author correctly shows the different methodological approach in comparison with the natural law approach of the manuals, although most of his stress falls on the different philosophical implications and not the theological implications treated here. However, Gremillion does not take up the question of eschatology and the tension between the imperfections of the present and the eschatological fulness to which we are all called in Christ Jesus. The article does mention sin; but the perfunctory treatment, which is primarily a long citation from the document itself, indicates that sin does not have a profound effect upon the world in which we live and struggle for justice and peace.[49]

Populorum progressio at times shows a more critical attitude towards the present reality of the world and also realizes the effect of sin in our world. Pope Paul, however, seems to imply that the individual development of the person is possible and so is the complete development of a true communion among all nations possible of achievement. Paragraph 21 supposes that the new humanism embracing this total development is possible, and this paragraph appears to be a foundational section of the encyclical. No mention is here made of sin preventing such total development

---

48. Joseph Gremillion, "The Church in the World Today: Challenge to Theology," in **Vatican II: An Interfaith Appraisal**, ed. John H. Miller, C.S.C. (Notre Dame: University of Notre Dame Press, 1966), pp. 521-544.

49. **Ibid.**, pp. 534-535.

nor the realization that the final development will never come until the end of time and outside history through the saving intervention of the second coming of Jesus. The foundational paragraph in the second part of the encyclical on the development of the human race in a spirit of solidarity speaks of the duty to form a true community among all nations based on a "brotherhood which is at once both natural and supernatural" and includes a threefold aspect: the duty of human solidarity, the duty of social justice, the duty of universal charity. Note that the terminology tries to overcome the division and separation between nature and grace, but there is in this foundational paragraph no mention of sin and of the fact that a "true communion" remains only an eschatological goal and hope.[50] Thus the later magisterial documents overcome the separation between nature and supernature, but fail to integrate this into a total Christian perspective especially because they fail to appreciate the finitude and imperfections of creation, the reality of sin, and the eschatological as a future now trying to transform the present but capable of fulfillment only as God's gift at the end of time. Catholic social ethics in the future needs a more realistic view of man and his life in this world which does not forget the finitude, limitations and sinfulness of the present as man strives for the truly human or the full development which will ultimately come only as God's gift at the end of time.

CATHOLIC SOCIAL ETHICS AND CHANGE

Change, even radical change, characterizes the present social, political, economic and cultural orders. In general, Roman Catholic social ethics in the past has not been equipped to come to grips with the reality of change. There are signs in the last decade, however, that social ethics as taught by the hierarchical magisterium is adopting a methodology more apt to cope with the reality of social change. The theoretical inability to deal with change

---

50. **Populorum progressio**, n. 44; **A.A.S.**, LIX (1967), 279.

and development is multiplied when one enters the practical arena of proper strategies to bring about social change. The problem becomes more acute because many people today are aware of the great changes which must take place in national and international life.

The papal social teaching of the past was not unaware of the changing conditions of economic, social, political and cultural life. Leo XIII began *Rerum novarum* by pointing out that the revolutionary spirit has influenced political and economic life.[51] To cope with these changes in the light of Christian teachings Leo wrote his many encyclicals. Pius XI realized that many changes had occurred since Leo's time, and he calls to judgment both the existing economic system and its most bitter enemy, socialism.[52] The very outline of *Mater et magistra* indicates Pope John's realization of the importance of past papal social teaching but also the historical changes which have occurred since that time. Part Two of that encyclical explains and develops the older teaching in the light of changed conditions, whereas Part Three examines new aspects of the social question.

At the same time there is another strand in the papal social teaching which methodologically hampers this teaching from dealing with the fact of change. In his encyclical on the state Leo XIII traces out what should be the form and character of the state in accord with the principles of Christian philosophy. Leo proposes a union of two powers, the ecclesiastical set over the divine and the civil set over the human, with each supreme in its own sphere and working together in a harmonious relationship. Just as in lower nature a marvelous order and harmony reign so that all things fitly and aptly work together for the great purpose of the universe, so too there must be a harmonious relationship between Church and state.[53] Leo understands the union of Church and state in this manner as reflecting the ever changeless

---

51. **Rerum novarum**, n. 1; **A.A.S.**, XXIII (1890-91), 641.
52. **Quadragesimo anno**, n. 98; **A.A.S.**, XXIII (1931), 209.
53. **Immortale Dei**, nn. 13-14; **A.A.S.**, XVIII (1885), 166-167.

law.[54] He then condemns that harmful and deplorable passion for innovation which has invaded philosophy and thrown confusion into the Christian religion. This innovation brings about that unbridled license which is at variance with not only the Christian but even the natural law.[55]

The somewhat negative attitude towards change manifested by Leo obviously has many partial explanations including the historical conditions of the time, but the methodological approach of natural law, seen now in its philosophical aspect, is a major contributing cause. The papal social teaching even in the encyclicals of John XXIII insists that the natural law proclaims an order for society in which all things should exist in harmony and unity. "Now an order of this kind, whose principles are universal, absolute and unchangeable has its ultimate source in the one, true God."[56] The natural law has these unchanging characteristics, and even the order shares in such characteristics. The impression arises that there is a hierarchically structured order in which all things form a harmonious whole with each having its proper function with regard to the whole. Such a notion of order with its correlative insistence on universality and immutability does not furnish an apt paradigm for change. A more adequate social ethic, while truly appreciating the need for order and structure, will reject a static approach which tends to deny the reality of change.

The danger also exists of identifying a particular historical ordering with this order in the mind of God whose principles are immutable and universal. This danger is heightened when theology loses the sense of the eschaton as calling into judgment every existing social order and institution. Both theologically and philosophically the papal natural law methodology had difficulty coping with the reality of historicity and change. The tendency of social conservatism arises not only from the unwillingness to accept change because of an overemphasis on order but also because the changes brought about in the present seem often to contradict

---

54. **Ibid.**, n. 22; **A.A.S.**, XVIII (1885), 169.
55. **Ibid.**, n. 23; **A.A.S.**, XVIII (1885), 170.
56. **Pacem in terris**, n. 38; **A.A.S.**, LV (1963), 266-267.

some past order which appears to be the order willed by God. A methodology proceeding from the concept of an immutable order in the mind of God which has been implanted in the heart of man easily adopts an *a priori* and deductive approach. As late as 1963, *Pacem in terris* builds its entire argument on just such a notion. Leo XIII had earlier pointed out that the Christian organization of civil society was "educed from the highest and truest principles confirmed by natural reason itself."[57]

A New Developement

Pacem in terris, however, also marks the beginning of a change which will ultimately embrace a more inductive methodology more open to change, development and even tension. The concluding paragraphs of the four main parts of the encyclical speak about: distinctive characteristics of our age, these requirements in our day, the fact that men are becoming more and more convinced of a certain reality, a commendation of the modern development of the United Nations Organization with its Universal Declaration of Human Rights.[58]

The Pastoral Constitution on the Church in the Modern World takes a further step toward a more inductive methodology more open to change, tension and perhaps even some disorder. *Gaudium et spes* begins with an introductory statement, originally intended to be the first part of the Constitution, which records the signs of the times. "Signs of the times" was a favorite expression employed by John XXIII, but the phrase itself appears very rarely in the final version of *Gaudium et spes* because some Council Fathers objected to the use of a term in a manner different from its primary scriptural meaning.[59] The Council thus acknowledges the rapid changes taking place in the modern world and tries to speak to them in the light of the gospel and of human expe-

---

57. **Immortale Dei,** n. 16; **A.A.S.,** XVIII (1885), 167.
58. **Pacem in terris,** nn. 39-45, 75-79, 126-129, 142-145; **A.A.S.,** LV (1963), 267-269, 278-279, 291, 295-296.
59. **The Documents of Vatican II,** pp. 201-202, footnote 8.

rience.[60] Each of the five chapters in the second part of the Constitution begins with a reading of the signs of the times in the particular area under consideration—marriage, culture, economy, politics, peace and international relations. Note that the signs of the times are now considered first and not last as in *Pacem in terris*.

Populorum progressio takes another step in this same direction. Paul VI, for the first time in a papal encyclical, cites contemporary authorities from other fields, a sign that some type of dialogue is truly taking place.[61] The earlier literary genre of papal encyclicals with its lack of specific references to other areas of science and knowledge and its frequent citations of "Our predecessors of happy memory" reinforced the *a priori* and deductive type of methodology which is antithetical to change. In the later documents there is no longer any question of beginning with the order which God has imprinted in the hearts of men from which the principles and order of society can be deduced.

In the future Catholic theology must develop a methodology which can grapple with change and even radical change, but Christian theology and the Churches should never uncritically baptize every change which occurs. A sound theological and philosophical methodology cannot be totally inductive in the sense that there are no criteria outside the present situation by which to judge it. A naively utopian theological perspective together with an unwillingness to rationally assess possible changes is obviously quite rampant in our society. This would be just as inadequate an approach to the problem as the Catholic natural law approach which in the past could not cope with the reality of change.

STRATEGIES FOR CHANGE

Christian ethics or moral theology considers not only the more theoretical question of the norms, values and goals for Christian

---

60. "Thus the human race has passed from a rather static concept of reality to a more dynamic evolutionary one." **Pastoral Constitution on the Church in the Modern World**, n. 5; A.A.S., LVIII (1966), 1029.

61. See the references in the following footnotes of the official text:

action but also the more practical question of the strategies for bringing about social change. Generally speaking Catholic theology, including the papal social teaching, has been very deficient in this area of strategies. Again there are implications in the older method-ological approach militating against developing a suitable strategy for the implementation of moral ideals, goals, and norms in social life. Catholic natural law stressed the order of God reflected in the world in which all things fit together in a marvelous hierarchical coordination and subordination. Such an approach could not easily accept the fact of change.

On the level of structure such an approach again emphasized a hierarchical ordering in which authority and power were invested in the office holders in the society, and all direction in the society (and what little change there could possibly be in the light of such a model) came from the office holders. Order and ordering in the theoretical realm became law and structure in the practical realm. Obviously the structure of the Roman Catholic Church well illus-trates this practical understanding. Change is brought about pri-marily through order or reason in the theoretical realm and through reason and law or structure in the practical realm. Such a method-ology has a built-in prejudice against change in the theoretical realm and almost totally bypasses the question of practical strategy for social change, since this would be accomplished in an orderly way by the office holders.

In practice, one must admit that Catholic social teaching was cognizant of the need for strategies in bringing about social change. The papal social teaching realized, despite its stress on hierarchical ordering, that there were also many tensions in society. The papal encyclicals were written primarily because of the disorders, im-balances and tensions existing in society either between the rich and the poor in a particular country or between the rich nations and the poor nations of the world.[62] Papal teaching realized that

15, 17, 22, 27, 29, 31, 44, 45, 46, 62.

62. E.g., **Rerum novarum**, n. 1; **A.A.S.**, XXIII (1890-91), p. 641; **Mater et magistra**, n. 122; A.A.S., LIII (1961), 431.

labor needed the right to strike as a means of trying to obtain justice from employers. The right to war has even been recognized often in Church documents. Even more recent writings of the hierarchical magisterium speak, although somewhat reluctantly, about revolution as a means of last resort to bring about social change, but caution against ever finding the proportionality commensurate to the harm caused by revolution.[63]

Changes in the theoretical approach to an understanding of Christian social ethics have already been mentioned. The emphasis on an *a priori* ordering involving a somewhat detailed plan of subordination and coordination of all the different parts as a reflection of the plan of God is beginning to disappear. More importance is given to historicity, change, tension, growth. These same changes will also affect the practical realm of strategies for social change. In the categories employed by Edward LeRoy Long, Jr., there will be a shift from a more institutional motif to a more operational motif on the level of strategy for the implementation of social justice. The operational motif gives less place to the role of structure or ordering and sees change coming about through the various influences present in any society.[64] Such a view also has a more realistic understanding of the existing social structures. Such institutions and structures are not necessarily a perfect reflection of the divine order produced by human reason. Rather they very easily reflect the power and influence of those who do have power in the society itself. Law and structure very often incarnate discrimination and injustice as well as some attempt at justice. Not only a more operational motif but also a theological realization of the sinfulness of man despite his resurrection destiny would come to the conclusion that existing social structures are not merely a rational reflection of the order of God.

In the future Roman Catholic theology must develop a more operational motif which can more adequately handle the problem of strategies in bringing about social change. For many people

---

63. **Populorum progressio**, n. 31; **A.A.S.**, LIX (1967), 272.
64. Edward LeRoy Long, Jr., **A Survey of Christian Ethics** (New York: Oxford University Press, 1967), pp. 167-251.

today, especially in the area of living the Christian life, the more important question remains the strategies by which social change can be accomplished. Many Christians today are convinced of the general framework of social justice and charity which should exist but are frustrated in their attempts to bring about corresponding change.

Among the many questions that Catholic theology will have to address is that of power which obviously is an important factor in the reality of social change and the strategies to bring about such change. As pointed out, the papal magisterium realized the need for power in its general attitude to strikes and in its realization that revolution could never be absolutely ruled out despite the many concomitant problems. Interestingly, the final version of *Gaudium et spes* in its consideration of the political community is less conscious of power as a means of social change than an earlier version. The 1964 Appendix I on the political community contained an entire section on public opinion. "More and more centers of moral power are cropping up in present day society; they exert influence on public opinion and change it. The effect of this new type of power is that more and more people are able to participate in social life."[65] Unfortunately this section was dropped and not included in the final draft.

The final draft of *Gaudium et spes*, however, does show some advantages over *Pacem in terris* pointing in the direction of a lesser influence of the structural and hierarchical ordering in society. In reality many nineteenth and twentieth century Church documents on political life considered only the aspect of political authority. *Pacem in terris* also gives first and primary consideration to political authority but points out that authority is a means in the service of the common good and the community.[66] *Gaudium et spes* first discusses the political community itself before going into the topic of authority, since the community obviously embraces more

---

65. The text is cited by Jean-Yves Calvez, S.J., "The Political Community," in **The Church Today**, ed. Group 2000 (Westminster, Md.: Newman Press, 1968), p. 198.

66. **Pacem in terris**, nn. 46-79; **A.A.S.**, LV (1963), 269-279.

than just authority. The Pastoral Constitution calls for the participation of all in the government.[67] Thus one can see a development towards a lesser role and function given to authority and structure in the understanding of society, which illustrates the emergence of a more operational motif.

In the future Roman Catholic social ethics must develop a more operational motif which includes power as a means of social change. Such a development should not totally deny the need for order and structure which has been the most significant aspect of Catholic social ethics in the past. The importance of both order and change must be recognized so that theology is truly critical about proposed changes. Likewise in developing a theology of power, power should not be seen primarily or exclusively in terms of sin. Catholic theology with its ontological pre-suppositions can see power as a necessary characteristic of being. A balanced theology of power will show that power stems also from the connection with the power of redemption. Power, understood in its relationship to the total Christian perspective of creation, sin and resurrection destiny, can never become the sole consideration of social ethics, but again must be integrated into the other elements of social ethics—justice, truth, love and freedom. These are the challenges facing the future of Roman Catholic social ethics.

INDIVIDUAL AND COMMUNITY

A perennial ethical problem, which will be of even greater importance in the future, concerns the relationship between the individual and the community. The growing interdependency and complexity of human existence will heighten tensions and possible conflicts between the individual and the community. In the area of population growth the question arises about the rights of the government to impose limits on family size. Discussions in the area of genetics occasion questions about the role of the community in the genetic planning of the future of man. Catholic social

---

67. **Pastoral Constitution on the Church in the Modern World**, nn. 73-75; A.A.S., LVIII (1966), 1094-1099.

teaching has lately admitted the legitimacy of government appro-
priation of large unused estates so that more people might share
in the ownership of the land.[68] On an international level trade
between nations cannot be dictated only by the market place
because the rich nations of the world will continue to exploit the
countries that export only raw materials.

On the other hand many in our society are more conscious
than ever of the rights of conscientious objection either to the
policies of the government or the military draft or the immoral
orders of a superior in the military. The cybernetic revolution has
brought about a situation in which the government can easily obtain
and preserve much data about the private life of its citizens which
seems to be an invasion of the privacy of the individual.

The teaching of the hierarchical magisterium on social ethics
retains, as would be expected, the tension between the individual
and the community, with a changing emphasis depending on
changed historical and cultural circumstances. The older approach,
however, did at least in theory lay heavy emphasis on the community, and especially the state.[69]

In general, Catholic social ethics views man as political and
social by nature. Society is a natural institution because of the
very nature of man. This is a constant theme recurring in Roman
Catholic social ethics, as exemplified in the following passage from
Gaudium et spes: "Individuals, families, and various groups which
compose the civic community are aware of their own insufficiency
in the matter of establishing a fully human condition of life.
They see the need for that wider community in which each would
daily contribute his energies toward the ever better attainment
of the common good. It is for this reason that they set up the
political community in its manifold expressions."[70]

The Protestant tradition generally sees the origin of the state

---

68. **Populorum progressio**, n. 24; A.A.S., LIX (1967), 269.

69. Heinrich A. Rommen, **The State in Catholic Thought** (St. Louis:
B. Herder, 1945).

70. **Pastoral Constitution on the Church in the Modern World**, n. 74;
A.A.S., LVIII (1966), 1095.

in the sinfulness of man, whereas Catholic theology understands the state as a natural society based on the very nature of man. Between these views there is not only a theological difference about the importance attached to sinfulness (which, as discussed previously, does not receive enough attention in Catholic thought) but also a metaphysical or philosophical difference in the understanding of man. The more classical stand in Protestant theology would tend to view man primarily in terms of his freedom, so that the state as a result of sin must compel man to act in accord with civic righteousness.[71] Catholic theology does not see man primarily in terms of freedom but rather as a being with a structure to which he must conform. In a sense freedom in such a Catholic view is only the freedom to correspond to and act according to man's essential structure. This is the primary reason Catholic social ethics did not originally stress the freedom of man.[72] The Catholic emphasis on order and structure thus understands the state as "an organic unit in which, under the preservation of their metaphysical, substantial equality and independence, the members of the moral organism in different, unequal, concrete functions form that organism. Thus the dignity of the person always exists even in the humblest function of the organic whole."[73] In this way Heinrich Rommen sees Catholic thinking overcoming a dichotomy or duality between the individual and society. Since the individual person is not understood primarily in terms of his liberty but also in terms of his natural relationship to the societal whole, there is not only an equality about man but also an inequality because each has different functions to fulfill in the social organism. The above description of the state in Catholic thinking does reflect the Papal teaching before Pius XI. In this context one can better

---

71. Jacques Ellul, "Rappels et réflexions sur une théologie de l'état," in Les Chretiens et l'etat (Paris: Mame, 1967), pp. 130-137.

72. For the contrast between the older view of responsibility and freedom and the newer view, see Albert R. Jonsen, S.J., Responsibility in Modern Religious Ethics (Washington/Cleveland: Corpus Books, 1968), pp. 11-27.

73. Rommen, p. 299.

understand the denial of the right of religious liberty even in the encyclicals of Leo XIII.[74] For the same reason, Leo XIII could call for the intervention of the state to overcome some of the evils associated with *laissez-faire* capitalism.[75]

Although even the older Catholic teaching in the nineteenth century upheld the dignity of the human person and thus rejected the socialism of the day, it was Pius XI who gave even greater emphasis to the dignity of the human person in his social ethics. In conflict with the totalitarian states of fascism and communism, Pius XI proclaimed the dignity and freedom of the individual person who cannot be sacrificed to the end of the state.[76] Obviously such a new stress in different historical circumstances opened the way for a development or change in the hierarchical teaching on religious liberty, which Vatican II based on the dignity of the human person which "has been impressing itself more and more deeply on the consciousness of contemporary man."[77]

This changing emphasis in the social teaching of the hierarchical magisterium has also been lately incorporated into the theoretical understanding of man and society. Part Four of *Mater et magistra,* for example, calls for a reconstruction of social relationships, indicates some false philosophical approaches, and then outlines the teaching of the Church on social matters as "having truth as its guide, justice as its end, and love as its driving force."[78] The heading of this final part of the encyclical, which is not a part of the official Latin text but is included in the translations supplied by the Vatican in other languages, reads: "Reconstruction of social relationships in truth, justice and love."[79] *Pacem in terris* indicates an important development by adding a fourth member—freedom—to this origi-

---

74. Pope Leo XIII, **Libertas praestantissimum**, especially nn. 18-47; **Acta Leonis XIII**, VIII (1888), 228-246; see also **Immortale Dei**.

75. **Rerum novarum**, nn. 32-42; **A.A.S.**, XXIII (1890-91), 655-661.

76. For the historical development in the teaching of the popes on the freedom of the individual, see John Courtney Murray, S.J., **The Problem of Religious Freedom** (Westminster, Md.: Newman Press, 1965).

77. **Declaration on Religious Freedom**, n. 1; **A.A.S.**, LVIII (1966), 929.

78. **Mater et magistra**, n. 226; **A.A.S.**, LIII (1961), 454.

79. **Ibid.**, n. 212; **A.A.S.**, LIII (1961), 451.

nal trio.[80] The fourfold basis for Catholic social teaching as proposed in *Pacem in terris* does not merely constitute one other
paragraph in the encyclical but rather serves as a foundational
point for the development of the teaching itself. Part Three on
the relations between states uses this particular fourfold schema
to develop its teaching. The section on liberty or freedom calls for
the developed countries to respect the liberty of the developing
countries in the promotion of their own economic development
and progress.[81]

Perhaps somewhat paradoxically, the decade of the 1960's
also witnessed a renewed realization of the intervention of the
state in the social order. *Mater et magistra* recalls that the multipli-
cation of social relationships is one of the principal characteristics
of our time. Greater complexity and interrelatedness call for an
added emphasis on man's role in community and also call for an
expanded role of the government itself, as well as the functioning
of other smaller groups in the society. In this light Pope John
developed his famous teaching on socialization.[82] Later writings,
especially *Populorum progressio,* have extended this concept even
to include at times government expropriation of unused large
estates.[83]

The social teaching of the hierarchical magisterium in the 1960's
reflects an insistence on both the dignity and freedom of the person
and the complexities of contemporary existence calling for a
correspondingly larger role of the state in social life. Catholic
theology with its traditional stress on order, hierarchical structure
and relationships has provided a theoretical basis for greater community intervention in the life of the society and of the individual
person. The dignity of the person and the self-transcending characteristics of the individual have been incorporated into this original

---

80. **Pacem in terris,** n. 35; **A.A.S.,** LV (1963), 265-266.
81. **Ibid.,** n. 123; **A.A.S.,** LV (1963), 289-290.
82. **Mater et magistra,** nn. 59-66; **A.A.S.,** LIII (1961), 415-418. See
Jean-Yves Calvez, S.J., **The Social Thought of John XXIII** (Chicago: Henry
Regnery, 1966), pp. 1-14; John F. Cronin, S.S., **The Social Teaching of
Pope John XXIII** (Milwaukee: Bruce, 1963), pp. 8-12.
83. **Populorum progressio,** n. 24; **A.A.S.,** LIX (1967), 269.

framework with a corresponding loosening of the way in which hierarchical ordering, structure and relationships are viewed. Interestingly, the freedom and dignity of the human person have thus accomplished the same general result as the realization of sin and the transforming power of grace mentioned in the first part and the historicity mentioned in the second part of this chapter.

The presuppositions of the hierarchical teaching have not abandoned their emphasis on order and structured relationships, but other elements are added which introduce greater flexibility, historicity and even tension and some disorder into this Catholic social teaching. The hierarchical social teaching in its understanding of man and society has now incorporated the realization of man's freedom as an important foundation for its teaching, but man is not viewed in terms of his freedom alone. The very fact that truth, justice, love, freedom and power form the basis for the understanding of man's life in society indicates the tensions that will exist now and in the future. With this somewhat balanced basis, one can better approach the social problems of our complex future existence.

The Future of Christian Social Ethics [1]

STANLEY HAUERWAS

As I understand it the primary case Father Curran makes against Catholic social ethics, at least as so far embodied in papal documents, includes these three distinguishable but interdependent points: (1) They are based on natural law (not just on a wrong conception of natural law); (2) they contain a far too optimistic and rationalistic understanding of man and society that pays insufficient attention to the reality of sin; and (3) they are too static and conservative as they ignore the eschatological dimension of human existence.

CRITIQUE OF NATURAL LAW

Father Curran objects to the natural law basis of the encyclicals for three primary reasons which might be characterized as the theological, the ethical, and the social. Theologically natural law is based on a view of the natural as an independent realm only "topped" in a hierarchical fashion by a supernatural realm. This fails to do justice to God's redemption of his created order and the dynamic relation between nature and grace. I take it Father Curran is trying to take into account for ethical reflection the critiques of De Lubac and Rahner of the nature-grace distinction found in much of Catholic theology. I am in full agreement with the negative force of this general position (though I am also sure that Thomas is not open to such a crude understanding of the relation of nature to grace), but I am not sure if an adequate

---

1. A response to the presentation of Rev. Charles E. Curran given at the College Theology Society Convention, St. Paul, Minn., April 13, 1971.

account of the positive relationship between nature and grace can be assumed to exist. For I am not sure whether either De Lubac or Rahner has been able to adequately state what kind of integrity the natural can have or actually has.

Secondly, natural law thinking tended to give credence to a two stage ethic—a common or lower morality for laymen and a more perfect one for religious and priests. I suspect that Father Curran also thinks this distinction often served as an ideology for an unwarranted authoritarian imposition by the hierarchy on the laity. Finally, natural law ethics is socially conservative as it absolutizes the relative by identifying the natural law with one historically contingent form. Though I assume this charge is true it seems to me we need good historical studies to show exactly to what circumstances this oft stated criticism applies.

Because of these failures Father Curran suggests that we dispense with natural law thinking and adopt the language of the "truly human." For such language (1) does not artificially separate nature-grace, creation and redemption into hierarchical spheres, (2) is based on a profounder theological basis as it affirms Christ as the ontological basis of the world, thus allowing for a positive appreciation of non-Christian social ethics as taken up in Christ, and (3) provides the basis for appeals to human experience not as an independent realm of "nature," but as the basic values and sense of justice embodied in all men that is at once "nature" and "grace."

What puzzles me about this suggestion is that it looks very much like a natural law ethic—perversions removed. For surely one of the primary insights of natural law is that Christians share basic moral convictions with all men whether they be Christian or not. Father Curran has criticized a conception of natural law that was interpreted as abstract principles perceived by the individual through a special super faculty called "reason." But it is not clear that natural law is necessarily "rationalistic" in that sense, for natural law is open to interpretation as the fundamental prerequisites for human interdependence. It is exactly the kind of affirmation Father Curran makes at the end of his paper about the basic sociality of man, that is that we are human only in so far as we are interdependently related by justice and the common good.

Moreover, I think Father Curran is quite right to say that this is a fundamental basis for any discussion of one of the basic issues of social ethics, that is particularly significant in our own day, namely the relation of the individual and community. For it is on such a natural law basis that an authentic conception of the common good can be explicated as it affirms that we are fundamentally social creatures with social goals. So understood, the common good is not simply the sum of our individual interests regardless of the content of those interests, but a genuine good of the whole. It is just such a conception of the common good that renders problematic the liberal individualism of most contemporary forms of social life and ethics. Moreover such a conception of the natural law provides the necessary condition for a morally substantive understanding of the political that raises the political order above simply the clash of interest groups. Thus, I am convinced if Father Curran rubbed his notion of "human experience," or perhaps better, if pushed to come clean on the normative content of such experience, it would possibly look very much like a natural law ethic.

Briefly, my other difficulty with Father Curran's exposition of the idea of the "truly human" is its theological basis. As an unrepentant Barthian I suppose I ought to rejoice in the kind of Christological basis he provides as a warrant for taking the "natural" seriously, but I must admit I am extremely uneasy with this. For if Christ is everything—if grace ultimately sustains all creation —what difference do such affirmations actually make or what do they tell us about reality? Put another way, what do these sweeping theological affirmations add to our ethical dispositions, attitudes, or judgments? Father Curran in another article entitled "Is There a Distinctively Christian Social Ethic?"[2] has argued that there is no distinctively Christian social ethic. Rather "personal acknowledgment of Jesus as Lord affects the consciousness of the individual . . . , but the Christian and the explicitly non-Christian can and do arrive at the same ethical conclusions and can and do share the same general ethical attitudes, dispositions, and goals." While

---

2. Philip Morris, ed., **Metropolis** (Notre Dame, Ind.: Fides, 1970), p. 114.

I think this is certainly descriptively true, I am puzzled what meaning consciousness has in this context and its relation to Christ since ethical attitudes, dispositions, and goals do not seem to be included within it. Thus I am trying to suggest that Christian ethics has a stake in maintaining the integrity of the natural, not only because it has integrity, but also because it is the necessary pre-supposition for any attempt to affirm distinctive obligation of the Christian that involves more than a *Gesinnung* ethic.

THE REALITY AND SIGNIFICANCE OF SIN

Father Curran is quite right to fault Roman Catholic social ethics for an insufficient understanding of the reality and power of sin. By this I take him to be referring to the assumption on the part of the encyclicals that what was at stake in social problems was an insufficient understanding of justice. Thus once the Holy See made these clear it was assumed that the employer would love the worker, everyone would find their rightful place in the social order, and the nations would make peace. Thus the papal teachings as well as some forms of the social gospel had a far too naive view of the moral potential of the political realms. They attempted to place too much faith in moral persuasion rather than the necessity of power and violence to effect the good. It does my Niebuhrian heart good to hear a Roman Catholic finally talking in this way, but I am afraid it comes at a time that my own Niebuhrian soul is filled with doubt. For if you really take sin as a fundamental reality then the keynote of your social ethics is not "how can the good be done?" but rather the essential question becomes "how can evil be prevented?" For many this means the Christian should view the political realm primarily as an arena where some less than salutary interests are balanced by other similar interests. The Christian would then side with the dispossessed in so far as they lacked power, but we should have no illusions about the virtue of the poor. Thus, for example, a consistent Niebuhrian while supporting blacks does not assume black men are inherently virtuous. Rather the blacks simply represent a necessary check on white demonic pretentions. But once having made it we expect the black man to buy in suburbia, get two cars, and worry about Jews moving in.

I think many of us are beginning to feel two rather fundamental difficulties with this kind of social ethic. We are increasingly aware that our "realism" tends to be conservative as it asks little from the political realm. We simply assume that a balance of interest is the highest good the political realm can accomplish. It limits us to the options of the going order for we fear being branded "idealists" or "utopian." Our perception of the predominant social ethical problems tends therefore to be what the current ethos says they are. We quite literally read the "signs of the times" from the *Times*. Secondly, we are beginning to question if our "realism" was not a cover or way of avoiding making clear what our fundamental principles or conception of justice were. That is, we are no longer so sure that "principles" or a fundamental view of the good society can be ignored for any basic political judgment. Reinhold Niebuhr got along pretty well on intuition, but we are not so sure we can continue to do so.

In this sense I must admit that I think that Father Curran's Catholic soul has intuitively felt this difficulty. For unless I miss entirely the fundamental tendency of his approach, he still wants to require more from the political than the limitations of evil. Order is not a good in itself but what must be risked is possible disorder in the hope of a more just society. The hard question thus is only begun once the significance of sin is recognized, for then one must go on to try to delineate the moral order that bounds sin in such a way that the forms and gradation of evil can be illuminated and dealt with in an appropriate manner.

Change and Eschatology

Finally Father Curran is critical of the difficulty of the Church in the past adjusting to the changing social conditions. He is, of course, not denying that the Church did not recognize change, but rather he is critical of *how* the Church tended to regard change in a negative fashion. The problem as he seems to see it is that the Church had locked itself into past models of society, in which the Church reigned supreme, and thus it had an institutional stake in preserving the status quo. I agree fundamentally with this point, but I cannot help but observe a historical irony about this. That there is embodied in Leo's encyclical an organic model of society is undeniable. Moreover, it is clear that in many ways Leo took feudal society to be paradigmatically normative for social arrangements. What is ironical about this is that when reasserted in the beginnings of a rationalistic-liberal social order it appeared positively radical. Thus Leo's conception of the family and the correlative notion of the just wage acts as a fundamental critique against liberal economic assumptions. In this respect there is a peculiar convergence between Marx and Leo as both are social conservatives trying to repeal the fundamental presupposition of the new order, namely, the division of labor.

In opposition to this failure to account for change Father Curran calls for a renewed appreciation of eschatology for Christian social ethics. By this he seems to mean that we must have a more positive appreciation of change as an affirmation of Christ's continued transformation of culture (H. R. Niebuhr). He does not wish, however, to warrant any conclusion that this can ever be completed or final in this form of existence. Rather I take him to be somewhat critical not only of Vatican optimism in this respect, but also of the contemporary theology of revolution in so far as it tends to identify change with God's will, revolution with the kingdom of God. Even though I agree strongly with his hesitancy in this respect, I must admit I am extremely puzzled in what sense or way Father Curran's understanding of eschatology differs from this position. I understand he wishes not to identify with any "realized eschatology" in preference to what must be something like a "realizing eschatology," but what I do not understand is how this actually helps illumine social ethical reflection or judgments.

What is needed are some criteria or models that help one identify the "signs of the times." From where do these come? Are they rooted in some fundamental conceptions of the structure of the kingdom of God? Or are they derived elsewhere? While I have no doubt that one's social ethics are ultimately dependent on one's eschatology the relationship is by no means clear, for there is no one doctrine of eschatology nor is there any one conception of social ethics. For example, traditional sectarian social ethics is strongly "eschatological" yet it warrants the churches' and the Christian's withdrawal from what Father Curran would regard as "responsible Christian social action." Moreover I think this indicates that a Christian social ethic ultimately cannot free itself from the past for the fundamental conceptions of the good society any social ethic ultimately must presuppose.

ECCLESIOLOGY AND ETHICS

I want to try to raise one last issue that I think is at the heart: I find presupposed and implied in Curran's social ethics a continuation of the Constantinian and Christendom assumptions of the social encyclicals. It is not my intention to argue that this is necessarily wrong, but rather what I wish to do is help us feel the oddness of this position and at least entertain the possibility that there are other alternatives.

First let me try to make clear what I mean. It has long been a fundamental axiom of those raised on Troeltsch that one's understanding of Christian social ethics is a correlate of one's ecclesiology. Thus the Church type has a fundamentally positive orientation toward the world and tries to sustain its social order. It willingly engages in the ethics of the lesser good or the lesser evil. The sect on the other hand negatively relates to the world and its powers, thereby rendering problematic the relative goods of our wider social involvement. In this context the reformation, especially in its Lutheran manifestation, never called into question the primary presupposition of the Roman Church's understanding of its relation to society. Rather it only solidified the independence of the created order by negatively relating it to the redemptive order as law is related to Gospel. The Roman Catholic Church was able to relate more critically to society as it positively regarded the social order as being infused with Christian values and spirit.

Father Curran is continuing in that tradition though he has rightly stripped it of its more triumphalistic aspects. Thus his call for the Church and Christians to pay more attention to the necessi-

ties of power and the "operational" (how to) means of the implementation of social justice. Though I am rather unclear exactly
how this is contrasted with the more institutional embodiment
of social justice, I take it basically to be a call for Christians to pay
much closer attention not to how justice ought to be accomplished
in terms of particular problems, but how it can be accomplished.
The Christian cannot think himself immune from the prerequisites
and necessities of effective social action—he must use the best
social knowledge and information available, he must exercise power,
he must coerce, he must finally kill. It is only when the Church
engages in this kind of reflection and action that her social ethics
will be more than platitudinous.

My question to this is simple—how do you do this and in any
meaningful way make clear that Christians affirm that God's
redemption is good and that they are in a hesitant way a redeemed
people? The constant difficulty of the Church type, the calls for
Christians to be responsible, is that in being such we become
the world. At this point I suspect the question of violence is *the*
question of Christian social ethics. For it strikes me that what
many contemporary theologians, Catholic and Protestant, are trying
to do is maintain under the general slogan of "people of God"
a sectarian ecclesiology with a Church type social ethic. Not only
do I think this theologically impossible; I am sure it is doomed
pragmatically.

Thus I suppose the upshot of these last remarks is to ask
Father Curran what kind of ecclesiology he thinks is implied in his
social ethic. I am sure by drawing the problems above in this
either/or fashion I am being somewhat unfair, but I think it at
least provides a framework for a discussion of what I take to be
a fundamental question. Also I suppose that I draw the issue
in this way because I am at least trying to suggest an affirmative
answer to Father Curran's question, "Is there a distinctively
Christian social ethic?" But it is affirmative not in the sense that the
Church possesses special insight or principles for effective social
action, but rather the form and nature of the kind of community

that is the Church is a social ethic. The Church's primary ethical responsibility is to be herself. In other words it may be that the Church's most relevant social ethic is her social irrelevancy occasioned by her refusing to take up the ways of the world even in the name of a good cause.

III

AMERICAN LIFE: SEEKING QUALITY

8   The Hermeneutic of the American "Now"

NATHAN R. KOLLAR

There is a great deal written on the subject of hermeneutics.[1] I do not intend to re-work the ground many times plowed and planted by the authors of these books and articles. Instead I wish to concentrate upon the hermeneutical event itself and the presuppositions which underlie it as event in contemporary America. What I am doing is using the principles of the modern hermeneutic on the hermeneutical event as it occurs in the United States. Two current writers demonstrate the importance of the problem I wish to consider. Fuchs, for instance, states that the hermeneutical principle is *that with which* the text is confronted to call forth from it what it has to say[2] and Gadamer states in his *Hermeneutik und Historismus*[3] that the point of departure for hermeneutics must be the great historical realities of society and state which are already determinative prior to every experience. My problem is

---

1. I would suggest as introductory books: P. J. Achtemeier, **An Introduction to the New Hermeneutic** (Philadelphia: Westminster Press, 1969), J. M. Robinson & John B. Cobb, **The New Hermeneutic**, New Frontiers in Theology Series, vol. 2 (New York: Harper & Row, 1964); R. E. Palmer, **Hermeneutics** (Evanston, Ill.: Northwestern University Press, 1969). Palmer is a history and excellent evaluation of all the present leaders in the field of hermeneutics; bibliography is comprehensive and excellent. Robinson & Cobb is a discussion between American theologians and European theologians about the hermeneutical problem. Achtemeier is a clear introduction to the thought of the new hermeneutics, especially that of Heidegger.

2. E. Fuchs, **Hermeneutik** (Stuttgart: R. Mullerschon, 1963) pp. 103-118.

3. Hans-Georg Gadamer, "Hermeneutik und Historismus," PhR IX (1962), p. 243. Gadamer's main work is **Wahrheit und Methode: Grundzuge einer philosophischen Hermeneutik** (Tubingen: J.C.B. Mohr, 1960), 2nd ed. This is one of the central theses in the modern hermeneutic.

to understand the "that with which the text is confronted" of Fuchs and the "great historical realities of society and state" of Gadamer as they occur in the concrete, now, in the United States.[4] This will be done by considering first the constitutive elements of the hermeneutical event, then the presuppositions of this event, and finally by examining specific methodological implications to the first two considerations.

The Hermeneutical Event

Hermeneutics is interpretation, is understanding. It is the understanding, in this instance, of something produced before the "now" of the interpretative event. The event is constituted by the interpreter, who may be an individual or a team; the work-done (e.g., a book) and the language of both interpreter and the work-done. These three elements are the historical concretization of various worlds. Each represents an interlocking history which comes to play within this event so as to realize something new which is the interpretation.

The interpreter is the front wave of his own historicity. His facticity at this moment in time evidences that "he was" as well as "he is." All of his actions are tainted by this historicity. As he stands present within this event he is representative of his past. The work done is also representative of a past, but not in the exact same fashion as the interpreter, for it exists in a frozen fashion. Within its horizon is its author, perhaps many centuries dead, its past history of interpretation, and most especially its present context. It is within its present context that it speaks meaning. I would note especially here that the present cannot be left in order to go into the past. The meaning of a past work cannot be seen solely in terms of itself. On the contrary, the

---

4. I would like to emphasize here that I am not concerned with the usual themes of the new hermeneutic. I am involved in the step between the philosophy of understanding of Gadamer, Fuchs, Ebling et. al. and the particular philological studies. I am asking what are the presuppositions to all of these investigations, be they philosophical or philological, in the United States.

"meaning" of the past work is defined in terms of the questions put to it from the present.

Language is the medium of understanding which binds the event together, gives it substance. Language is both personal and communal. It is personal inasmuch as it is the medium of the interpreter's understanding. It is his personal gesture filled with his meaning. However the language, which is medium, is also communal. It is not created *de novo* by the interpreter but rather is part of the given of his situation in time and space. Man has "world" and lives in "world" because of language. Language then is symbolic of the person and the person's total historicity which includes the universe of discourse handed down to him. In speaking, he realizes both the communal universe of discourse and his own personal stance within the event.

These (interpreter, language, work-done) are the actors in the hermeneutical event. One last fact must be mentioned before examining the presuppositions of the present hermeneutical event. We must be aware that this is event, that is, that it happens in time: it draws upon the *past* of the interpreter, language, work-done by a question fashioned in the *present* for purposes of *future* living. History forms the backdrop to this event.

What happens in the event is very simple. Someone is working on a project. He is attempting to understand a text or artifact of some kind. All at once he understands, he is able to interpret this text to himself and hopefully to others. The hermeneutical event has occurred. There is meaning, the understanding grasps a specific intelligibility in the essential reciprocal interaction of whole and parts. As event it is representative of the history of all those involved and in turn influences the respective historicity of each. In some way these respective histories can be seen in the concrete resultant of the event, for instance in the article which is written, which in turn influences others outside the specific event.

PRESUPPOSITIONS TO THE EVENT

In the event, as event, there are both implicit and explicit factors at work. One of these factors is the presuppositions held by the society which forms the context of the event as well as the context for the person(s) participating in the event. In our society I see these presuppositions as five: the purposiveness of knowledge, the over-confidence in the organic development of history, the transitory character of the contemporary world-view, the loss of the faith-dimension of man, and the individual person as the ultimate criterion for the interpretation of the event.

The first is the purposiveness of knowledge. Within our society the purpose of knowledge is twofold: a) first and most important its purpose is knowledge. "Abstraction," "intellect," "mind," "thought"—these are some words which describe the knowing process. Perhaps this is better understood by saying that it is presupposed in the scientific investigation of truth that one investigates and interprets not by dance, music or painting but by some word abstraction. We understand when the thought is thought, not danced. b) The second intent of knowledge is that knowing itself is seen as a good, something that should never be opposed. Ideas themselves are never evil, only the one who understands them can be evil. We presuppose that any knowledge discovered, any thought thought should be allowed the freedom of the market place.[5]

The second presupposition is the organic development of history. "We stand upon the shoulders of those who have gone before us," said Newton. "History is interconnected in such a way that to understand an historical event one must reconstruct the question for which the historical actions of persons were the answer" (Collingwood). But is there such organic growth and inter-connectedness in man's history? Does man always depend upon those who have gone before him, or the circumstances which surround him? Is it possible that instead there may be quantum leaps of freedom which reach out of present history to new levels of life?

The third presupposition is the transitory character of the contemporary world view. This transitory character is based upon a symbolic process of mythologization and de-mythologization.

---

5. Cf. M. Novak, The Experience of Nothingness (New York: Harper & Row, 1970), ch. 4.

There is a constant de-mythologization of past and present events in which man's cognitive descriptions of reality are re-fined and re-defined. At the same time there is an unrecognized building anew of new myths, which are the models or images into which and against which all the relativities and partial realizations of human knowledge and life are projected.[6] The total resultant is a continual building up and breaking down of man's view of the world and of himself.

Concretely the process of de-mythologization has taken place in our understanding of religion itself, in the understanding of the foundational books of religion, in the dogmatic component of religion. The history, sociology and anthropology of religion are explained without a reliance upon the transcendent.[7] The concept of scripture as a source of propositional truth or as a source of the life of Christ is long past. The result of this de-mythologization is that the authority of these documents as foundational for the dogmatic component of religion has been eroded. A stable, normative and universal religious statement can no longer be made. As the de-mythologization has taken place a consequent mythologization has occurred. Accepted without question are the ideals of community, equality, pluriformity of life style and a unified world. Just as the relativity of our world is accepted without question, so these ideals are accepted and form the unchallenged horizon of all investigation.

The fourth presupposition is the loss of the faith-dimension of man. Belief of some sort is part of mankind, just as myth is always evident in our world. Implicit and not recognized is a genuine loss of faith. There is change of faith's expression and because of this a change in faith.

Man is constituted by his relationship to the world around him. He is not a body-soul duality. His faith does not remain in his soul while his body and his world change. On the contrary, man

---

6. Cf. J. F. Hayward, "The Uses of Myth in an Age of Science," **Zygon** (June 1968).

7. Cf. J. M. Yinger, **The Scientific Study of Religion** (New York: Macmillan Co., 1970), ch. 1.

is a unity. A change in man's relationships is a change in man and faith is one of these relationships. For example, if a person continually acts the clown and suddenly becomes serious and reflective, do we not say he is changed? It is much the same for faith. When one's religious expressions change or the former religious expressions no longer exist, neither does his faith. The faith-expression (modality) of man is new. This too is implicit in all of modern man's actions. He has a different faith than before. Expression of faith and faith are one. They are such that man, the questioner, stands faith-filled in a different way than before. The result is our fifth presupposition, that the individual person is the criterion for interpretation.[8] What is the norm of this hermeneutical event?—I am.

Is there an internal coherence to my understanding of the event? Only if it is real for me. No matter what verbal or logical barrage is waged against my understanding, it must beat down what I see as making sense to me. If it does not, then it is useless. If, ultimately, others do not believe in me and what I propose as true, I can always rest behind the walls of my presuppositions, resisting all attack since these presuppositions are "mine." They make sense, to me.

These, then, are the presuppositions of the Hermeneutic of the American "Now." I am not saying that I see them as good. I make no value judgment in regard to them. I merely state that they exist as implicit in every interpretative event as it occurs in the United States. In the event, as it occurs, they are representative of the present unity or chaos in American culture, and they are effective of further unity and chaos.

IMPLICATION FOR METHOD

What are the implications for method of these presuppositions? Since method is concerned with interpretation the implications for method must be looked at in the examination of the hermen-

---

8. Cf. L. Gilkey, **Naming the Whirlwind: The Renewal of God-Language** (New York: Bobbs-Merrill, 1969), p. 255.

eutical event. I would see these implications as twofold: speculative and practical.

In regard to the speculative implications for method of these presuppositions I would make three claims:

First, that where disorganization and chaos are implicit in the event, so these will be present implicitly or explicitly in the outcome. The purpose of knowledge as presupposed in the American "Now" is narrow because it neglects the fact that man understands with his whole body: emotions, will, health—the whole man. There are varying influences in man, to some extent beyond control. When we say "give us time; we'll figure it out," we turn our backs on the fact that we may not have time, that the backdrop of chaotic emotion may wipe out all that mind discovers or attempts to build. When we state that a knowledge of history is a knowing perspective upon present action we forget that man can say "no" to his own history and destroy it in the chaos of death. When we de-mythologize a past event to tell it "as it really is" without a consideration of the present myths, we build upon sands that will shift when others de-mythologize our myths. When we posit that presuppositions cannot be attacked, we creep into an individualism which in itself leads to further chaos. It is suggested, therefore, that the present hermeneutic is representative of the present historical chaos and also productive of further chaos. The chaos is ontologically part of every being. Second, and this is my main point, chaos is present in the historicity of all those involved in the event because our culture is chaotic. This chaos, of both types, only leads to further chaos.

My second claim for method is that where coherence is implicit so will the outcome be coherent. In the present hermeneutic this is found principally in the building up of myth. Langer in her *Philosophy in a New Key* states that every era works with a certain world-view, certain presuppositions upon which all agree (though implicitly) as normative.[9] Such agreement does not exist today. However there is what I would call a "feeling around for the

9. S. Langer, **Philosophy in a New Key** (New York: Mentor Books, 1948), ch. 1.

proper myth." By this I mean that people are trying on various world-views, myths, interpretations of reality. Sometimes these are discarded as soon as they are tried, because they just do not fit. But because man is a myth making animal, I think that somewhere behind this "trying on" a new myth, a new unity is being born. What are some of these new myths? I will not play the prophet but I will quote from those who enjoy the role. Novak would see a culture where everyone was respectful, willing to learn and responsive as one myth that should be a-growing;[10] Wheeler would see man as non-belligerent, technical, and living in a democratic theocracy as another myth which is coming to prominence in our society.[11] For my purposes, though, it makes no difference what the specific myth or myths are. My claim is only that they are present in the hermeneutic event because they are present in our culture and that they offer points of unity which are derivative from the hermeneutical event.

The third and final claim is that where the individuals involved in the hermeneutical event betray disorientation, its traces will be evident in the outcome of the event. In our fifth presupposition we stated that the individual was seen as the ultimate criterion. If this is so, then the individual disorientated person's interpretation will also be disorientated. This claim is merely stating that people are involved in interpretation and that they can bend the interpretative event to fit their own purposes for good or for evil. Their final interpretation will reflect the individual's personal likes and dislikes.

These speculative claims, in regard to the present hermeneutic, result in very concrete, practical consequents for the academic study of religion.

First, one's own personality must always be considered in the work being done. In any interpretative process, whether carried out in the classroom or in the study, one's personality will color the final outcome of the event. If one is aware of his own feelings

---

10. M. Novak, "The Enlightenment is Dead," **The Center Magazine** 4 (March/April, 1971), p. 20.

11. H. Wheeler, "The Phenomenon of God," **ibid**, pp. 11-12.

and thoughts and takes these into consideration in his own work a deeper recognition of the interpretation can take place.

Second, there must be a recognition that historical research is limited. One should not claim more for the past than is its due. The present cannot be left in order to go into the past. The meaning of a past work cannot be seen solely in terms of itself. On the contrary, the "meaning" of the past work is defined in terms of the questions put to it from the present. Because of this fact one should be aware that his claim that tradition speaks a specific truth or scripture says something is also dependent upon the present question. Many times the past says nothing of the sort that we are claiming for it. We should admit this and let our present teaching stand or fall on its own merits and not on the merits of some hidden past authority. The questions of the present are not always the questions of the past.

Third, there will always be chaos in the interpretative process. As long as man searches for answers, as long as he questions, there will be chaos, disorder. There will never be a systematic unity of answers to one question, just as there will never be one question to ask of reality. This is not something to be feared. What it tells us is that man cannot solve his problems by intellectual interpretation alone. Something more is always needed. Human knowledge is not the sole solution to human problems.

Fourth, and last: human acquiescence to argumentation depends upon more than its logical consistency. From the presuppositions mentioned above and also from the chaos which results from these presuppositions, it must be recognized in every interpretative event that your interpretation does not necessarily lead to the conviction of others. Your interpretation is not someone else's interpretation. There may be logical consistency for you. You may have complete coherence to your argument but there is always that added extra of the individual's will, to see as you see, that makes the difference.

SUMMARY

Understanding our own presuppositions is necessary. Understanding the presuppositions of our culture is important. Whether our understanding has effects upon our actions we only know in practice. The "now" is changing. Where it goes, we do not know. We can only hint at what is happening. I have given some hints by suggesting that the hermeneutical event itself should be seen as a whole. A symbolic whole which will be representative of its culture and also influential in creating a new culture.

9   The Crisis In American Culture— A Religious Interpretation

WILLIAM E. MURNION

The crisis in American culture may not be so evident today, now that campuses and ghettoes are quiet once again. Yet even the establishment knows better than to think that the threat of revolution which hung over America for the last few years has vanished and left us, nevermore to return. Last year, a special issue of *Life* on "The New Shape of America" quoted the results of a Harris poll of 26 million Americans between the ages of fifteen and twenty-one which purported to show that "young people are surprisingly traditional in their basic values and beliefs," so that we might expect that "after a long and nasty interlude, the conflicting elements in our society are edging toward accommodation."[1] In the same issue, though, the writer of the main article had to admit that "America isn't returning to anything; it is in the process of emerging into something else," for "many Americans are persuaded that something is enormously wrong."[2] Likewise, in the cover story in which *Time* announced "The Cooling of America," it had also to admit that "some fundamental assumptions have been altered," and "most of the trouble that breeds violence is still there," so that the cooling-off period we are now enjoying is but "an opportunity for America to get on with the much-delayed business of rebuilding itself."[3] Small wonder, then,

---

1. **Life,** January 8, 1971, p. 22.
2. **Ibid.,** p. 86.
3. **Time,** February 22, 1971, p. 10.

that in his State of the Union message President Nixon should have blurted out, "Let's face it. Most Americans today are simply fed up with government at all levels. They will not—and should not—continue to tolerate the gap between promise and performance." Then he called for "a new American revolution—a peaceful revolution in which power [is] turned back to the people."[4] Quite justifiably, Emmet Hughes could deride this speech by "the era's most resolute antirevolutionary" as the fitting climax to the "Age of Rubbish," Richard Hofstadter's epithet for the sixties, but the fact that the era's most consummate politician felt it necessary to echo the call for revolution does show just how deepset and widespread the sentiment for revolution has become.[5]

What the establishment acknowledges as a threat, the intelligentsia proclaims as a prophecy. The descriptions may vary: "generation gap,"[6] "new radicalism"[7] "the New Left,"[8] "the counter culture,"[9] "rebellion,"[10] "the pursuit of loneliness,"[11] "the expe-

---

4. **Ibid.**, February 1, 1971, p. 11.

5. Emmet John Hughes, "From the New Frontier to the New Revolution," **The New York Times Magazine**, April 4, 1971, p. 25.

6. Margaret Mead, **Culture and Commitment:** A Study of the Generation Gap. (New York: Natural History, 1970).

7. Paul Jacobs and Saul Landau, **The New Radicals** (New York: Random House, 1966); M. Novak, **A Theology for Radical Politics** (New York: Herder & Herder, 1969).

8. Mitchell Cohen and Dennis Hale, **The New Student Left: An Anthology** (Boston: Beacon Press, 1966); Priscilla Long, ed., **The New Left: A Collection of Essays** (Boston: Sargent, 1969); Carl Oglesby, ed., **The New Left Reader** (New York, Grove Press, 1969); Massimo Teodori, ed., **The New Left: A Documentary History** (Indianapolis-New York: Bobbs, Merrill, 1969).

9. Theodore Roszak, **The Making of a Counter Culture:** Reflections on the Technocratic Society and Its Youthful Opposition (Garden City, New York: Doubleday, 1969).

10. William O. Douglas, **Points of Rebellion** (New York: Random House, 1970); Stephen Spender, **The Year of the Young Rebels** (New York: Random House, 1969).

11. Philip Slater, **The Pursuit of Loneliness** (Boston: Beacon Press, 1970).

rience of nothingness,"[12] or "the greening of America."[13] But in every case the event is the same: a transformation of consciousness among white, middle- and upper-class American college youth. They are rejecting the American way of life in the name of the professed values of America; that is, they are rejecting technocracy, the Protestant ethic, and capitalism in the name of life, liberty, and the pursuit of happiness. Now it may be, as the Bergers rather cynically argue, that all this cultural revolution will produce is a hardening of the class structure along with an exchange of roles, as lower middle-class and working-class youth assume the positions in industry and government now being forfeited by the upper-class and middle-class youth who are turning toward careers in art and the social sciences or else dropping out of the system altogether.[14] But it is at least as likely that it means, as Jean-François Revel maintains, the beginning of a new world revolution, for never before have economic, political, social, and cultural motives for revolution been welded into a united front, centered in such a large, affluent, and educated body, empowered by the new revolutionary technique of dissent and dedicated to ending the aggressive dominance of the nation-state for the sake of world peace based on global order.[15]

If America is indeed facing a cultural crisis of potentially global import, a religious person naturally looks for a religious explanation. I propose, therefore, to sketch some of the factors in the crisis to bring out the religious dimension in it; then I shall advance the interpretation that the Christian faith is the ultimate

---

12. Michael Novak, The Experience of Nothingness (New York: Harper & Row, 1970).

13. Charles Reich, The Greening of America (New York: Random House, 1970).

14. Philip L. Berger & Brigette Berger, "The Blueing of America," The New Republic, April 3, 1971, pp. 20-23.

15. Jean-François Revel, Ni Marx ni Jesus: De la seconde révolution américaine à la seconde revolution mondiale (Paris, 1970), pp. 9, 14, 219, 226, 228, 234. For confirmation see Tom Wicker, "The Politics before Us," New York Review of Books, February 11, 1971, pp. 14-18.

reason for the crisis; and, finally, I shall reflect upon some of the presuppositions of such an interpretation. For it is my belief that this crisis is essentially a crisis in the Christian religion, and as such it signals the need for a transformation in the religious consciousness of Christians.

FOUR FACTORS IN THE CRISIS

Four factors in the crisis in American culture are revolution in politics, renewal in education, rebellion among youth, and reform in the Church. Each of these motives for change has precipitated a movement that began as an effort to correct abuses in the system and then, as participants in it came to realize the abuses were systematic rather than accidental, turned into resistance to the system itself. These movements have fed into one another, and taken together they indicate a change of heart in America.

The revolution in politics means that needy minorities now realize they cannot achieve a just share in the goals of the system that denies them justice. The first to move have been the blacks. For a while, after the Supreme Court decision of 1954, it seemed that blacks could count on nonviolent protest to prompt the legislation which would prohibit segregation in schools and housing and discrimination in jobs and public facilities. They thought then they could rely upon police enforcement of such legislation to guarantee their enjoyment of civil rights. It quickly became clear, though, North as well as South, that whenever blacks insisted upon their rights, they would have to face police violence and that no amount of legislation would overcome the deep and pervasive racism of American society. The long hot summers from 1964 to 1967, climaxing in the paroxysm of rioting after Martin Luther King's assassination on April 4, 1968, revealed a black rage born of long frustration.[16] King lived long enough to see his leadership challenged by black nationalists, to know blacks had come to

16. Report of the National Advisory Commission on Civil Disorders (New York, 1968); Jerome Skolnick, The Politics of Protest (New York: Simon & Schuster, 1969), pp. 125-209.

repudiate his theory of nonviolence in favor of black power, and to fear the movement for civil rights would become a movement for black separatism.[17] Now, it seems, all ethnic groups, the Indians and Chicanos whom the blacks inspired, as well as the Italians and the Polish whom the blacks threaten, show more faith in violence than in politics to gain or to protect their rights.[18]

Likewise, the peace movement has become revolutionary. What was once a protest movement against the political decisions leading to American involvement in Southeast Asia has become resistance to the American government itself. Trials of draft-resisters, destroyers of Selective Service files, alleged conspirators in draft resistance, destruction of government property, kidnapping of government officials, and incitement to riot show not only that the movement has become revolutionary but that the government recognizes it as such. Daniel Berrigan has been quoted as saying that no one can be a Christian and obey the laws of this country.[19] The Weathermen, now underground, have taken to bombing public buildings, including the Capitol in Washington. More significant, perhaps, than any of these other actions is the ballooning movement of tax resistance among the middle class.[20] This classical American revolutionary tactic is a practical response to the raft of well-documented attacks on the military-industrial complex now in control of the American government.[21]

---

17. See Martin Luther King, **Where Do We Go from Here: Chaos or Community?** (Boston: Beacon Press, 1968).

18. Skolnick, **op. cit.**, pp. 210-292.

19. See "The Resistant Priests," Newsweek, August 17, 1970, p. 94.

20. Peter Barnes, "Withholding War Taxes," The New Republic, April 10, 1971, pp. 15-17.

21. Robert Perrucci and Marc Pilusik, **The Triple Revolution: Social Problems in Depth** (Boston: Little Brown Co. 1968) pp. 3-172. Richard Barnet, **Economy of Death** (New York: Atheneum, 1969); Sidney Lens, **Military-Industrial Complex** (Philadelphia and Kansas City: Crowell, 1970); Adam Yarmolinsky, **The Military Establishment; Its Impact on American Society** (A Twentieth Century Fund Study: New York, 1971); Richard Kaufman, **The War Profiteers** (Indianapolis-New York: Bobbs-Merrill, 1971); James A. Donovan and David Shoup, **Militarism, U.S.A.** (New York, 1970). See the review article by I. F. Stone, "In the Bowels of Behemoth," **New York**

As yet, the poor have not been able to organize as effectively as either blacks or pacifists, perhaps because the poverty of their culture has deprived them of the self-respect necessary for group consciousness. Still, the poor have shown signs of radicalization. So vigorous was their response to the provision for maximum possible cooperation in the programs of the Office of Economic Opportunity that the Johnson administration had to quickly clamp down on the programs and the Nixon administration has all but dismantled the Office. Representatives of the poor disrupted the 1969 White House Conference on Food, Nutrition, and Health and then formed a rump session at the follow-up to the conference in February of last year (1971). All along, Saul Alinsky has had success in organizing the poor to seize power when and where they have had a clearcut grievance. And an ideology for a revolution of the poor lies waiting in the writings of John Kenneth Galbraith, Richard Elman, Michael Harrington, Benjamin Seligman, and Gabriel Kolko, all of whom argue that the capitalist economics of the United States have produced poverty and serve to keep the poor in their place. But the real radicalization of the poor needs no ideological base: it is to be found in the spiraling crime rate, especially in inner-city ghettoes. For criminality becomes a way of life, Daniel Bell has argued, for those who cannot attain the normal economic benefits of society by legitimate means.[22]

Review of Books, March 11, 1971, pp. 29-37.

22. Daniel Bell, "Crime as an American Way of Life," The Antioch Review, 13 (June, 1953), 131-154. His theory is based upon Robert K. Merton's thought in "Social Structure and Anomie," Social Theory and Social Structure (London, 1957[2]), pp. 131-160. See also The Epidemiology of Delinquency and Crime" in Donald R. Cressey and David A. Ward, eds., Delinquency, Crime and Social Process (New York, Evanston & London: Harper & Row, 1969), pp. 243-418, and Fred P. Graham, "A Contemporary History of American Crime," in Hugh Davis Graham and Ted Robert Gurr, The History of Violence in America: Historical and Comparative Perspectives (New York-Washington-London: Praeger, 1969), pp. 485-504; Ramsey Clark, Crime in America (New York: Simon & Schuster, 1970).

What is important to realize about the revolution in politics coming from the blacks, the pacifists, and the poor is that it means not just a change of tactics, but a shift in strategy. It now aims not at getting a share of the benefits promised under the present economic system but at changing the political system to provide for a new kind of economics, one that will enable racial equality, peace, and common prosperity.

Besides the revolution in politics, America is also facing renewal in education. For years, radical critics of the educational system had been saying that from kindergarten to graduate school it failed to educate, in the most basic sense of enabling students to develop their human potential. But no one listened until the revolution in politics backed up into education. Then it became evident that the schools, instead of providing a base from which to liberate blacks, end the war, and eliminate poverty, served rather to enforce the *status quo*. One study after another showed that schools taught blacks to become stupid and violent, that the research facilities of the larger universities were in the pay of the military, and that colleges functioned as training schools for government, industry, and the armed services.[23] At Berkeley in 1964 the students there discovered that they would have to transform the university before they could hope to use it as a base to transform society. Teach-ins, protests against government- and industry-recruiters, leadership in peace demonstrations, all tended to politicize the university, not in the sense that it now entered the political life of the country, but in the sense that it now had to acknowledge its responsibility for the political system. The student take-over at Columbia in 1968 made it evident that the university could no longer function under the absentee land-

---

23. E.g., Ronald and Beatrice Gross, **Radical School Reform** (New York: Simon & Schuster, 1970); Charles Silberman, **Crisis in the Classroom** (New York: Random House, 1970); Henry J. Aiken, "The American University" (a review article of Daniel Bell's **The Reforming of General Education**; James Perkins' **The University in Transition**; and Herbert Shoup's **Bureaucracy in Higher Education**), **New York Review of Books,** October 20 and November 3, 1966; idem, **The Predicament of the University** (Bloomington, Ind: Univ. of Indiana, 1971).

lordship of trustees representing moneyed interests, but had to become an active society of the administrators, faculty, and students who were actually engaged in the process of education.[24] The moratorium of the spring of 1970 confirmed the impression that there would never be peace on campus until America ended its involvement in Vietnam and concentrated its energies upon solving the problems of the blacks and the poor at home.[25] Yet President Nixon was right to insist that the university must heal itself before blaming all its ills upon him, for even the baneful effect of government policy upon campus life had become possible only because the university had made education into a means for its own enrichment instead of treating it as an end in itself. The renewal that has begun is based on the assumption that education as the process of facilitating human growth-and-development is an end in itself with its own internal dynamism and its own fulfillment.[26]

The change of heart in America is not confined, though, to revolution and renewal; it is also found, perhaps most poignantly, in the rebellion of the young. For no matter how successful revolution or renewal may prove to be, the white, middle-class youth of America have already decided that neither of these movements is adequate to their needs. They have begun to form a counter culture that prefers to preserve nature instead of polluting it, to play instead of work, to enjoy sensuality instead of repressing

---

24. See Crisis at Columbia: The Cox Commission Report (New York, 1968); A. Etzioni, "Confessions of a Professor Caught in a Revolution," New York Times Magazine, September 15, 1968; J. L. Avron et al., Up Against the Ivy Wall (New York: Atheneum, 1969); "Annual Education Review," The New York Times, January 9, 1969, pp. 49-80.

25. See "Peace on Campuses: New Survey," U.S. News and World Report, November 16, 1970, p. 66 (on the Report of the President's Commission on Campus Unrest); Immanuel Wallerstein and Paul Starr, eds., The University Crisis Reader (2 vols. New York: Random House, 1971).

26. Philip H. Phenix, Education and the Common Good (New York: Wiley, 1961); Robert Wolff, The Ideal of the University (Boston: Beacon Press, 1970); Robert Nisbet, The Degradation of the Academic Dogma: The University in America, 1947-1970 (New York: Basic Books, 1971); Paul Goodman, New Reformation: Notes of a Neolithic Conservative (New York: Random House, 1970).

it, to promote community instead of individualism. By exalting art over science, intuition over calculation, involvement over detachment, subjectivity over objectivity, they are attempting to recover that primordial unity of man with his environment, of human beings with one another, and especially of man with himself that has largely been lost in the modernization of Western culture.[27] Their recourse to drugs, to rock, to exotic clothing, to Eastern religions and occultism manifests an effort to escape from Western culture, and so far escape seems to have been the closest they have come to freedom. But women's liberation and gay liberation, because they affect the psyche at its profoundest depths, may yet prove to be the levers that will turn escape into a constructive and programmatic search for freedom.[28] Then the rebellion of youth will be on its way to achieving its aim of personal self-appropriation in all its dimensions.

Important as revolution, renewal, and rebellion are to the crisis in American culture, the most significant factor of all is reform in the Church. For reform means ultimately a revision of ultimate values, and that entails the reconception of an entire culture. The reform in the American church seems to have been precipitated by the Second Vatican Council. Before that the Catholic Church had little identity of its own; it had attempted to be as Roman as possible in theology and liturgy and as American as possible in bureaucracy and style, thus becoming both a religious ghetto and also indistinguishable from American society. But the stringent self-examination of the Church in Vatican II came just as American culture was under attack, and the stir of reform that resulted in the Catholic Church in America encouraged efforts at reform in Protestant and Episcopal churches. In this reform, just as in any other, the leadership has come from

---

27. Theodore Roszak, **op. cit.**, pp. 205-238; see Mitchell Goodman, ed., **The Movement Toward a New America** (Philadelphia and New York: Knopf, 1970); William Hedgepeth and Dennis Stock, **The Alternative: Communal Life in America** (New York: Macmillan, 1971).

28. Mary Daly, "After the Death of God The Father," **Commonweal,** March 12, 1971.

those who have abandoned their positions in the established structures in order to form new ones: the laity who have joined underground churches and started their own associations, the nuns who as individuals have left their convents or as groups have renounced the control of local bishops and of the Roman curia over their apostolate, the priests who have either laicized or else formed voluntary associations within the official ministry. Thus the counter-reformation within established structures has depended for its success upon the threat of further loss to the Church of some of its most active and dedicated members. But the issue of reform is joined not between those within and those without but between those who think the Christian religion can transcend the limits of Western culture to become truly a world religion and those who believe the Christian faith is indeed on the verge of inaugurating a new era but the Christian religion is wed to Western civilization, and specifically to that form of Western civilization known as Christendom.[29] The former regard reform as an adaptation of ecclesiastical structures to new demands; the latter consider it a transformation of the religious consciousness comparable to the emergence of Christianity from Judaism.

These, then, seem to be the main factors in the crisis in American culture—revolution in politics, renewal in education, rebellion among youth, and reform in the Church. The question arises—if these are the elements of the crisis, what does it really mean? It might be interpreted politically as the emergence of a New Left, psychologically as either purposeful schizophrenia or futile oedipal rage, sociologically as the normality of conflict in the process of change, historically as the decadence of a civilization, philosophically as part of the destiny/downfall of Western metaphysics, or theologically as the death of God in the modern world. Each of these interpretations has something to recommend it and altogether would provide a fairly comprehensive picture

---

29. For the latter view see Arend Th. Van Leeuwen, **Christianity in World History: The Meeting of the Faiths of East and West** (New York: Charles Scribner's Sons, 1966); idem, **Development through Revolution** (New York, Charles Scribner's Sons, 1970).

of the situation, but by reducing the crisis to a more general category they also seem to impose a meaning upon the crisis from without rather than draw one from within it. If we look at the motives of those who have precipitated the crisis, it becomes apparent that the crisis is basically religious in nature. It is obvious that those who are engaged in the reform of the Church are inspired by religious motives, and we have only to recall the leadership of Martin Luther King, the Berrigans, and Cesar Chavez in the revolution in politics to realize just how much it has been animated by the same motivation. Likewise, Joseph Califano has described campus turmoil as a crisis of belief,[30] and Paul Goodman has diagnosed it as a New Reformation,[31] so that it is evident that the renewal of education entails religious motivation. Both Michael Novak and Theodore Roszak have shown how youth in their rebellion are prone to apply religious criteria to their critique of American culture and eager to find some religious meaning in life if only through Eastern religions or occultism.[32] Therefore, I think it is much more natural to define the crisis in American culture as a heresy against what Robert Bellah has called the civil religion of America: the more or less conscious belief that America is the realization of the Kingdom of God on earth.[33] For the crisis has occurred precisely because those engaged in revolution, renewal, rebellion, and reform have denied the ultimate value of one or another American institution or belief in such a way as to disrupt the fundamental consensus necessary for a unified civil religion.

---

30. Joseph Califano, **The Student Revolution:** A Global Confrontation (New York: W. W. Norton & Co., 1970).

31. Paul Goodman, **op. cit.**

32. Michael Novak, **A Theology for a Radical Politics**, pp. 17-29, 99-128; Theodore Roszak, **op. cit.**, pp. 124-154, 239-268.

33. Robert Bellah, "Civil Religion in America," **Daedalus**, 96/1 (1967), 1-21; reprinted in D. Cutler, ed., **The Religious Situation 1968** (Boston: Beacon Press, 1968) pp. 331-56; see also Sidney Mead, **The Lively Experiment** (New York: Harper & Row, 1963); H. R. Niebuhr, **The Kingdom of God in America** (Chicago: Harper & Row, 1937).

An Explanatory Hypothesis

If the crisis in American culture is truly religious in both intent and effect, then the only adequate interpretation of it must also be religious. Thus it is my contention that, while the crisis entails a rejection of religion, even of the Christian religion insofar as it is the source of the civil religion of America, it is nonetheless a crisis which the Christian faith has caused, since in Western civilization the Christian faith has been the source of the revolution, renewal, rebellion, and reform which have engendered the crisis in America. In other words, my hypothesis is that the Christian faith has shaped the Christian religion through a process of revolution, renewal, rebellion and reform, but when the Christian religion proved inadequate to realize all the potential of these impulses, the faith itself generated the secular culture of modern times as an alternative mode of self-propagation. Hence, what we are now experiencing in America is the culmination of the process of secularization provoked by the Christian faith.

To anyone who thinks of the Christian religion as identical with the Christian faith and of the Christian faith as an immutable essence, such a transformation of it must appear incredible. But to anyone who is aware of the history of the Christian faith such transformations seem to be of the essence of it. For, in the first place, the Christian faith originated from a progress in revelation which prompted a change in religious perspective from people to world, from law to love, from apocalypse to eschaton, from monotheism to incarnation—a change so marked it could not be contained within the same religious tradition. With the establishment of Christianity, progress in revelation hardly ceased, if the mission of the Spirit to the Church means anything at all, but at that point it became a development of dogma, which created the propositional realism of Western philosophy by adapting Hellenistic thought, in all its materialism, naturalism, and essentialism, to an explanation of the meaning of the redemption.[34] And though the development of dogma did not end with the Council of Chalcedon, if the *magisterium* of the Church is to be recognized as authentically Christian, by that time it had begun to generate a history of theology, as the great speculative minds of Christendom attempted to understand the dogmas of the faith in some systematic way. Finally, the history of theology as an independent science did not end with Aquinas or Calvin or Hegel, if the scientific study of religion is to be taken seriously, but with the emergence of the modern world it has been sublated into a fundamental hermeneutic, the study of the conditions for the possibility of faith in the dynamic structure of human consciousness. Thus, the history of the Christian faith is the story of the basic transformation by which it has been constituted as what it is.

Now it would be possible to demonstrate that the Christian faith is the source of revolution, renewal, rebellion, and reform in Western civilization by tracing each of these movements back to its origin in the Bible, but it will be more convenient, I think, to demonstrate the results of such retrospection by beginning with the origins of each of these movements in the biblical revelation, then following their developments through the formation of the Christian religion, into the onset of secularization in modern times, up to their influence upon the present crisis in American culture.

REVOLUTION

By revolution, I mean the effort to obtain equality among men in the enjoyment of the resources of the earth. This economic interpretation is justified, I believe, on a number of grounds: modern revolutions have arisen for economic reasons and have resulted in economic benefits;[35] the Marxian notion of world

---

34. See Bernard J. Lonergan, "The Origins of Christian Realism," (mimeographed notes of lecture at Regis College, Ontario, September 8, 1961).

35. Crane Brinton, **The Anatomy of Revolution**, (New York: Peter Smith, 1952[2]), pp. 28-71, 254-61, 266-68, 278-80, 291.

revolution is economic; the revolution in the Third World is based upon economic grievances; and revolution threatens our own country because of the economic injustices of our foreign and domestic policies. To understand the meaning of revolution, therefore, it will be necessary to discover the inspiration of the search for economic equality in Western culture.

That inspiration is to be found in biblical messianism. For in Israel the king functioned as Yahweh's anointed to protect the promised land from invasion and to assure justice within it for all (2 S 7:14). The infidelity of kings to their mission led to the institution of prophecy, for it was the duty of the prophet to recall the king to his responsibility to the poor of Yahweh, but finally the prophets began to place their trust in a Messiah anointed by the Spirit to bring to the poor the good news their day had come (Is 11:1f; 61:1f).[36] At Nazareth, Jesus attributed the fulfillment of this prophecy to himself (Lk 4:16; cf. Mt 11:2-6); in the Sermon on the Mount he told the poor to rejoice for the Kingdom of God was theirs (Mt 5:3; Lk 6:20) and in the Eschatological Discourse he promised that at the last judgment the King would admit to the kingdom of his Father only those who had recognized him in the poor (Mt 25:31-46). There is some basis then for believing that Jesus himself interpreted his messiahship in terms of the Suffering Servant,[37] and almost none for believing he thought of himself as a leader of violent revolution.[38] The primitive Christian community took his lead by identifying his lordship over creation with his death in the form of a servant (Phil 2:9). They emulated Christ's identification with the poor by surrendering all personal possessions (Acts 4:32), and under

---

36. Wilhelm Zimmerli and Joachim Jeremias, **The Servant of God** (S.B.T. 20: London and Napierville, Ind., 1957), pp. 79 ff.; cf. R. Fuller, **The Foundations of New Testament Christology** (New York: Charles Scribner's Sons, 1965), pp. 102-141, esp. pp. 115-119.

37. Oscar Cullman, **Jesus and the Revolutionaries**, trans. G. Putnam (New York-Evanston-London: Harper & Row, 1970) vs. S. G. F. Brandon, **Jesus and the Zealots** (New York: Charles Scribner's Sons, 1968).

38. David Stanley, **Christ's Resurrection and Pauline Soteriology**, Analecta Biblica (Rome, 1961).

the guidance of Paul they came to conceive of their own mission as an identification with Christ in the fellowship of his sufferings (Phil 3:10).[39] Thus the biblical conception of power became identified with service to the poor.

This conception became part of the tradition of the Church insofar as the counsel of evangelical poverty became recognized as a condition for leading a life of perfection in monasticism. The only difficulty with this conception of poverty was that it tended to divorce it from power, for once the Church became established after the Peace of Constantine, the ordinary laity were not expected to lead a life of poverty, nor was political power employed to eliminate either slavery or the causes of poverty. What is more, the hierarchy's assumption of political power marked its distance from any identification with poverty. By the time of the Cluniac reform it had become virtually impossible for a monastery to have any effect upon the larger society without succumbing itself to the corruption of wealth. It may be too much to assert that the heresies of the ancient Church were disguised social movements, but there is no denying that the major heresy of the twelfth-century Poor People's movements led by Arnold of Brescia and Peter Waldo was their threat to the vested interests of papacy and hierarchy.[40] Only through the rise of the friars, Franciscans and Dominicans, in the thirteenth century did the power structure of the Church institutionalize within itself, if only for a while, the ideal of evangelical poverty.[41]

---

39. Yves Congar, **Power and Poverty in the Church,** Garden City, N. Y.: Doubleday, 1964).

40. A. H. M. Jones, "Were Ancient Heresies Disguised Social Movements?" (**Facet Books,** Historical Series, 1: Philadelphia, 1966); H. G. Beck, K. A. Fink, J. Glazik, E. Iserloh, H. Wolter, **From the High Middle Ages to the Eve of the Reformation (Handbook of Church History,** H. Jedin and J. Dolan, eds., Vol. IV: New York, 1970), pp. 98-104. The legal basis for the Inquisition began to be laid when Innocent III, on March 25, 1199, condemned heresy as **"crimen laesae maiestatis,"** the identical charge that had been made the basis for persecuting Christians in the Roman Empire during the second century.

41. Jurgen Moltmann, **Religion, Revolution, and the Future** (New York:

By realizing the identification of power with poverty, the friars became the originators of the social and intellectual revolutions that ushered in modern times. Joachim of Fiore (b. 1260), a Spiritual Franciscan, called for a new era, inspired by the Spirit, to succeed the era of the Church, so that the poor could have the Gospel preached to them unencumbered by the burden of the hierarchy.[42] In the radical Reformation, Joachim's ideas became the stimulus for aiming at a new social order that presumed the equality of all men before God. This kind of populist Christianity provided through the English Revolution of 1648 and 1688 the religious sanction for modern revolution by countenancing regicide as a means of achieving economic equality for all.[43]

Likewise, it was the friars, Dominicans at Paris and Cologne and Franciscans at Oxford, who initiated the intellectual revolution of modern times. At the universities in those cities, they began to use the experimental method that became the basis of modern science, they cultivated the development of rational inquiry that enabled the establishment of modern philosophy, and they compiled the records that led to the origins of modern history. The motivation for the emergence of these new intellectual disciplines was a desire for control over nature. The methodical pursuit of these disciplines became the means for a knowledge of the world apart from the authority of the Church, which had through the abuse of its power forfeited any right to stewardship over nature.

By the end of the eighteenth century, the social and intellectual revolutions the friars had begun five centuries earlier had culminated in an Age of Revolution, beginning with the Industrial Revolution in England and the political and social revolution in France. For the remainder of the nineteenth century, Europe

---

Charles Scribner's Sons, 1969), pp. xii, 26; a more critical assessment is to be found in Eric Voegelin's **The New Science of Politics** (Chicago: Univ. of Chicago, 1966[2]), pp. 110-117.

---

42. George M. Trevelyan, **The English Revolution 1688-1689** (Oxford, 1946[2]).

43. Herbert Butterfield, **The Origins of Modern Science 1300-1800** (New York: Free Press, 1958[2]).

was periodically racked with revolution: in 1830, again in 1848, and finally in 1870. By that time, the bourgeoisie had replaced in power both hierarchy and aristocracy by gaining control over commerce and industry, the levers of economic might, but they had communicated the spirit of revolution to a new class, the proletariat, who had emerged in the course of revolution itself.[44]

Thus, while Marx at first regarded his thought as the necessary theory for future revolutionary practice, after 1844 he came to realize that it was really the articulation of the revolutionary practice of the proletariat.[45] It is now commonplace to recognize in Marx's thought a secular messianism, to detect in it influences of the radical Reformation, to note the constitutive effect upon it of the intellectual revolution in science, philosophy, and history, and to remark on the derivativeness of his realization of the revolutionary significance of the proletariat. To that extent Marx's thought was an articulation of the past even more than he realized, but what was truly original was his discovery of the significance of work—his realization that the poor are powerful precisely because they are the ones whose work enables a control of nature and, thereby, the possibility of man's enjoyment of the earth. Thus Marx's vision of the power of the proletariat to bring about a world revolution, after which everyone would work as he was able and receive what he needed, was a secular transformation of the good news the Christian faith had first proclaimed to the poor.

Hence, the Christian response to Marxism in the social encyclicals, in the thought of Ernst Troeltsch, and in the Social Gospel is but the recognition of the revolutionary mission of Christianity. And the Christian-Marxist dialogue which has ensued is grounded not only on the need to work together for the future but also

---

44. E. J. Hobshawm, **The Age of Revolution 1789-1848** (Cleveland: Praeger, 1962), pp. 114, 121 ff., 200-216 (esp., 204 ff.).

45. Nicholas Lobkowicz, **Theory and Practice: History of a Concept from Aristotle to Marx** (Notre Dame, Ind. and London, 1964) pp. 271-292; Robert Tucker, **Philosophy and Myth in Karl Marx** (Cambridge, 1965), pp. 113-118.

on the recognition of a common source in the past.[46] The need for world revolution—in the sense of a universal effort to obtain equality among all men in the enjoyment of the resources of the earth—has never been greater. It is that need, first inspired by the Christian faith and now articulated in Marxism, that is behind the threat of revolution in our own country. To that extent the Christian faith is the cause of the revolution in politics that has contributed to the crisis in American culture.

RENEWAL

By renewal, I mean the effort to establish society on a rational basis. Taking this basis as the natural community already existing among men, those engaged in renewal try to formalize the bond through the creation of law and order. Thus the proper medium of renewal is rational discourse and the underlying dynamism, democracy. In such a course of action the only adequate perspective is a thorough-going humanism. For renewal supposes that fraternity is a natural right as well as an ultimate value. To understand the meaning of renewal in Western civilization, therefore, it will be necessary to locate the source of the ideal of fraternity that has inspired the continual efforts to give society a rational order.

That source is to be found in the biblical notion of covenant.[47] For the significance of the Mosaic covenant was that the Hebrews realized they had become the people Israel only through the mercy of God and could remain a people only through His fidelity (Ex 23 and 34). To preserve this covenant, though, they had to respond to God's mercy and fidelity by loving Him with their whole heart and soul and strength and by loving their neighbors as themselves (Dt 6:5; 10:12; 26:16ff). Thus, when they violated the covenant, they began to disintegrate as a people: first, they

---

46. Roger Garaudy, **From Anathema to Dialogue** (Intro., L. Dewart: New York: Random House, 1966); Ernst Bloch, **Atheismus im Christentum** (Frankfurt, 1968).

47. K. Baltzer, **The Covenant Formulary in Old Testament, Jewish and Early Christian Writing** (Philadelphia: Fortress, 1970).

split into two kingdoms; then, one after the other, the kingdoms were conquered by the Gentiles; and, finally, Israel went into exile in Babylon. Even then, however, Yahweh remained faithful to the covenant. Through Ezechiel he promised a new covenant to last forever (Ez 16: 59-63), sealed as it would be through a circumcision of the heart (Jer 4, 4). It was this new covenant that Jesus instituted at the Last Supper through the sacrifice of his own body and blood as a sign of God's utter love for men (Mt 26:28; Jn 15:13); to this initiative on God's part there corresponded on men's part obedience to the new commandment that they love one another as Christ had loved them (Jn 13:34; 15:12; cf. Mt 5:43; 22:34-40). Thus, with the descent of Christ's Spirit upon his disciples at Pentecost, the bond among them became their brotherhood in the breaking of bread (Acts 2:42). Paul conceived of the community which resulted as the Body of Christ (1 Cor 12:12f), living in love (1 Cor 13) and dissolving all distinctions "between Jew and Gentile, slave and free, male and female" so that all became "one in Christ Jesus" (Gal 3:28; Col 3:11).[48] The catholicity of such a community enabled Christianity to break the bonds that bound it initially to one people and to spread East and West, first among subjugated peoples and plebians but eventually throughout all the classes of Roman society. By the time of Constantine the Christian faith had become the real bond of unity in the Empire, and the Christian Church, the established religion.[49]

The consequence of this event was, as Christopher Dawson has so cogently demonstrated, that the Christian religion became the basis of Western culture.[50] Already the Apostolic Fathers and

---

48. J. A. T. Robinson, **The Body: A Study in Pauline Theology** (S.B.T. 5: Napierville, Ind., 1957); L. Cerfaux, **The Church in the Theology of St. Paul, Christ in The Theology of St. Paul,** and **The Christian in The Theology of St. Paul** (New York: Sheed & Ward, 1959 and 1968).

49. Robert M. Grant, **Augustus to Constantine: The Thrust of the Christian Movement into The Roman World** (New York-Evanston-London, 1970).

50. Christopher Dawson, **Religion and The Rise of Western Culture** (Garden City, N. Y.: Doubleday, 1958²); **The Historic Reality of Christian**

the Apologists had appropriated Hellenistic thought as the patrimony of Christianity, in their minds the only true philosophy. Clement and Origen had established the pattern, later to be followed by most of the Fathers, most strikingly by Augustine, of using Neo-Platonist and Stoic thought to express the dependence of world order upon the Word of God, who had created everything in its proper nature and, moreover, had enabled man, through his mind, to share actively in the resultant universal rationality.[51] As the demands of understanding the implications of the incarnation of the Word led in ecumenical councils to the development of Christian realism, so also the demands of governing the orthodox Christian community necessitated the organization of local churches through communion with the church of Rome into one catholic Church. So strong was communion with Rome that even when the Empire broke under the onslaught of the barbarian invasions, the Church retained its identity, converted the barbarians, and expanded throughout what was to become Europe. By the time of the crowning of Charlemagne, however, on Christmas day, A.D. 800, the breach between Western and Eastern halves of the Church had become irremediable, however many attempts were later made to heal it. Thereafter, Catholic and Orthodox, which had once had the same meaning, now designated two different churches, and the Catholic Church became the social and cultural form of Europe, which from its beginnings was known as Christendom or, more simply, the Church.[52]

Though Christendom had become separated from its origins in the East, it returned to Hellenism whenever it wished to recover the rational bases for the establishment of civil society.

Culture (New York: Sheed & Ward, 1960); **The Formation of Christendom** (New York: Sheed & Ward, 1968).

---

51. A. H. Armstrong and R. A. Markus, **Christian Faith and Greek Philosophy** (New York: Sheed & Ward, 1960); Jean Daniélou, **Message évangélique et culture hellenistque** (Tournai, 1961); Henry Chadwick, **Early Christian Thought and the Classical Tradition** (Oxford, 1966).

52. Christopher Dawson, **Understanding Europe** (New York: Sheed & Ward, 1960[2]), esp. pp. 13-50.

Any advance in learning was always based upon the study of classical texts preserved from antiquity, and education consisted largely in the assimilation of the significance of such authoritative texts for a new social context. Thus the Christian humanism that developed tended to regard the very process of understanding as the revival of tradition.[53] The culture of Christendom became, therefore, a tradition of classical renaissance: the sixth century renaissance at the New Academy under Boethius, the Carolingian renaissance of the ninth century, the Frankish renaissance of the twelfth, and, finally, the Italian renaissance of the fifteenth century. Every three centuries, it seemed, Christian humanism needed a renewal from the classical sources that had given it its original shape. In the process, the renewal had turned from a dependence upon Platonist thought to Aristotelianism, then back again, when the study of Aristotle had degenerated into a subservience to the text instead of leading to rational analysis of the world. By the time of the Italian renaissance, the humanist perspective of renewal had become objectified into the study of man himself; now man, instead of a classical authority, became the measure of orthodox thought.[54]

The recovery of self-confidence which this independence of mind implied was no small advance in human culture, but in the process of continual renewal, Christendom had forgotten the dependence of culture upon grace. The Church had become so immured within civil society as to have become indistinguishable from it. If previously Europe had been the Church, now the Church became the Papal States, and Julius II more a petty prince than a pope. Thus the unity which the Church had given Europe through one religion exploded when that religion became the pretext for almost interminable internecine struggle. The Age of Discovery in the fifteenth century had already opened the eyes

---

53. M. D. Chenu, **Introduction a l'etude de Saint Thomas d'Aquin** (Montreal-Paris, 1954²), pp. 22-28, 106-131.

54. Jacob Bronowsky and Bruce Mazlish, **The Western Intellectual Tradition: From Leonardo to Hegel** (New York: Harper & Row, 1960), pp. xv to xvl. To this extent the Burkhardt thesis seems to be correct.

of Europe to cultures that had never known Christianity, and when the Wars of Religion (1560-1648) that followed the discovery of the New World and the Reformation of the Old pitted country against country in the name of the same God, reasonable men began to look for a purely rational basis for human society, one that would enable them to include men who had never been Christian and to exclude the constant strife the Christian religion seemed to have engendered among them.

Thus the Enlightenment was the first attempt at renewal in Western history to turn to pagan antiquity more for its religion than for its philosophy.[55] The philosophers laid the ground-work for dispensing with the hypothesis of God in any science, while there appeared a raft of sciences unknown to antiquity: the human sciences of biology, linguistics, and economics.[56] Following the French revolution, the rise of liberalism marked the effort to make civil society free of any interference from the Christian religion. Freedom of conscience, separation of Church and State, and universal education became the signature of the nation-state as it was constituted by liberal bourgeoisie.[57] The positivism of a self-constituted society created sociology to replace religion as the arbiter of values.[58] As liberals saw their program put into effect, they had reason to consider the nineteenth the most progressive of centuries. They assumed that public education would make inevitable the progress needed to banish forever the social ills still lingering from the dark ages of Christendom.[59]

55. Peter Gay, The Enlightenment: An Interpretation, Vol. I: The Rise of Modern Paganism (New York: Knopf, 1966), esp. pp. 59-71.

56. Michael Foucault, The Order of Things: An Archaelogy of the Human Sciences, (New York: Pantheon, 1971).

57. Martin Marty, The Modern Schism: Three Paths to the Secular (New York: Harper & Row, 1969), pp. 18-58.

58. Alvin Gouldner, The Coming Crisis of Western Sociology (New York: Basic Books, 1970), p. 24.

59. J. Bury, The Idea of Progress: An Inquiry into Its Origin and Growth (New York: Peter Smith, 1932²); Christopher Dawson, Progress and Religion (Garden City, N. Y.: Doubleday, 1960²), esp. pp. 13-61, 143-161.

Many who remained Christian recognized the value of these efforts to give society a rational basis. Lammenais for one, though he failed to convince the Catholic Church of the superiority of the modern state to the *ancien régime*. Schleiermacher, however, was extremely successful in his project of locating religion in a natural instinct within reason itself, and a generation of Protestant theologians proceeded to explore the implications of considering the Christian religion a creation of civil society. Catholic modernists who took the same tack, however, were quickly and severely condemned. Yet it has become recognized in Catholic circles as well as Protestant that the scientific study of religion, as the structure of ultimate values in society, can be applied as well to Christianity as to any other religion. And the renewal of Catholic theology sparked by the Second Vatican Council has consisted essentially in an attempt to assimilate liberalism as openly and fully as the early Church assimilated Hellenism.

Liberal Christianity has begun to demonstrate the ability of the Christian faith to renew society by collaborating in the renewal of education going on today. Education needed such renewal because it had become the instrument of nationalism, that other child of liberalism. The inherent defects of nationalism have become more than evident in two World Wars and one Vietnamese war. What is now needed for world peace is for Christianity once again to demonstrate the dependence of any covenant among men upon a covenant with God.[60]

REBELLION

By rebellion, I mean the effort to achieve perfect freedom. This effort stems from a decision to lead a life in perfect conformity to one's ideals, regardless of the consequences. The rebel chooses this way because he must be true to himself in the

---

60. That does not mean an attempt to restore the Christian culture of the Middle Ages, but rather the sort of fraternal collaboration in establishing bonds of brotherhood which was evident in John XXIII's **Pacem in Terris** and Vatican II's **Constitution on the Church in the Modern World.**

chamber of his conscience.[61] Since civil society always puts restraints upon freedom by demanding compromise and conformity, rebellion requires either the overthrow or the abandonment of civil society. As a consequence, the rebel seeks to find or to found a community based upon the exercise of complete freedom. To understand the meaning of rebellion, therefore, it is necessary to discover the source in Western civilization of the ideal of a community in which one can enjoy complete freedom.

That source is to be sought in biblical apocalyptic.[62] The revelation of God's judgment upon human history originated with the visions constitutive of the prophetic mission (Ex 19; Is 6). But after the Exile, during the days of Seleucid and Roman domination, apocalyptic became distinctive as a belief in the imminence of God's judgment, to come on a Day of the Lord heralded by a Son of Man, who would reward the remnant of Israel with a millennium of perfect peace.[63] By the time of Christ, the most vivid belief in an imminent apocalypse was to be found in the Qumran community living off by itself near the Dead Sea. Jesus confirmed such apocalyptic hopes inasmuch as he announced the kingdom of God was close at hand (Mt 3:2; 4:17; etc.), actually in the midst of his listeners (Lk 17:21). If he did not consider himself at the crucifixion to be the Son of Man heralding the Day of the Lord, at least his disciples did (Mt 26:64).[64] Thus disciple-

---

61. Albert Camus, **Rebel:** An Essay on Man in Revolt, trans. A. Bower (New York: Random House, 1954).

62. H. H. Rowley, **The Relevance of Apocalyptic:** A Study of Jewish and Christian Apocalypses from Daniel to the Revelation (London, 1963³).

63. Bruce Vawter, "Apocalyptic: Its Relation to Prophecy," **Catholic Biblical Quarterly,** 22 (1960), pp. 33-46.

64. F. H. Borsch, **The Son of Man in Myth and History** (New York: Westminster, 1967); Norman Perrin, **The Kingdom of God in the Teaching of Jesus** (London: Westminster, 1963); idem, **Rediscovering the Teaching of Jesus** (New York: Harper & Row, 1967); H. E. Todt, **The Son of Man in the Synoptic Tradition** (New York: Westminster, 1965); F. Hahn, **The Titles of Jesus in Christology: Their History in Early Christianity,** tr. H. Knight and G. Ogg (New York, 1969); R. Funk, ed. "Apocalypticism, **Journal for Theology and the Church,** 6 (1969).

ship to Jesus demanded the purity of heart appropriate to one expecting imminent judgment,[65] and it manifested itself in charisms designed to encourage the faithful remnant in its ultimate trials.[66] According to *Revelations,* these trials occupy the entire career of the Church.

It was this belief that made Christians martyrs to the faith. No compromise with idolatry was possible if God was about to judge them; no earthly kingdom could have the hold on their consciences the kingdom of God exerted. The faith that demanded martyrdom also inspired mysticism. Stephen, Paul, Ignatius, Polycarp—all were martyrs because they were mystics. Thus from the earliest days of Christianity, the mystical realization of God's immanence to the souls of the faithful has given assurance of the imminence of his judgment upon the world. At times of severe crisis, mysticism has sustained Christians as the social order about them has collapsed. In the fourteenth century, therefore, there was a sudden upsurge of mysticism when the medieval world disintegrated before the combined impact of the Avignon captivity and the Black Death.[67]

At the same time millenniarism was rampant. Whole communities, entire cities believed they were the faithful remnant to whom the millennium had been promised. This specious form of apocalyptic derived from Gnosticism, a mirror-image of the Christian religion from its very beginning.[68] Those who were disillusioned to discover that the coming of the Kingdom was marked

---

65. E. Schweizer, **Lordship and Discipleship** (S.B.T. 28: London and Napierville, Ind.).

66. Karl Rahner, **The Dynamic Element in the Church** (Quaestiones Disputatae 12: New York: Herder & Herder, 1964); H. von Campenhausen, **Ecclesiastical Authority and Spiritual Power in the Church of the First Three Centuries** (Stanford: 1967).

. 67. H. G. Beck, K. A. Fink, J. Glazik, E. Iserloh, H. Wolter, **op. cit.**; pp. 291-390; Hilda Graef, **The Story of Mysticism** (New York: Sheed & Ward 1960), esp. pp. 185-217.

68. Norman Cohn, **The Pursuit of the Millennium:** Revolutionary Messianism in Medieval and Reformation Europe and Its Bearing on Modern Totalitarian Movements (New York, 1961²), cf. E. Voegelin, **op. cit.**

by martyrdom for the faith escaped to a private world where they presumed an esoteric knowledge of a spiritual redeemer would preserve them from contamination by the material world.[69] In a paradoxical combination of severe asceticism and extreme eroticism, this belief kept cropping up throughout the history of Christianity, as either Mandaeism or Manicheeism or Catharism, no matter how vehemently it was repressed. The millenniarism of the fourteenth century seems to have been fueled by vestiges of Manicheeism brought back by Crusaders from Moslems who had adopted elements of it.[70]

Millennial expectations did not die because the millennium failed to appear. They animated certain sections of the radical Reformation, and they became spiritualized in Jansenism.[71] But, more significantly, they became secularized in utopian thought.[72] Now there was no longer any expectation of human perfection being reached through the advent of the Kingdom of God, but a Thomas More could speculate about the happiness that would be possible if only men could be made to be perfect. Jean-Jacques Rousseau transformed this speculation into a vision of the natural innocence and goodness of man before he had become corrupted by civil society. His romanticism became the inspiration for a series of abortive attempts by utopian reformers—Proudhon, Saint-Simon, Fourier—to establish communities where the natural goodness of men might be given the freedom to flourish.

One of Fourier's disciples, Robert Owen, transplanted his

---

69. Robert M. Grant, Gnosticism and Early Christianity (New York: Columbia, 1959).

70. Stephen Runciman, The Medieval Manichee (Cambridge, 1947); Denis de Rougement, Love in the Western World (New York: Pantheon, 1956).

71. Norman Cohn, op. cit., pp. 209 ff.; D. F. Durnbach, The Believers' Church: The History and Character of Radical Protestantism (New York: Macmillan, 1968); Ernst Bloch, Thomas Munzer als Theologe der Revolution Frankfurt, 1962²).

72. J. O. Hertzler, The History of Utopian Thought (New York: Cooper Square, 1923); R. R. Ruether, The Radical Kingdom: The Western Experience of Messianic Hope (New York: Harper & Row, 1970).

utopian designs to America.[73] Here, if ever, utopia should have happened. For from the time of the first settlements by radical Protestants, immigrants have been enthralled by the opportunity of making a New World in the virgin wilderness.[74] The subsequent history of America is a story of disillusionment, but it also shows the persistence of a stubborn radicalism among a creative minority. There have always been those who have refused to believe civil society should be allowed to stifle the God-given rights to life, liberty, and the pursuit of happiness. Pacifism, abolition, free-thought, socialism—each of these movements has been a rebellion against deadening conformity to bourgeois values.[75] Even much of the dreadful violence in American history is evidence of impatience with anything less than a perfect order.[76] It is easy to understand, therefore, where the rebellion of today's youth has its origins.

The danger in such rebellion, however, is clear from the direction it took in Europe during and after the French Revolution. For Rousseau's dream of man's recovering his natural state of perfect freedom became the stimulus not only for utopianism but also for anarchism and totalitarianism.[77] The common ground

---

73. J. Harrison, **Quest for the New Moral World:** Robert Owen and Owenites (New York: Charles Scribner's Sons, 1969).

74. R. Nash, **Wilderness and the American Mind** (New Haven: Yale, 1967); D. W. Noble, **The Eternal Adam and the New World Garden** (New York: Grosset & Dunlap, 1968); E. L. Tuveson, **Redeemer Nation: The Idea of America's Millennial Role** (Chicago: Univ. of Chicago, 1968); S. Lens, **Radicalism in America** (New York: T. Y. Crowell, 1966); S. Lynd, ed. **Intellectual Origins of American Radicalism** (New York: Pantheon, 1968 and 1969).

75. Stoughton Lynd, ed., **Nonviolence in America:** A Documentary History (Indianapolis and New York: Bobbs, Merrill, 1966).

76. R. M. Brown, "Historical Patterns of Violence in America," in Graham and Gurr, **op. cit.,** pp. 45-83; **cf. et.** Parts II, III, IV of the same work.

77. Rousseau's responsibility for totalitarianism: J. L. Talmon, **The Origins of Totalitarian Democracy** (New York: Praeger, 1960²); idem, **Political Messianism: The Romantic Phase** (New York: Praeger, 1961). His responsibility for anarchism: Marshall Berman, **The Politics of Authenticity:**

for both of these political philosophies was the belief that if civil society was responsible for man's loss of perfect freedom, it had no reason to exist. They differed in that, according to anarchism, men would become perfect if only they were allowed to be free, while according to totalitarianism, men might become free if they were forced to be perfect. In either case, it was thought justifiable to use whatever violence was necessary to destroy civil society. Thus the consequences of presuming that man can bring the Kingdom of God to earth was a switch from a readiness to suffer to a willingness to kill. Terror instead of martyrdom became the index of rebellion when it abandoned its roots in the Christian faith.

REFORM

By reform, I mean the effort to reassert and augment within man the image and likeness of God in which he has been created.[78] Begun when a man first repents of his sins and turns to God, reform is a process of conversion that continues as long as a man lives. Thus the social dimensions of reform primarily affect religious institutions, always in need of being saved from the corruption flesh is heir to. Insofar as reform applies to secular institutions, it presumes they will be only as good as are the men who create and operate them. Because reform is essentially a religious mode of social change, it is impossible to understand its significance in Western civilization except by referring to its source in biblical revelation.

That source is to be found, as has already been noted, in the notion that though God has created man in his own image and likeness, male and female, to master the earth (Gen 1:26ff), yet

---

Radical Individualism and the Emergence of Modern Society (New York: Atheneum, 1970).

---

78. Gerhard Ladner, The Idea of Reform: Its Impact on Christian Thought and Action in the Age of the Fathers (New York and Evanston: Harper & Row, 1967²), p. 35; cf. S. Otto, Gottes Ebenbild in Geschichtlichkeit: Ueberlegungen zur dogmatischen Anthropologie (Munich-Paderbon-Vienna, 1964).

man has by his sin repudiated this relationship, so that he stands in need of redemption (Gen 3).[79] If there is a central motif to the Bible, it is the contradiction between God's paternal love for his people and their refusal to honor him for it. So prone were they to adore false gods that worship in the Old Testament seems to alternate between idolatry and sacrifice for sin. No wonder, then, that Christ came calling men to repentance (Mt 3:2). He depicted God as a loving Father awaiting the return of his prodigal son so that he might forgive him (Lk 15:11ff.). It is not too much to say that Christ's mission was to enable men to know his Father (Mt 11:27) so as to call upon Him as their own (Mt 6:7ff.).[80] Thus the power Christ shared with Peter and the Twelve was to forgive sins in order to eliminate any barriers to communication (Mt 16:19; 18:18). Hence, Paul could conceive of the Christian life as a death to sin in baptism, with a re-creation of man to the image of Christ.[81] The whole point of the Church then was to foster the continuous effort needed to retain that image.

As a consequence, entrance into the Church demanded a complete reform of morals. It is too much to say that Christianity came on the scene as a new moral code but not that it succeeded in converting the Roman Empire to a new moral life.[82] The idea of reform in the Fathers of the Church was grounded securely upon the notion of man as made to the image and likeness of God. The Greek Fathers interpreted this notion to mean a kind of return to the state of Adam at creation, but the Latin Fathers, particularly St. Augustine, thought of reform as a re-creation

79. J. De Fraine, **Adam and The Family of Man,** trans. D. Raible (Staten Island, N. Y.: Alba House, 1965); H. Renckens, **Israel's Concept of Beginning:** The Theology of Genesis I-III, trans. C. Napier (New York: Sheed & Ward, 1964); S. Lyonnet, **De peccato et redemptione** (2 vols.: Rome, 1957, 1960).

80. W. Marchel, **Abba, Père: Le prière du Christ et des Chrétiens** (Analecta Biblica 19: Rome, 1969).

81. G. Ladner, **op. cit.,** p. 59; C. Spicq, **Dieu et l'homme selon le nouveau testament** (Lectio Divina 29: Paris, 1961).

82. A. D. Nock, **Conversion:** The Old and the New in Religion from Alexander the Great to Augustine of Hippo (New York [s.d.]).

of man in the image of Christ.[83] Augustine gave a psychological base to the image-metaphor by locating the reason for it in man's mind. Then he took the mind and made it the analogy for understanding the relationship of the Persons to one another in the Trinity, before reversing the process to make the missions of the Persons in the Trinity the scheme for understanding human history.[84] No less brilliant was Augustine's reliance upon monasticism to implement the reform implied in his conception of the God-man relationship.[85]

Thereafter, in the West, the theory of reform was Augustinian and the practice, monastic. The reform of Gregory the Great, the Merovingian efforts at reform, the Cluniac and Cistercian reforms were all attempts executed by monks to convert men's minds to the moral consequences of having been created in God's image and likeness.[86] In the process, the papacy became organized specifically as an agency of reform. The high point, and at the same time the beginning of decline, came in the reform of Gregory VII, who brought about a moral regeneration of the Church by freeing papacy, hierarchy, and clergy from lay interference. The unintentional consequence was a secularization of the hierarchy as it became a self-serving bureaucracy and a sacralization of lay authority as it assumed control of all but the liturgical life of Christendom.[87]

By the time of the Avignon captivity, it had become evident that the papacy, instead of being an agency of reform, needed itself to be reformed if it was to make the Church a force for good. The conciliarist crisis of the fifteenth century arose from the papacy being too weak to reform the Church but too strong for

---

83. G. Ladner, op. cit., pp. 63-283.

84. J. F. Sullivan, The Image of God: The Doctrine of St. Augustine and Its Influence (Dubuque, Iowa: Priory Press, 1963).

85. G. Ladner, op. cit., pp. 319 ff.

86. J. Deccareaux, Monks and Civilization: From the Barbarian Invasions to the Reign of Charlemagne (London, 1964).

87. B. Tierney: The Crisis of Church and State 1050-1300 (Englewood Cliffs, N. J.: Prentice-Hall, 1964); W. Ullman, Growth of Papal Government in the Middle Ages (New York, 1970[3]).

anyone else to reform it.[88] John Wycliff and Jan Hus tried unsuccessfully to cut the Gordian knot by taking reform to the laity. Thus they set the scene for Martin Luther, the Augustinian monk, to call for a reform of the Church "in head and members." He rejected both the papacy and monasticism because they had failed in the mission for which they had been conceived, but his call to repentance appealed to the traditional sources of Christian reform in Paul and Augustine.[89] Without necessarily having to subscribe to Weber's thesis of the Protestant ethic being the spirit of capitalism, one must admit that the Protestant reformers did succeed in conceiving of a mode of reform appropriate to the lay life of the modern world. By recognizing commerce, industry, and government as "good works," they attributed to profane activities the moral seriousness once reserved for the sacred, thus making them subject to reform.[90]

Within the Roman Catholic Church, the counter-reformation did indeed correct some of the excesses of the Protestant Reformation, and it eliminated many remaining abuses of the power to forgive sins. Once more, the papacy began to function as an agency of reform, largely because of recovering its moral stature, and as a result it became more powerful than ever. It is in this light that the promulgation of the dogma of papal infallibility of the First Vatican Council is to be understood.[91] This council, though, was the high-water mark of the Counter-Reformation. Thereafter, the futility of polemics and the scandal of division

---

88. F. Oakley, **Council over Pope? Toward a Provisional Ecclesiology** (New York: Herder & Herder, 1969).

89. J. Todd, **History of the Reformation:** A Conciliatory Assessment of Opposite Views (New York and Paris, 1964).

90. R. H. Bainton, **Reformation of the Sixteenth Century** (Boston: Beacon Press, 1956); cf. S.N. Eisenstadt, ed., **The Protestant Ethic and Modernization:** A Comparative View (New York and London: Basic Books, 1968).

91. Church historians dispute about the proper parameters for interpreting Vatican I, but from the careful study H. J. Pottmeyer has made of the preparation of the constitution **"Dei Filius"** in **Der Glaube vor dem Anspruch der Wissenschaft** (Freiburg, 1968), it is evident that the Fathers regarded Protestantism as the source of all their troubles.

became increasingly obvious to both Protestants and Catholics. Protestant churches were the first to promote a kind of ecumenism among themselves, but at the Second Vatican Council the Catholic Church attempted to reform itself so it could join in the ecumenical endeavor. By now it has become evident that if the Church is ever to fulfill its mission of reforming the modern world, it must first reform itself to the image and likeness of its Founder.

PRESUPPOSITIONS AND CONCLUSIONS

From this survey of the course of revolution, renewal, rebellion, and reform, it has become evident, I trust, that the Christian faith has been the source of social change in Western civilization. It should be clear, in fact, that the kinds of change the faith inspired determined the shape the Christian religion took. Only when the Christian religion proved inadequate to continue to mediate the impetus from the faith for revolution, renewal, rebellion, and reform did these movements break away from the Church and turn against it. At certain points, then, in the history of Western civilization, these four movements of social change assumed a secular form, and it is this form that is operative today. Thus the crisis these four movements have provoked in American culture, though it has been precipitated by the secular form they eventually took, derives ultimately from the Christian faith which initially generated them.

The only adequate verification for this hypothesis is a consideration, such as we have already made, of the historical events it is supposed to interpret. In these days of hermeneutical sophistication, however, we realize that the perspective with which we view events determines the way they appear to us. Thus the conception we have of them is actually an articulation of the way they appear to us according to our outlook upon them. In order, therefore, to evaluate the significance of the hypothesis I have proposed for the roots of the crisis in American culture, it will be necessary to reflect upon the outlook implicit in it. Such a reflection will make evident the presuppositions I brought to my study and the conclusions I wish you to draw from it.

In the first place, the course of Western history, as I have described it, has been a dialectic of secularization. The biblical revelation at the base of the Christian faith secularized the world by clearly distinguishing it from God and subordinating it to His good will. Then, in the process of shaping Western civilization, the Christian faith itself became secular by taking the specific institutional form of the Christian religion. While such secularization is intrinsic to religion, it had the unfortunate consequence of making the Christian religion worldly, in the pejorative sense of perverting its mission from God into a concern for its own interests. The ensuing disillusionment with sacred forms of the Christian faith became the context within which the ineluctable dynamism of the faith gave rise to secular forms of revolution, renewal, rebellion, and reform. It may even be, as Martin Marty has argued, that at a certain point in the nineteenth century, between 1830 and 1870, Western culture became definitely and irrevocably secular, in the specific sense that it no longer had any use for the Christian religion.[92] It is true at least that at that time the prophets of the end of the modern world—Marx, Darwin, Freud, and Nietzsche—all proclaimed, in one way or another, that God was dead. These iconoclasts did indeed topple what had become the idol of the Christian religion, but if the resulting secularization of culture is a new mode of divine revelation, the experience of nothingness which it has left us is an almost unbearable tragedy.

Now if revolution, renewal, rebellion, and reform remain operative in secular culture as well as religious, then—and this is our second presupposition—it would seem they are the basic categories of human consciousness. This becomes more evident if we consider both the horizon to which they refer and the viewpoint from which they derive. The horizon to which they refer is constituted by the objects to which man is related. Thus the object of revolution is man's relationship to nature as his environment; the object of renewal, man's relationship to his fellowman

---

92. M. Marty, op. cit., pp. 11 ff.

in human society; the object of rebellion, man's relationship to himself in the privacy of his conscience; and the object of reform is man's relationship to God as the source, ground, and goal of his being. Since there do not seem to be any other objects to which man can be related, there does not seem to be any other form of consciousness he can have. It is the same story when we turn to the viewpoint from which they derive. This viewpoint is constituted by the temporality of human subjectivity. Thus the perspective of revolution is the past as the promise of cyclical return; the perspective of renewal, the present as the ground for inevitable progress; the perspective of rebellion, the future as the possibility of radical innovation; and the perspective of reform is eternity as the motive for ultimate transcendence. Since there do not seem to be any other dimensions to time, there does not seem to be any other form of consciousness man can have. Thus revolution, renewal, rebellion, and reform seem to be the basic forms of human consciousness.[93]

Now if the basic forms of human consciousness are modes of change, then—and this is our third presupposition—man is

---

93. Often enough, revolution, renewal, rebellion, and reform are used interchangeably to mean, without distinction, all four forms of social change; or, if they are distinguished from one another, the meanings I have given them are interchanged; in addition other terms are used to mean the same as they do, such as "evolution" for "renewal" or "radicalism" instead of "rebellion." To a large extent therefore, the fourfold framework I have chosen to interpret social change is merely a heuristic structure. Nevertheless, the specific terms I have chosen do seem historically appropriate to the specific modes of change they are supposed to signify since they articulate the very intentionality of those engaged in each movement and also enable clear distinctions to be made among consistently diverse kinds of change. As a coordinated framework of interpretation, they suggest the historical sources for the abstract categories of relationship used in process philosophy and of subjectivity used in existential philosophy. Since the function of the framework is essentially dynamic, anthropological, and phenomenological, the framework itself seems to represent the self-mediation of man-in-the-world. Therefore the value of this fourfold categorization of consciousness verges on being ontological: the self-interpretation of man through reflection upon his history.

fundamentally in process. Moreover, as is clear from the forms themselves, this process is the dynamism of the structure of human consciousness. From the past, we gain an experience of nature through sensory data, whose meaning we formulate in language; from the present, we get an understanding of reality that we attain within human society and articulate in thought; from the future, we are impelled to the judgment we render upon history and implement in culture; and from eternity, we derive the wonder we bring to being and carry into action. Therefore, the basic structure of human consciousness is constituted of experience, understanding, judgment, and wonder.[94] Now since this structure is always in process of development from the stimulus of data upon experience and the evocation of wonder by being, then human consciousness is fundamentally dynamic, as in process toward self-transcendence.

Now if human consciousness is a process of self-transcendence then—and this is our final presupposition—it is essentially a possibility for faith. For faith is a commitment to wonder about experience. It is the realization that in our heart of hearts we are questioners, bound to search, as long as we live, for the meaning of being. The confidence to go on searching when we can find no answer is something Christians get from the Spirit of Christ. It is Christ who has inspired us to call the object of our wonder, "Father." Before Christ, the philosophers who openly and delib-

94. This conception of the structure of human consciousness is, of course, based upon Bernard Lonergan's (cf. "Cognitional Structure," Spirit as Inquiry, a special issue of Continuum, 2/3 August, 1964), 530-542; reprinted in Collection: Papers by Bernard Lonergan, S. J. (F. Crowe, ed.; New York: Herder & Herder, 1967), with the significant modification that I consider the final level to be "wonder," not "decision," since even the capacity for decision, as well as originality in any of the other levels, derives from the primordial wonder at the source of consciousness. Moreover, I would contend that this reconception of Lonergan's position is not only psychologically sounder than his conception, but also that it represents a more authentic development from the sources of his thought in St. Thomas Aquinas's work, and even that it is demanded by the logic of Lonergan's own conception of the dynamism in cognitional structure.

erately wondered about the meaning of being were overcome by despair. And today, those who have rejected Christ along with the Christian religion are filled with anguish. But for those who have found faith in Christ, there is much to wonder about, little to despair of. In this crisis of American culture, the Christian faith still has the power to enable us to preserve whatever is valuable from the past and to create whatever is necessary for the future.

IV

THE QUALITY
OF RELIGIOUS EXPERIENCE

10   Death and Dying: Life and Living

PETER H. BEISHEIM

RELATION OF DEATH TO THE QUALITY OF LIFE

One of the major obstacles to man's search for greater quality of living is the underlying fear of death, both individual and collective. Psychotherapy has been one of the principal sources of detecting this fear by encountering individuals unable to cope with this "fact of life," thereby indicating that these fears are possibly societal as well as individual.[1] While every society has traditionally demonstrated itself capable of explaining death—its origin and meaning, our society presently implies, through its nuclear attitudes, music, funeral practices and sexual emphases, that death may well be the enigma of our age. Funeral directors and practices, over the past few years, have been scrutinized by social commentators who interpret "repose," "slumber" and "grief-therapist" as obvious manifestations of society's inability to face dying, death, undertaker and grave.[2] Concealment, whether it be verbal or cosmetic, becomes a pathological condition when society denies a reality with which all must come to terms. The vicious circle continues when the funeral director reflects the wishes of society and society leaves funerals solely to the "experts." This circle, however, can be broken by individuals reflecting upon and arriving at some type of acceptance and posture towards dying and death. Superficial attacks upon funeral customs, i.e., wakes and open caskets, tend to deny the positive aspects (social and

---

1. Rollo May, **Love and Will** (New York: W. W. Norton & Co., Inc., 1969), p. 19.
2. Jessica Mitford, **The American Way of Death** (New York: Simon and Schuster, 1963).

psychological) of mourning and grief that are absolutely essential for the survivors' readjustments to their new situation.

Pointing to contemporary rock music is not an attempt for relevancy; for one of the truest indicators of a culture's fears, values, priorities and myths is its aesthetic dimension. If death is becoming a significant theme in music today, more than just what the normal emphasis would be, then it may be a result of fear—fear of nuclear destruction. This nuclear destruction includes not only the other and his world, but ours as well. Enveloping sound, popping pills, turning off—escape from reality? What reality—Death?? Liberation from the past, present and future, to exist only in the NOW, may reflect along with psychotherapy findings that death is gradually being understood as cessation, nothingness, annihilation. These fears inhibit human development and freedom both individually and collectively.

The crushing burden of sexuality which appears to be an inhibitor, rather than a positive liberating element of an individual's being, may also be linked to the underlying fear of death.[3] Victorian backlash may not be the exclusive or even major explanation of society's obsession with nudity, obscenity and genital-sexuality. The experience of loss or separation in a child's initial awareness of death may account for the emphasis in later years on sexual acrobatics, frequency and orgasm rather than risking interpersonal involvement. By not taking the risk, one never loses. Is this "fear of loss" the basis for the contraceptive mentality which fails to take into account that integrative-sexuality must be open to the possibility of new life? How this "new life" is to be understood is not altogether clear, since it may refer either to new offspring or to the new personal relationship between the individuals or both.

These few aspects of the problem merely indicate the constitutive relationship of death to life—of dying to living. The following sections shall deal with some of the insights developed by varied disciplines and how these may affect a developing theology of death.

---

3. Rollo May, op. cit., ch. 4.

INTERDISCIPLINARY INSIGHTS INTO DEATH

Dichotomy, even though it tends towards artificiality, is necessary in order to grasp the specific problems and contributions of the disciplines in developing an overview of the phenomenon of death.

Bio-Medical. Scientists in the bio-medical field, who are attempting to re-define death due to the breakthroughs in organ transplantation and mechanical devices to sustain vital organs, are recognizing the need for a deeper understanding into the meaning of "life" and "spirit of man" in order to avoid reducing the person to a mere problem in bio-chemistry.

Two major questions (beyond the myriad of ethical questions) have arisen: (1) Are functioning organs life? and (2) are these medical advances prompted by an underlying fear of Death? The former question is being discussed in context defining the criteria for determining death.[4] The profession apparently is divided as to whether the criteria should rest solely on the examination of one vital organ—the brain—or a number of organs.[5] Those who lean to examining a number of organs or systems view this in deference to life as the integration of "many factors," even though it is somewhat narrowly conceived. On the other hand, those who tend to view the brain as the key organ to be examined do so because they regard this organ most constitutive for life. While organ transplants have raised new ethical dilemmas for doctors, they have influenced directly the problem at hand—the definition of death. Many donors have been declared dead because they will never recover to their former selves or near normal selves, indicating an objective decision being based on subjective criteria— "Life is. . . ." Who defines life, the meaning of life—individuals,

---

4. Paul Ramsey. 'Updating Death," in **Updating Life and Death,** ed. by Donald R. Cutler (Boston: Beacon Press, 1969), pp. 31-54.

5. "A Definition of Irreversible Coma: Report of the "ADHOC" Committee of the Harvard Medical School, under the chairmanship of Henry K. Bucher, M. D., to examine the Definition of Brain Death," in **Updating Life and Death.**

medicine, jurists, theologians, philosophers, or society in general? Apparently organ transplants do not in themselves cause difficulties; but there are arising many voices calling for "Christian generosity" in the donation of organs and even possible social legislation demanding the organs after death, so that organ banks for eyes, inner ears, hearts, kidneys and others would be kept supplied. But what about the ultimate transplant?

The ultimate transplant to be performed is the brain or head, which is considered possible with present skills.[6] Where do the problems lie—lack of volunteers, societal unreadiness, psychological unknowns, or that ability does not impel oughtness? It may mean that this ultimate operation indicates that society is unable to cope with reality—that it is natural to die, that man can choose or not choose to die with dignity, grace and in control of his human condition.

An allied solution proposes the wider use of cryonics [7]—the freezing of people as soon as they die in the hope that science will determine how to unfreeze them at some future date. If we disparage this type of study, do we reflect a pessimistic fatalism toward man's truly controlling his future—that is, controlling his biological nature? The philosophical questions about matter, spirit, personhood are infinite. If a response to this is rejection because it reflects a very mechanistic standpoint, is it not possible that this rejection indicates a limiting standpoint concerning man's creativity and destiny?

If a man's death is not answered solely in terms of his organic structure, then it may impel society to redirect its energies not in efforts of quantity (as prolongation) but quality of living. Quality or quantity of life brings to the forefront the need of some investigation into the insights raised from a sociological stance toward death.

Sociological. Life can be understood as a process of personal development and social integration. The process of social integra-

---

6. Alan Harrington, **The Immortalist** (New York: Avon Books, 1969), pp. 201-213.

7. **Ibid.**, pp. 214-229.

tion consists of an ever-expanding circle of inter-relationships and experiences stemming from birth, reaching its fullest capacity through maturity and then slowly contracting in the waning years of the individual's life.[8] This process of slow contraction in old age has been termed "anticipatory socialization"[9] in which the person entering old age views life from the standpoint of the grave and begins severing acquaintances, relatives and other relationships that do not have real meaning or depth, while simultaneously curtailing the accumulation of new experiences as new.

The main difficulty in fully understanding this process is whether the basic dynamism lies in the person or in the social forces, although life is basically the interaction of the two. From the standpoint of the individual, the search for meaning and the understanding of self lies in our relations with others. Because of this, one of the most frequent proposals today regarding the dying is that the remaining span of time be spent within the circle of loved ones at home, if at all possible.

On the other hand, it is quite possible that the contraction of relationships is initiated through society which determines the value of the individual. Reaching maturity, the individual's worth is rated proportionately to his economic productivity and social conformity, which is supposed to be reward enough in itself, and through these his search for meaning in life will be realized. Contradicting this value, however, is the harsh treatment of the elderly in our society. We appear to be a people who value little the age, experiences and wisdom of the old as evidenced by the recent uncoverings of the unhealthy conditions of nursing homes, hospitals for the chronically ill and housing for the elderly. In effect, the individual contracts his life process through isolation rather than intensification of life through love, by society categorizing him as non-person. In hospitals, this process becomes quite evident

---

8. W. Lloyd Warner, **The Living and the Dead** (New Haven: Yale University Press, 1959), ch. 9.

9. Ernest Q. Campbell, "Death as a Social Practice," in **Perspectives on Death**, ed. by Liston O. Mills (Nashville: Abingdon Press, 1969), pp. 211-218.

when the patient takes on death-like characteristics such as supine position, open mouth, staring eyes, and body rigidity, even though living or existing.[10] Thus the process of anticipatory socialization, which should be the culmination of a fulfilling life-process, ends rather dejectedly with the individual fearing the process of dying as one of isolation and awaits death when this isolation, alienation, rejection and non-living will cease.

These disconcerting social attitudes and conditions are reinforced by the latest results of psychological investigations into the phenomenon of death.

Psychological. Dr. Kubler-Ross of the University of Chicago[11] has determined that terminal patients undergo a process of dying which encompasses five stages not so easily dichotomized as would appear:

Denial: "No, it can't be!"

Anger: "Why me?" "Why not him?"

Bargaining: "If I do this, will. . .?"

Depression: Introspective silence and isolation.

Acceptance: Coming to terms with the reality.

Even more important than these, however, is the keeping alive of hope—a hope which is twofold: first, a hope in the possibility of some type of cure or treatment which may arrest the illness or ease the pain for a significant period of time; and second, even more important than the first, the fostering of a real atmosphere of awareness that the individual is a person neither rejected nor forgotten by the staff and the family. Hundreds of cases have been reported and studies have shown that the death rate increases in situations where the prevailing conditions foster an attitude on the part of the staff that the patients are things that merely occupy one's time whether it be dispensing a pill or

---

10. Robert Kastenbaum, "Psychological Death," in **Death and Dying** ed. by Leonard Person (Cleveland: Press of Case Western Reserve University, 1969), pp. 8-14.

11. Elizabeth Kubler-Ross, **On Death and Dying** (New York: Macmillan, 1969), pp. 34-121.

wrapping a morgue sheet.[12] Expediency and inconvenience are two of the many characteristics which appear in this type of situation. But the blame does not rest solely on the staffs of hospitals, clinics and homes, since the social milieu expresses a denial of death; and when confronted with this fact, society's first reaction is to remove the "fact," namely, the dying individual, from our midst. A small number in the medical profession is emphasizing the fact that hospitals exclusively for the terminally ill should not exist—that general hospitals should handle all patients. The fact that segregated hospitals do exist indicates a fear of death by society in general and that its solution is to hide the reality.

The greatest pain in the process of dying is the pain of loneliness which may possibly account for the heavy sedations of the chronically ill, which suppresses the isolation and alienation. Most people who reach the stage of acceptance do so through the interpersonal relationships with family, friends and staff who care, who see their lives as having been enriched from patients having "lived." This is dying with dignity. However, dignity has come to mean that which is associated with the lack of inconvenience, that is, the staff being able to proceed routinely without any undue pressure of moans, demands, weeping, etc.; and the family not having to spend great amounts of time, money and energy coping with the individual's fears, wants and demands of attention. If a conscious search for meaning in life has not begun previous to this stage in life, the individual is placed in a position of constructing some meaning in his past which may be an illusion since there is nothing else left. The search for meaning raises one of the many paradoxes of life—a person who lives life to the fullest accepts death most willingly; one who doesn't fears it the most.

Would this paradox indicate that regardless of the desire for life after death, the meaning of a man's life is to be fulfilled in this span of time: birth to death? Does the search for meaning cover the entire life-span or only that mature span between youth

---

12. David Sudnow, **Passing On: The Social Organization of Dying** (New Jersey: Prentice-Hall, 1969), chs 3, 4.

and old age during which time the individual may be at the peak of his social integration? Fulness of life does not necessarily mean prolongation of life, but rather achieving the intensity of meaning through love and selfless concern for others. One of the therapy techniques being utilized in hospitals today is the interview with a dying person.[13] The individual is usually approached and most apt to consent when the emphasis is placed on the theme—"Teach me to die." Why? Why should a person expose to me their most intense and personal feelings, fears and thoughts? Is it possible that the five stages of dying coincide with the life-span of an individual, that the "aging" process is entered into sooner than expected because of the immanent death? Is it possible that Erikson's category of generativity (seventh of the eight stages of life) in which the old need the young in order to avoid stagnation by transmitting wisdom, experience, and love, can account for the success of the interview-therapy?[14]

The previous three disciplines have raised many questions related specifically to their field of endeavor, but many of them are fundamentally philosophical.

Philosophical. All of the questions raised in this section are not necessarily *the* fundamental questions for every person, but they do indicate the problem areas regarding death. An underlying premise for the interview-therapy sessions appears to be that insights (rational and/or non-rational) into the experience of dying may be communicated to one another. Many react negatively to this premise, at first, because of the confusion surrounding the process of dying and the polar concept of death as end or death as beginning. If death can be seen as the end of dying, a process which begins at conception, then we need not view death as the problem. Dying as life-process now becomes the problem, and insights into life are regarded as possible.

What does it mean when psychologists claim that man cannot

---

13. Kubler-Ross, **op. cit.**, ch. 10.
14. Erik H. Erikson, **Childhood and Society** (New York: W. W. Norton, 1963), pp. 266-268.

conceive of his death? Will "I" continue to exist? The "I" evolves through self-expanding love with others within a process of continual physical dissolution to the point of cessation. In other words, what is the reciprocal relationship of maturity and aging? Can I will myself to remain open to change, or is it intrinsic to my nature to become rigid and closed? If a person is looking for certainty of an existence-after-death, could not this assurance stem from a history of man which reveals a tradition of beliefs in an existence-after-death; if it doesn't, this may reflect an a-historical stance. How does this historical posture relate to an "objective" reality? It would seem that a trans-historical and trans-cultural belief in an existence-after-death would reinforce the position that "I" do not really die alone. Or has the stress on individuality so weakened historical continuity and personal identification with Man, past, present and future, that I really *do* die alone?

Regarding the future, does the belief in the continuation of the "I" exist only as long as the individual believes in the continual historical existence of Mankind? Then immortality, whether it be family, reputation, achievements or whatever, rests primarily in the continual presence of man which is being threatened by nuclear warfare. Does this strengthen the posture toward life as being absurd?

DEVELOPING A THEOLOGY OF DEATH

Theologizing about death begins with the individual and the human condition. For the individual the process only begins when he is confronted with the fact of his death and what this means in terms of his human condition. In integrating this realization, my dying, with the least amount of anxiety, I realize that the belief in a life-after-death becomes problematic. It may be enigmatic regarding the moment of death, after-death, and how these are related to the death and resurrection of Jesus. An attitude may then be encouraged which possibly lessens the value of the individual's life-span and may also account for the apparent unconcern regarding the process of dying and its relationship to the quality of life.

In the Old Testament, death ends all bodily and religious activity, so that "Sheol" appears as a vague abode of suspended spirits—existing but not living. Judgment, however, exists in one's life as reward (prosperity and longevity), or punishment (poverty and an early demise), so that the future-life is not understood as continuation or development on some other level of reality. Death in the New Testament is less fearful because Jesus has conquered the "ultimate enemy of man"; yet this does not necessarily mean living-after-death. Equating life-after-death *as* one of the constitutents of Revelation is generally accepted as a later development arising from historical philosophical systems.

My approach shall be one which accepts life-after-death as an unknown, and its objective reality is not necessarily constitutive for understanding human nature, the human condition, or Christian revelation. Although it cannot be ignored either. Therefore, in light of the insights into death from the other disciplines, what can we say about a theology of death?[15]

Meaning in Life. If individuals fear dying without meaning rather than non-existence after death, then Christian revelation must be interpreted in this light instead of proving a life-after-death. This in no way devalues the meaning of Jesus and the redemptive function of His dying. Death is the culmination of my life, not in the sense of looking to the future, but that, in the fact of death, the meaning of all the decisions of my life leave me accepting them or despairing of them—which is the judgment. To live is to lose oneself. The development of the individual is one leading from the consciousness of "I", to Personhood, yet for the Christian, this development finds its complete fulfillment in the giving of the "I" for another (process of Kenosis). Isn't this the search for the genuine community today? Genuine community may mean the total integration of individuals, all losing

15. Ninian Smart, "Some Inadequacies of Recent Christian Thought About Death," in **Man's Concern with Death**, ed. by Arnold Toynbee (St. Louis: McGraw-Hill, 1969), pp. 133-137.

self for the others instead of keeping barriers and inhibitions intact so as not to lose their individuality which may be the source of alienation (original sin?) and isolation in today's society. Meaning in life, then, is realized in the process of humanization, which can be seen as "becoming Christ-like." In the process of kenosis by which one "becomes like Christ," the fear of dying and death is overcome. The individual is reborn, is capable of truly living.

Death of Jesus. Jesus died, I am going to die—what does this mean? Accepting the fact that I am going to die can liberate me in such a way that I can really be free to live, to enjoy each moment, to see each moment as a possibility for concern, care and love. The imperative of the message is the *Now*. I love my brother *now*—not later, for there may not be a later. Thus the freedom really becomes a burden because now the risk of lost opportunities makes despair a real possibility. It is possible that Jesus died because only in dying can one love passionately, can one risk being rejected and hated all the while losing oneself in love. Thus, in dying, my true creative capabilities and powers are realized—that I am what I have become, or I am not what I truly could have been. This is the risk of living, of loving and of losing self. That is the paradox of Jesus.

Resurrection and Ascension. Christ did not die. The Resurrection can be interpreted as the symbolic assurance of man's transcendence over the fear of death; that death is truly conquered when one lives his life to the fullest. When one loses his life for the other, he does not die. Because in the losing or giving, communion with one another is achieved and cannot be severed by death. Christ's dying for man establishes communion with His followers which is symbolized by the Resurrection. Christ becomes one with the community, so that in dying, one really lives and in the giving of ourselves, we *really* live. Only in dying and in death is new life created, and "the death of death" through faith and trust in Jesus frees one to be alive, to be raised from the human condition. The Ascension would appear to symbolize the ratification of the Resurrection. Ascension myths have been interpreted by historians of religion as indicators of man's desire to transcend his human condition.[16] Therefore, the Ascension emphasizes the fact that Jesus did transcend the human condition—that is, the fear of death; and that death is not the final or ultimate moment, but merely the last moment in a continuum which has or does not have meaning.

Ecclesial Dimension. If these problems appear to be somewhat individualized—how does the ecclesial community react to the fact of dying, the reality of death? If the ecclesial community has traditionally pointed to life-after-death by means of the Sacrament of Anointing, must it continually do so?

Anticipatory socialization and the psychological needs of man when confronting his death would imply that beyond preaching the message of Christ, the community must somehow, in practice, overcome the growing isolation of the dying person in which he is left to face this human event alone. Changes in the form of the rites of anointing which would allow each to share in the others' moments of suffering and joys of life could be initiated, thereby strengthening the communal aspect. Instead of the sacrament of anointing being administered as a routine action which one receives because of a particular condition, much like administering a pill, it may, rather than reassuring a member of his communal existence, alienate him all the more because the communal aspect may be entirely lost.

Possibly other types of activity would allow people to come to terms with this "fact of life," such as emphasizing the Christian obligation (not solely relegated to clergy) of visiting the sick as service to and by the community. Hospitals which are controlled by ecclesial communities should allow all who are ill to be housed under one roof in order not to hide that reality (death) which for us is continually present. Thus the ministry to the sick and dying can be participated in by the sick, dying and healthy, thereby building a community which is truly a community of love.

There is no conclusion, because there can only be an evolving standpoint regarding this phenomenon. As I progress in dying

---

16. Mircea Eliade, **Myths, Dreams and Mysteries** (New York: Harper & Row, 1967), pp. 99-115.

toward the moment of death, my posture will either be one of liberation or despair. The questions and problems confronted will depend upon where I am in the continuum of maturity. The Christian attitude, to be achieved in a fearful society, is one which does not fear death, but sees it as the last human act to be participated in by me—as a human being, as a person, as a Christian.

11 Quality of Sacraments — Quality of Life

BRENDAN ROSENDALL

Sacramental theology has stopped at the level of "Jesus-Encounter." To some, rather than being an alarming remark, this statement is going to represent the epitome of success in sacramental theologizing, the culmination of many years of intensive labor in reorienting the People of God relative to an understanding of the sacraments. Great progress has been made in recent decades in understanding the sacraments as well as in their liturgical realization, but it becomes alarming if because of this progress it is not recognized that an impasse has been reached, that sacramental theology has "stopped at" and not just "arrived at" the level of "Jesus-Encounter."

Alvin Toffler, among others, has helped to make people aware that progress and change are part of the human condition. He has also suggested that what we need if we are to stay "on top" of the situation is "cope-ability," a certain speed and economy with which to adapt to change.[1] This requires feedback, discussion, re-evaluation, critical analysis, refinement, open-ended planning, ongoing innovation, experimentation, new directions, and new and flexible interaction. It is the type of adaptive ability resulting from all this which will not only make life tolerable in the future, but which will even make it possible to continue to improve upon it.

The sacraments are for man. "They are from God, but their

---

1. Alvin Toffler, **Future Shock** (New York: Random House, 1970), p. 357.

thrust and intent, their institution and result, are for man."[2] The sacraments respond to the human condition; they need, therefore, the same adaptive ability that man himself needs today in the fact of the change and progress occurring relative to the human condition. In short, the sacraments must also participate in "cope-ability," at least, if they are to remain effective forces in the pursuit of a fuller humanity. That means, in effect, that those same factors which enable man to develop "cope-ability" must also be a part of sacramental development. Several of them would appear to be already a part of that package; one might mention in this regard "feedback," "discussion," and "critical analysis." But it is even easier to suggest, and to prove, that sacramental development has not been touched by "open-ended planning," "ongoing innovation," "experimentation," and most importantly, by "new directions." Such, at least, is the implication of sacramental theology having "stopped at" the level of "Jesus-Encounter."

A bold, new understanding of the sacramental reality was reached with the realization that the sacraments are the personal saving acts of Christ. With this understanding, and especially in the context of the liturgical reorientation consequent upon it, it was possible to reaffirm the importance of the sacraments in building a Christian life, and even their impact upon the quality of Christian existence. In restoring the idea of Christ and Church as sacraments, this stage of sacramental theology actually brought back into focus the broader facets of sacramentality. Since it also called for a personal type encounter, it was responsible for introducing the personalist approach into the sacramental dimension. This is the sacramental legacy of Schillebeeckx, Rahner, Davis, and others, and it represents a very high level of sacramental reflection and theologizing. As a legacy it contains principles which all future sacramental reflection will have to respect.

But the important question is *where do we go from here?* Do we keep pace in our reflection relative to the sacraments with

---

2. E. J. Fiedler, and R. B. Garrison, **The Sacraments: An Experiment in Ecumenical Honesty** (Nashville and New York: Abingdon Press, 1969), p. 11.

the pace of the world about us? And if so, what new directions need to be taken? That new directions do need to be taken should be evident to all. As one of the authors of the fascinating little book *The Sacraments: An Experiment in Ecumenical Honesty,* so aptly put it: "... we have begun to learn a costly lesson, and to safeguard falling into the same mistakes again, these signs and symbols, these sacraments must be kept in a dynamic state. They must communicate truly, but in a living way. God may lead us ... to the use of basic symbols, but the church must assure the dynamism of their expression. We are just beginning to emerge, hopefully, from a long static stage in accepting this responsibility."[3] The brief reflections presented here seek to participate in the search for new directions, as well as in the task and responsibility of the Church to keep the dynamism of sacramental theologizing alive.

As a very important corollary to our theologizing in the "Jesus-Encounter" tradition, we can state that the quality of the sacramental realization is paramount in promoting the quality of the Christian life. The Fathers of the Second Vatican Council certainly recognized the relationship involved here.[4] Corollaries, however, frequently appear in groups of two or three, and it appears legitimate to inquire if certain possibilities have not been overlooked in the present context. Does not, perhaps, the quality of the sacramental representation, that is, the liturgical realization, extend its qualitative effect to all the dimensions of human life; or to put it another way, are the sacraments responsible agents in determining the quality of human existence in a secular as well as a Christian mode? And what of the quality of life? Can't it in some way also affect the sacramental representation?

These questions are not as irresponsible as one might at first suppose. They are similar in effect to the questions asked a number of years ago by Terrence Toland at the close of an article on the

---

3. **Ibid.**, p. 31.
4. "Constitution on the Sacred Liturgy," **The Documents of Vatican II,** ed. by Walter Abbott (New York: Guild Press, 1966), p. 137.

sacraments as signs and experiences.[5] Two of the questions asked
at that time still seem very pertinent today in the search for new
directions for sacramental theologizing. They are: "Does not our
response to a religious symbol depend more than we might suspect
on our response to all symbols, especially the elements of nature?,"
and "Do we need new symbols?"[6] The answers given then were
affirmative, but they were very soft-spoken, and they have remained rather soft-spoken as the years have passed. Today, they
ought to be answered with more than that mumbled "yes." The
principles upon which those questions were founded are the basic
insights of the "Jesus-Encounter" level of sacramental thought,
and they, along with an additional principle, that of secularization,
provide the basis for these reflections. It is therefore expedient
that those principles now be sketched.

The first principle is the sacramental principle itself: matter
channels spirit. The external, the visible, outward reality signifies
and actualizes the internal, the invisible, the inward reality. The
invisible world of the spiritual affects man's innermost being
by means of outward symbol and visible, material reality. Because
of man's basic makeup, the supernatural, the spiritual makes its
impact upon man in a material, a bodily way. The principle
derives quite simply from a restoration of the genuine and broader
meaning to the word "sacrament." In speaking of the Church,
the Second Vatican Council recognized that the word "sacrament"
has "a meaning that stretches beyond the seven sacraments as
we know them. The word refers to a transcendent reality, invisible
in itself, but manifested in ways that belong to this earth."[7] Contemporary theologians have made extensive use of the notion in
their reflections upon Christ the Sacrament and the Church as

---

5. Terrence Toland, "Christian Sacrament: Sign and Experience,"
Readings in Sacramental Theology, ed. by C. Stephen Sullivan (Englewood
Cliffs, N. J.: Prentice-Hall, 1964), pp. 18-30.

6. **Ibid.,** p. 28.

7. "Preface," **The Sacraments in General,** ed. by Schillebeeckx and
Willems, **Concilium,** vol. 31 (New York: Paulist Press, 1967), p. 1.

sacrament, and it provides, moreover, the primary basis for the reflections to be made here.

The theology of encounter provides a second foundation for these reflections. "Encounter" is a word bearing significant personalized overtones, for it denotes a face-to-face meeting. Its use with reference to the sacraments is witness to the fact that at least for contemporary man the best expression of the sacramental structure is to be effected in terms of interpersonal relationships; its highest formulation, at least in a Christian context, in terms of an interpersonal relationship with Jesus himself. E. Schillebeeckx, who is largely responsible for the restoration of this personalist dimension to sacramental theology, shows how it reveals to us the structure of human and personal encounter inherent in the sacramental action. He has pointed out the consequences of the "tendency towards a purely impersonal, almost mechanical approach" to the sacraments, and has helped us to recapture in this way the reality of religion "as a saving dialogue between men and the living God."[8] The sacraments are to be viewed as personal acts, as a sacred experience of a person-to-person encounter with God. On this basis, it is possible to delineate and explain some of the intensely personal and human activity which the sacraments demand. The sacraments are "presenced" symbols; symbols embodying the presence of another. It is not necessary at this point to detail the dynamics of encounter; the principle which does need elaboration here is simply that a sacrament does imply such an interpersonal relationship.

A third principle recognizes the process of secularization. Secularization means that men must be allowed to be themselves before God. As there would seem to be no reason for removing cultic celebration from under the influence of this principle, one can assume that there must be a secular dimension to cult, to liturgy, and in short, to our realization of the sacraments. Moreover, it should never be forgotten that it is from the world that the Son of God "takes some elements for his sacraments, so that, acting in and

---

8. E. Schillebeeckx, **Christ the Sacrament of Encounter with God** (London and New York: Sheed & Ward, 1963), pp. 1 & 2.

through them, he may transform men's hearts."[9] George McCauley
has already attempted to theologize about the sacraments in this
vein. In his work, *Sacraments for Secular Man,* he gives explicit
recognition to the fact that the sacraments are "secular gestures,"
that "they deal with secular reality," even that they "promote
a greater secularity than we are accustomed to associate with
human existence."[10] On this basis, McCauley has sought out the
secular dimension of the Christian sacraments, elaborated upon it,
and suggested, especially relative to the sacramental realization
in the liturgy, certain changes. He concludes with a question:
why is it that the sacraments' "secular and humanistic dimension
is neglected in the lives of Christians?"[11]

The same question forms the starting point for the suggestions
now to be proposed here; suggestions based, as was already indicated, on the principles just elaborated. If there is difficulty in
perceiving the harmony between the sacraments and human life,
it is because the sacraments themselves are too simple and poor,
or because they are totally foreign to the contemporary mentality.
And if this is true, it is because the principles just outlined have
not been taken seriously enough. Sacramentality is the means
by which every generation keeps in contact with God. The sacraments need to utilize elements and activities out of the present
world condition if they are to make other worldly realities alive,
operative, and meaningful to the constituents of the present community of men. Recently, Christopher Kiesling made an eloquent
plea for a fuller recognition of the "sacramentality of all created
agents and activities." He said that "a sacramental theology which
does not approach the sacraments within the horizon of the religious
rites of non-Christian religions and secular activities of every kind
is no longer adequate for a true explanation and evaluation of the

---

9. H. Richards, and P. De Rosa, **Christ and Our World** (Milwaukee:
Bruce, 1966), pp. 15 and 16.

10. G. McCauley, **Sacraments for Secular Man** (New York: Herder &
Herder, 1969), p. 15.

11. **Ibid.**, p. 105.

Christian sacraments."[12] On this basis, Kiesling seeks to demonstrate that the seven sacraments are but paradigms intended to help recognize the sacramentality of all created agents and activities. Certainly, recognition of the overall sacramentality of things is essential if we are ever to see clearly the role of sacraments in promoting the quality of human life, but at the same time it might be wondered if the present attachment to the seven sacraments does not obscure rather than help this recognition. The possibility of transcending the seven sacraments by the creation of new sacraments for the express purpose of realizing this paradigmatic function of the sacraments now needs to be probed.

Reflection and research is making plain the conclusion that the relationship between God and men must be very closely related to the experience, aspirations, and culture of the human participants in that relationship. The symbols intended to express and foster that relationship need, then, to participate in those experiences, aspirations, and in that culture; they need to reflect the present reality of the human condition.

Reality becomes then the starting point for a reassessment of the sacraments. But what is reality for modern man? Without attempting to be exclusive, it might be suggested that in its general modes it is centered on two dimensions of the present human condition: a concern for the environment and a concern for the human person. These embody in a special way the experience and aspirations of modern men, and they speak not just to the sophisticated, but to the masses as well. Moreover, the objects of concern, nature and person, possess in themselves a certain mysteriousness, almost an incomprehensibility for contemporary man, which make them better than average partakers in the dimensions of "mystery-symbols," or sacraments. The reality itself is mysterious; the task at hand is to make it more intelligible.

One way in which to make this reality more intelligible is to explicitly endorse this reality as sacramental. Both nature and person are sacraments. Moreover, it might be argued that they

---

12. C. Kiesling, "Paradigms of Sacramentality," **Worship**, August-September, 1970, pp. 422-23.

are the most opportune sacraments for the "now generation."
The whole ecological package projects nature very readily into
this role. Nature is expressive of the Creator, but the message
of nature has become ambiguous. It is more easily abused than used,
more easily misread than read aright.[13] All of creation is capable
of supernatural instrumentality, but for the most part only certain
privileged parts of creation have been so instrumentally commissioned. Certain natural symbols have been granted "sacramental
squatter's rights," whereas in reality the whole world is in God's
hand and "expressive of his creative power and finesse."[14] The
biblical message about the earth is quite clear: man has an inevitable responsibility for the environment. But this responsibility is
frequently shirked; in interpreting his dominion, man has in the
present systematically devastated the earth. Man has indiscrim-
inately exploited the earth; he has made over "large sectors of the
land-mass, effecting radical environmental changes"[15] which in
their turn will affect the human species and the very quality of
human life. If the present pattern is not to continue, and the "now
generation" gives every evidence of being concerned that it should
not, then some new emblem of the world as expressive of its creator
is needed. It is time for a sacrament of the earth, or of nature.

Albert Camus, who has so frequently been applauded in many
areas for his pin-pricking of the human conscience, might now
also be given belated accolades for speaking to the present ecological crisis. His insight was a sacramental one. Camus, according
to Thomas Hanna, felt that when "one feels that the natural world
about him is God's world and is expressive of God's nature, then
this world obtains a certain value and holiness which tends to
eradicate any impatient contempt for nature and any desire to
subjugate it to the realization of historical goals."[16] Camus recog-

---

13. Toland, art. cit., p. 24.

14. Fiedler and Garrison, op. cit., p. 23.

15. Donald Imsland, Celebrate the Earth (Minneapolis: Augsburg
Publishing House, 1971), p. 62.

16. Thomas L. Hanna, "Albert Camus and the Christian Faith,"
Camus: A Collection of Critical Essays, ed. by G. Bree (Englewood Cliffs,
N. J.: Prentice-Hall, 1962).

nizes an explicit sacramental nature in the world—it is "expressive of God's nature" and possessive of "a certain value and holiness." For which reason, care must be exercised in evaluating the uses to which the natural goods of the world are subjected, and attention must be directed to the world's symbolic importance relative to God. In effect, Camus is saying that we must have a careful regard for nature that we do not destroy its sacramental value. From Albert Camus, then, we have one of the first and most eloquent pleas for a sacramental approach to ecology. Teilhard de Chardin is another who might be mentioned as having basically a sacramental insight into the world, and the names of Bonhoeffer, Cox and many others could also easily enough be added to the list. Given the insight of these men, and the firm foundations outlined for it previously, where is our sacrament of the earth, especially when there is a generation urgently crying out for just such an emblem reflecting their aspirations and goals?

And where is the sacrament of person? Certainly, a similar argument can be construed relative to this facet of modern reality. The whole package of inter-personal relationships projects person very readily into the role of sacrament for the "now generation," for the human person is expressive of God in so far as man is made in "the image of God." Moreover, person is already an element of the privileged part of creation which has been instrumentally commissioned to fill a sacramental role, at least the Person of Jesus Christ. God is giving himself and transforming men "as they go about their trite tasks of daily life, participate in various communities, commit themselves to human ideals and noble goals, share their lives and goods with others, converse with them, enter into friendships and marriage, care for others, sacrifice their own desires, goods, and even life for others."[17] If God gives himself to men in these "trite tasks," most of which center around other persons, is he not then encountered symbolically in these other persons? Certainly, this is the reality to be found as the basis for the sacramental nature of marriage. But personal encounters are most assuredly not limited to marriage, and again the "now

---

17. Kiesling, op. cit., p. 428.

generation" wants some emblem expressive of the values and dignity they have discovered in the human person. It is time for a sacrament of person.

As McCauley has pointed out: "that which should shape our thinking and appreciation of the sacraments is, beyond the material symbols used, the words spoken. Or rather, the discourse that takes place, since the words only have meaning as part of a discourse between persons about someone or something."[18] In the natural human situation discourse is most adequate at the level of person-to-person encounter, for it is then that a person most fully opens up to another individual, and becomes most truly free. And from that freedom comes openness to other people and a concern for racial justice, for world hunger, and for peace. So again, given the foundation laid above for recognition of the sacramentality of person, and a realization of the affirmation of human life and freedom which such recognition would contain, it is legitimate to ask *why is there no sacrament of person?*

The concern of modern man with the quality of the environment and with the value and dignity of the human person is a concern with the quality of life. If the sacraments are to be viewed as effective agents relative to the quality of life, then the possibility of sacramentalizing the present concerns of man about the quality of life needs to be explored. That there is at least a legitimate basis for beginning that investigation is hopefully what has been presented here. But it would be extremely naive to suppose that the present suggestions leave no room for further reflection. Objections to the proposal set forth here, as well as the task it sets for the future, are two facets of the present discussion which seem to demand greater clarification, and it might be well to conclude with just a brief remark along those lines.

The sacraments cannot be deprived of their secular meaning, but at the same time can one remove from them every vestige of Christianity? Cyril Vollert has stated that a "sacrament is primarily

---

18. McCauley, **op. cit.**, p. 28.

and basically a personal act of Christ,"[19] and it is extremely difficult to conceive of the sacraments without a "Christ-context." But what does the "Christ-context" mean in the secular world of today? Must it of necessity preserve the explicit links to the Christ-mysteries as has thus far been supposed? And do the sacraments of nature and person really ignore a "Christ-context"? In terms of Paulinian Christology and in the Teilhardian concept of the "universal Christ" or "Christ-Omega" all things, the earth and persons included, constitute the "cosmic body" of Christ. Or again, an encounter with a Christian person is obviously an encounter with Christ, and in terms of the concept of "anonymous Christians" an encounter with any person may constitute a Christian encounter. The sacraments of nature and person cannot be faulted for their lack of a Christ-dimension.

The principle of sacramentality embraces the use of matter unreservedly in the sacramental role, whereas in reality only a very limited number of material objects have ever been sacramentalized. The restriction is an artificial one, imposed by a principle of convenience developed in the early Middle Ages. Trent stated that there are but seven sacraments, but both "Scripture and comparison with other religions and cultures show that the point here is not the number as quantity but rather the number seven as a symbol of plenitude." [20] Nature and person reflect a fullness which could make the present sacramental enumeration obsolete. The sacraments should always speak to today, but they are not going to if artificial and non-essential restrictions are placed on them.

Where the real task, vaguely hinted at here, actually begins and ends, as well as the possibility of its overall feasibility, are difficult to state. Obviously what is called for is a radical rethinking and revamping of the entire sacramental system, a radical moving away from the present sacramental center with its built-in "hang-

---

19. Cyril Vollert, "The Church and the Sacraments," **Readings in Sacramental Theology**, ed. by C. S. Sullivan (Englewood Cliffs, N. J.: Prentice-Hall, 1964), p. 92.

20. E. Schillebeeckx, (ed.), "The Sacraments in General," **Concilium**, Vol. 31. p. 2.

ups," for example, the number seven, in order that new creative possibilities to restore the dynamism of the sacraments can be exercised. Surely, there must be a great deal more theological reflection both of the specific suggestions made here as well as of other creative possibilities which have so far escaped the imagination. There is the necessary consultation of liturgists as to how the suggested sacraments are best to be ritualized. The canonist will find his challenge in the present revision of the law which must be opened enough to allow for the suggested changes not just now, but at all relevant moments in the future. But the greatest involvement will undoubtedly be required of the academic proponents of religion and theology. These persons will experience a two-fold task: that of providing the "feedback" from reality which will indicate the new directions the sacramentalizing process must assume, and that of on-going education of all people as to the relevancy of the process.

The process is not just one of renewing and revising the sacraments; it is a process of refounding them. Schillebeeckx in particular provides the theoretical basis upon which this can be done when he elaborates upon the role of the Church relative to these rites.[21] But it will always remain theory unless the individuals who are the Church and are competent to undertake the task suggested here make the effort to move it from the planning board to existential reality. Since the quality of human life and existence is at least indirectly affected, the effort, although burdensome, should not lack motivation.

---

21. Schillebeeckx, **op. cit.**, pp. 142-163.

12 The Quality of Life in Prophetic Vision

A. JOSEPH EVERSON

"Next time the fire!" This message, spelled out with a great variety of powerful poetic imagery, is at the heart of the prophetic words of both Amos and Isaiah.[1] Both men lived and struggled amid the international turmoil of the latter half of the eighth century, B.C., turmoil that was intensified by the presence of a new factor in the ancient near east, the rise of the world empire of Assyria. Amos addressed his message to the northern kingdom of Israel in the years shortly after 750 B.C., while Isaiah ben Amoz addressed the concerns of Jerusalem and the southern kingdom of Judah over the last four decades from 740-700 B.C. and apparently remained active until about the year 687 B.C.[2] Both men seem to have struggled and suffered for most of their adult lives with the awesome and intensely frightening conviction that the people to whom they were speaking, kings and common folk alike, were following a course that could lead only to national suicide. Unless there was radical change in the national style or mode of life, the prophets were utterly convinced that destruction was coming for their countries through the horrors of war. The interesting fact is that Isaiah looked upon the world empire of Assyria not as an enemy, but rather as the instrument of punishment in the world. This is an important perspective, for it reminds

---

1. Cf. Amos 1:4, 7, 10, 12, 14, 2:2, 5 and the discussion of this theme in Amos in James Mays, **Amos** (Philadelphia: Westminster Press, 1969).

2. See John Bright, **A History of Israel** (Philadelphia: Westminster Press, 1959).

us that the prophets understood their Lord, Yahweh Sebaoth, as the creator and imperial sovereign of all nations and empires in the world, who ruled from his heavenly council and who commissioned the prophets to speak to the nations as his heralds or spokesmen.[3] Assyria, as the rod or tool of Yahweh, would effect judgment upon various nations of the world according to Yahweh's design. The awesome fact was that the design included judgment also for Israel and Judah.

We shall attempt in this study to explore some of the dimensions of the motif of judgment for nations as it is set forth by Amos and Isaiah. Primarily we will examine the reasons why these prophets interpreted events of war and other catastrophes as punishment. In recent study of the prophetic literature, great emphasis has been placed on distinguishing properly the two basic parts of the oracles of judgment—first, the *basis* and then the actual *announcement of judgment*.[4] Consideration of the first part, the *basis,* where the causes of judgment are set forth, is of central importance because there we can discover a great deal about the prophet's concern for human life and the nature or quality of life intended for man by his creator. The reasons cited by the prophets as the cause of punishment may in fact be the key for understanding the entire prophetic interpretation of history.

The Day of Yahweh in the Proclamation of Amos

It has long been recognized that the *Day of Yahweh* tradition stands at the heart of the prophetic message concerning judgment and the future.[5] Because this is so, it is possible to survey the announcements of judgment in Amos and Isaiah by focusing on

---

3. Cf. G. Ernest Wright, "The Nations in Hebrew Prophecy," **Encounter,** Vol. 26, (Spring, 1965), pp. 225-237.

4. See particularly C. Westermann, **Basic Forms of Prophetic Speech,** tr. Hugh Clayton White (Philadelphia: Westminister Press, 1967), pp. 84ff.

5. See G. von Rad, **Old Testament Theology,** Vol. II., tr. D.M.G. Stalker (New York: Harper & Row, 1965), pp. 119-125.

their use of this theological tradition. In chapter 5:18-20, Amos declares to the people of northern Israel:[6]

> Trouble for those who are waiting so longingly
>   for the day of Yahweh!
> What will this day of Yahweh mean for you?
> It will mean darkness, not light,
> As when a man escapes a lion's mouth, only to meet a bear;
>   he enters his house and puts his hand on the wall,
>   only for a snake to bite him.
> Will not the day of Yahweh be darkness, not light?
> It will all be gloom, without a single ray of light.

Whatever else he intended, Amos was here declaring that the coming Day of Yahweh event would not be what the people expected it to be. Apparently the Day of Yahweh tradition was already an established part of the popular religious thinking of the people addressed by Amos. If Gerhard von Rad is correct, the tradition originally heralded the triumph of Yahweh over his enemies and emerged from the traditions of holy war connected with the eras of conquest and judges in ancient Israel.[7] The new element in the proclamation by Amos is not the fact that the Day of Yahweh event will be a time of darkness and destruction; rather, the new element is the striking announcement that the darkness and destruction are coming upon Yahweh's own people, Israel.

And that destruction came with terrible consequences for the northern nation of Israel. In 721 B.C., after several decades of rebellious activity by the political leaders in Israel, Sargon II of Assyria sacked the capital city of Samaria and resettled large numbers of the population in other parts of his empire. Later

---

6. Biblical quotations are from **The Jerusalem Bible** unless otherwise indicated.

7. G. von Rad, **op. cit.**, p. 123 and "The Origin of the Concept of The Day of Yahweh" **Journal of Semitic Studies**, Vol. IV (1959), pp. 97-108.

generations of people in southern Judah could understand this destruction of Samaria and the end of the northern kingdom in 721 B.C. as the bitter fulfillment of all that Amos had earlier announced. The historical events of 721 B.C. thus constituted the Day of Yahweh for northern Israel. Her time of punishment had come. We must recognize, however, that this prophetic understanding of history was based on theological reflection; it was an interpretation in retrospect through the eyes of faith. The tragic history of Judah in the years after 721 B.C. and the witness of Isaiah and other later prophets offer telling evidence that the prophetic perspective concerning northern Israel was not understood or accepted as valid by most of the political officials or by the masses of the people in Judah.

The Day of Yahweh in the Proclamation of Isaiah

Although Amos is not mentioned by name in the collection of Isaiah, one cannot escape the conclusion that the fall of Samaria, and perhaps the actual words of Amos, must have had a deep impression on Isaiah. If, by chance, he did not know of Amos, then the similarities between their proclamations of judgment are all the more striking. Already in 735-34 B.C., Isaiah was actively involved in the national affairs of Judah, counseling Ahaz not to call in Assyrian troops against the coalition headed by Pekah and Rezin, the "smoldering stumps" in northern Israel and Syria.[8] Again, during the years of crisis from 720-711 B.C., Isaiah spoke sharply against reckless national policies of further rebellion in league with Tyre, Egypt or Ashdod.[9] It seems clear that by the latter decades of the eighth century, Isaiah had come to understand that Judah was heading for exactly the same end that had come upon northern Israel. At the center of the poem recorded

---

8. See Is 7:1-9 and the related texts in 2 K 16:1-20 and II Chr 28:16-27.

9. Cf. Bright, op. cit., pp. 263-271 concerning the historical events of this era.

in Isaiah 2:6-22, which appears to date from the era before 701 B.C., Isaiah announces judgment for Judah, declaring that a Day of Yahweh is coming also for the southern kingdom.

The references to the cedars of Lebanon, the oaks of Bashan and the ships of Tarshish are included not as geographical designations but prevalent symbols of power and might in the world. In the crisis that was coming for Judah, Isaiah foresaw the humbling of all that was high and lofty including the arrogance of men.

And these awesome words also came to pass. In 705-701 B.C., Hezekiah became involved with other vassal nations in a conspiracy to withhold tribute, and the new Assyrian emperor, Sennacherib V, responded by leading a military force against the various rebellious countries. Behind him he left a trail of desolate cities and exiled populations. The available historical evidence indicates that in the year 701 B.C., Sennacherib surrounded Jerusalem with earthworks and kept a military siege of the city in effect for some time while systematically completing the task of destroying the smaller cities of Judah. Concerning this campaign, the famous Annals of Sennacherib report:

> As to Hezekiah, the Jew, he did not submit to my yoke. I laid siege to 46 of his strong cities, walled forts and to the countless small villages in their vicinity, and conquered (them) by means of well-stamped (earth-) ramps, and battering-rams brought (thus) near (to the walls) (combined with) the attack by foot soldiers, (using) mines, breeches as well as sapper work. I drove out (of them) 200,150 people, young and old, male and female, horses, mules, donkeys, camels, big and small cattle beyond counting, and considered (them) booty. Himself I made a prisoner in Jerusalem, his royal residence, like a bird in a cage. I surrounded him with earthwork in order to molest those who were leaving his city's gate. His towns which I plundered I took away from his country and gave them (over) to Mitinti, king of Ashdod, Padi, king of Ekron, and Sillibel, king of Gaza. Thus I reduced his country, but I still increased the tribute and the katru-presents (due)

to me (as his) overlord which I imposed (later) upon him
beyond the former tribute, to be delivered annually.[10]

The account continues by describing at length the tribute imposed by Sennacherib upon Hezekiah as the price of surrender.
The text of 2 Kings 18:13-16 is in striking agreement with the
account in Sennacherib's Annals. The critical problems relating
to the various military campaigns of Sennacherib are numerous.
But the agreement between the text in 2 Kings and the report
in Sennacherib's Annals builds a very strong case for the view
that both refer to events of 701 B.C., while the adjacent accounts
in 2 Kings 19 and in Isaiah, chapters 36-39 probably relate to later
events.[11] What seems apparent from the accounts cited above is
that Isaiah understood Sennacherib's invasion of Judah and siege
of Jerusalem in 701 B.C. as the fulfillment of his own oracle in
2:12-17.

Looking back on the invasion and reflecting on the cities
of Judah in ruin, Isaiah wrote:

Your land is desolate, your towns burnt down,
    your fields—strangers lay them waste before your eyes;
    all is desolation, as after the fall of Sodom.
Daughter Zion is left like a shanty in a vineyard,
    like a shed in a melon patch, like a besieged city.
Had Yahweh not left us a few survivors,
    we should be like Sodom,
    we should now be like Gomorrah.[12] (Is. 1:7-9)

In light of these texts, it seems clear that Isaiah's oracle in
chapter 22 is also to be understood most properly as a reflection

---

10. J. B. Pritchard (ed.), **Ancient Near Eastern Texts** (Princeton:
Princeton University Press, 1950), p. 288.

11. Cf. Bright, **op. cit.,** Excursus I. "The Problem of Sennacherib's
Campaigns in Palestine," pp. 282-287.

12. Read "Daughter Zion" following W. F. Stinespring, "No Daughter
of Zion: A Study of the Appositional Genitive in Hebrew Grammar,"
Encounter 26 (Spring, 1965), 133-41.

on the events of 701 B.C. There, again in retrospect, Isaiah describes the bitter events which had come upon Judah, now calling those events the Day of Yahweh:

> For the Lord, Yahweh of hosts, has had a day of tumult,
>   trampling and confusion in the valley of vision;
> Kir was shouting, and Shoa was at the mountain!
> Elam took up the quiver, with chariots and horsemen,
>   and Kir uncovered the shield.
> Your choicest valleys were full of chariots,
>   and horsemen took their stand at the gates.
> And He took away the covering of Judah.[13] (Is. 22:5-8)

Just as the destruction in Samaria in 721 B.C. had been a day of Yahweh for northern Israel, so also the massive destruction in Judah in 701 B.C. and the narrow escape of Jerusalem were now looked upon in retrospect in the prophetic perspective as Judah's Day of Yahweh.

The Reasons for the Coming of 'Day of Yahweh' Events

Despite certain basic differences in their articulation of judgment, Isaiah and Amos are in striking agreement concerning the causes or reasons for understanding events as punishment for their nations. Both prophets denounce abuses in several areas of national life. In the first place, justice could not be administered because dishonest men were in positions of authority. In both Israel and Judah, the legal systems had become distorted to serve the interests of the rich and the powerful.[14] In a second area, both Amos and Isaiah declare that worship practices have become meaningless, hollow rituals because of the hypocrisy of priests and people. Like the legal structures, the religious establishment appears to

---

13. My own translation. The preterite understanding of verse 5a is consistent with the references to earlier events throughout this chapter.

14. Amos 2:6-8, 5:6-7, 10-15, 6:12; Is 1:21-23, 24-26, 3:13-15, 5:23, 10:1-4.

have become a tool in the hands of the ruling political powers.[15]
A third area of common concern for the prophets was the arrogance of the rich and the affluent. The wealthy and landed peoples
appear to have been preoccupied only with the pursuit of greater
luxuries, their women asking for greater stores of ornaments and
fine perfumes. For Amos and Isaiah, the attitudes and actions
of this group stand in radical contradiction to the quality of
human life that is pleasing to Yahweh.[16] It is impossible for
Yahweh to tolerate such conditions and still be a Lord of justice
and righteousness.

I would suggest, however, that another theme in Amos and
Isaiah should be viewed, not as a fourth area of concern, but
rather as the underlying or central theme which influenced what
the prophets said in all other areas. This fundamental theme is the
situation of the poor in a society. If individuals and nations wish
to know the basic reason for the coming of judgment, they are
to look at the condition of those in the lowest levels of their society
—the poor (‘anāyim), the afflicted (dalîm) and the needy (’ebyônîm).[17] There they will see most clearly the truth about their
own real concerns in life. More than any other factor, the condition
of the poor and the afflicted people in a society lays bare the selfish-
ness (i.e., lack of faith) of the upper classes of a nation. Repeatedly
Amos refers to the weak, the poor, the afflicted and the righteous
(i.e., innocent) as a particular group within a society. Of this
group, James Mays has written:

> Their suffering is the arresting circumstance that discloses
> the situation of the entire nation before Yahweh. The weak

---

15. Amos 2:8, 3:14, 4:4-5, 5:4-5, 21-24, 25-27, 7:10-17; Is 1:10-17,
2:20-22.

16. Amos 3:9-11, 13-15, 4:1-3, 5:11, 6:1-3, 4-7, 11-14, 8:4-6; Is 3:
13-15, 16-4:1, 5:8-10, 11-12, 18-19, 20, 21, 22-23, 32:9-20.

17. See references to the "poor" (‘anāyim) in Amos 2:7, 8:4 and Is
3:14,15, 10:2, 11:4, 14:32, 25:4, 26:6, 29:19 and 32:7; to the "afflicted"
(dalîm) in Amos 2:7, 4:1, 8:6 and Is 10:2, 11:4, 14:30, 25:4 and 26:6
and to the "needy" (’ebyônîm) in Amos 2:6, 4:1, 5:12, 8:4,6 and Is
14:30, 25:4, 29:19 and 32:7.

are being sold into slavery (2:6), dispossessed (2:6, 8:6), exploited (8:5, 5:11), and ignored (6:6). The prophecy of Amos can be heard as Yahweh's response to their cry, for the weak and poor are the special objects of Yahweh's compassion and concern; the obligation of his people to protect and respect the weak in their helplessness is a theme of every survey of covenant norms preserved in the Old Testament.[18]

I further suggest that the same central concern for the welfare of the poor is also at the heart of the message of Isaiah. In chapter 32:7, Isaiah denounces those who leave the hungry man's cravings unsatisfied and refuse drink to the thirsty, who devise wicked plots and ruin the poor with lies. In chapter 3:13-15, Yahweh identifies himself with the poor and announces his complaint in the form of a legal lawsuit. With the imagery of the song of the vineyard in chapter 5, Isaiah announces Yahweh's complaint against the elders and the princes:

You are the ones who destroy the vineyard and conceal what you have stolen from the poor. By what right do you crush my people and grind the faces of the poor? It is Lord Yahweh Sebaoth who speaks. (Is 3:14b-15)[19]

Concern for the poor is also central in the visions of the future time of peace. Offenses committed against the lowly in society will then be righted as Zion becomes a place of refuge for the afflicted (14:32); in Zion, the poor shall obtain fresh joy and shall exult in their Lord (29:19). The ruthless will be brought under control, the scoffer will be silenced and all who seek to do

---

18. Mays, op. cit., p. 10.

19. In v. 13, read the plural "nations" or "peoples" with the Hebrew rather than the singular "his nation" or "his people" with the Syriac and LXX. Yahweh is here not the accuser of his people, but is rather their advocate (cf. the "my people" of 15a). See further J. Limburg, "The Root rib and the Prophetic Lawsuit Speeches," Journal of Biblical Literature, LXXXVIII (Sept., 1969), pp. 291-304.

evil will be destroyed (29:20). As with the plumbline imagery in Amos, Isaiah declares that in the new community, justice will be the 'line' and righteousness the 'plummet' by which the community will live (28:16). Then wars among nations will come to an end, and grievances will be settled by arbitration (2:1-4).

At the center of this city will stand the ideal leader, the Messianic king of the Davidic line. As the model of a good governmental ruler, he will bring peace with justice precisely because of his concern for the poor and his fair judgments for the meek of the earth (11:3-5).

During the national crisis in 735-34, Isaiah chided Ahaz for his lack of faith (Is 7:1-9, 10-17). Judah was needlessly about to become an occupied country because of the king's immediate fears and his short-sighted self-interests. In similar fashion, Isaiah was certainly thinking about the total welfare of the people of the land when he counseled Hezekiah in 714-711 and again in 705-701 against reckless policies of revolt against Assyria, which could lead only to disaster. The political leaders were being irresponsible with the lives of their soldiers and ultimately with the lives of the entire population.

Possibly the clearest picture of Isaiah's concern is found in the opening chapter of his writings. After deploring the utter hypocrisy of the people who bring multitudes of sacrifices and preoccupy themselves with questions about proper ritual washings, the word of Yahweh is sounded:

> Wash (yourselves), make yourselves clean!
> Take your wrong-doing out of my sight.
> Cease to do evil.
> Learn to do good, search for justice, help the oppressed,
>   be just to the orphan, plead for the widow.
>   (Is 1:16-17)

Orphans and widows are singled out because they were specific groups within society which were cut off from access to the economic structures; without care these persons were the prey of thieves and were subject to starvation. The concern for the poor, and specifically for widows, orphans and the homeless, is not something new that appears in Israel with Amos and Isaiah. Rather, their central concern for the poor continues a sacred tradition that is as old as the ancient Book of the Covenant in Exodus 20:22-23:33.

There is one further aspect of the concern for the poor in the writings of Amos and Isaiah that should be recalled here. Punishment for crimes against the poor is not set out in Amos or Isaiah as the exclusive reality of history for the religious community of faith or as the exclusive reality for the nations of Israel and Judah. Instead, this prophetic understanding is set forth as the universal principle of history for all nations, great empires and small city-states alike. Assyria, the world power, is responsible before Yahweh for a wise and careful stewardship of her tremendous power.[20] Smaller nations are responsible according to their size and power. In Amos, indictments are announced for Syria, Gaza, Tyre, Edom, Ammon and Moab.[21] Isaiah announces judgment for these nations and adds oracles of judgment for Egypt, Arabia, Sidon, Philistia and the empire, Assyria.[22] In this international perspective, war, wherever it appears in the world, is understood by the prophets in one way or another to be the inevitable outcome of the arrogant use of power by kings and emperors. The nations are indicted for slavery, for violations of common international norms of morality, for excessive cruelty in warfare, for violations of covenant agreements, for deceitful conduct and most of all, I would submit, for their failure to be concerned with the poor of the earth. As the result, times of punish-

---

20. See esp. Is 10:5-11, 12-19. Because of her arrogant use of power, Assyria will in turn be punished.

21. See Amos 1:3-5, 6-8, 9-10, 11-12, 13-15, 2:1-3.

22. See Is 14:24-27, 28-32, 15:1-16:14, 17:1-6, 18:1-20:6, 19:1-15, 20:1-6, 21:11-12, 13-17, 23:1-18. No oracle is directed specifically against Ammon in Isaiah; the other nations indicted by Amos are also indicted by Isaiah.

ment or "days of Yahweh" are coming for the various nations and empires.[23] Whether they recognize him or not, Yahweh is the Lord of all men and nations of the world. He is the creator and sovereign of kings and the poor alike.

In Isaiah 25:4-5, the closing lines of a prayer of thanksgiving can perhaps summarize our basic concern here. The words call us to the prophetic task of examining our national and individual priorities as we seek the quality of life that is pleasing to the Lord.

> You (Yahweh) are a refuge for the poor,
>> a refuge for the needy in distress,
>> a shelter from the storm, a shade from the heat;
>> while the breath of pitiless men is like the winter storm.
>
> Like drought in a dry land
>> you will repress the clamour of the proud;
>> like heat by the shadow of a cloud
>> the singing of the despots will be subdued.
>
>> (Is. 25:4-5)

---

23. The oracles against foreign nations have frequently been interpreted in the context of the oracles of salvation because they appear to imply salvation for Israel in the situations in which they were uttered. See Westermann, op. cit., pp. 204ff. Such a perspective does not seem broad enough, however, in light of evidence such as is present in Amos 2:1-3 where Moab is indicted for a crime against Edom and in Is 10:5-19 where Yahweh is set forth as universal Lord and judge of all nations. Specific Day of Yahweh terminology is used in oracles addressed to foreign nations in Jer 46:2-12 (Egypt), Ez 30:1-9 (Egypt), Is 13:1-22 (Babylon), 34:1-17 (Edom and all nations), 63:1-6 (various nations), Joel 1-4 (various nations), Obadiah (Edom), and Zech 14:1-21 (various nations).

13 Faith in Crisis: A Lesson from Samuel

JAMES W. FLANAGAN

The critical problems of the Books of Samuel are manifold. Among the more perplexing are the inconsistencies surrounding the institution of the Israelite monarchy in 1 Sam 7-12. There, Samuel functions as kingmaker as he guides Israel through the crisis of faith that accompanied the collapse of the tribal league. Israel believed in the first commandment and had structured a government that expressed that belief.[1] The superiority of the Philistines forced the people to reassess their faith and to choose between annihilation and a strong, permanent leader such as a king.

In the past, critics have attacked the problems found in chapters 7-12 with various methodologies, but no one has been successful in recovering a unified view of the monarchy that completely explains the presence of both anti-monarchical and pro-monarchical traditions in the same narrative. In recent years, several important investigations have been made into the historical role of Samuel.[2] With their help and with a new look at the literary

---

1. John Bright, **A History of Israel** (Philadelphia: Westminster Press, 1959), p. 128.
2. Edward Robertson, **The Old Testament Problem. A Reinvestigation** (Manchester: Manchester University Press, 1950); William F. Albright, "Samuel and the Beginnings of the Prophetic Movement," in **Interpreting the Prophetic Tradition**, ed. Harry M. Orlinsky (New York: Ktav Publishing House, 1969); Artur Weiser, **Samuel. Seine geschictliche Aufgabe und religiöse Bedeutung** (Göttingen: Vandenhoeck & Ruprecht, 1962); John L. McKenzie, "The Four Samuels," **Biblical Research**, 7 (1962), 3-18.

structure of the chapters, we are now able to move toward a clearer understanding of the view of the compiler of 1 S 7-12 and therefore to appreciate more fully the quality of life in ancient Israel.

The present arrangement of the institution narrative is obviously the work of a compiler, and, along with the rest of 1 and 2 Samuel, it now stands as part of the broader history compiled by the Deuteronomic historians.[3] Since it is generally agreed that the Deuteronomists were not the original compilers of the Books, our investigation may begin by removing the Deuteronomic redactions. These must be looked upon as literary insertions which have been imposed upon the earlier narrative in order to modify or accentuate its theology by making it more compatible with the views of the redactors. Because one can be tempted to explain away all the problems of the institution narrative by labelling them Deuteronomic, caution must be taken to single out only those units that contain definite and easily recognized literary signs of Deuteronomic style.

The Deuteronomic sections of chapters 7-12 are: the chronological reference to twenty years in 7:2; Samuel's admonition against service to the Baals and Ashtaroth in 7:3-4; the expansive description of the dangers of monarchy in 8:9, 11-18, and possibly a remark that introduces the description in 8:5; the isolated reference to the "law of the king" in 10:25; the report of Saul's battle with the Ammonites in 11:1-11; the covenant formula which extols the victories of the judges in 12:6-15; and finally some reworking of 11:12-15 and 12:19-25 in order to make the last two units fit their present contexts. When each section is studied in detail, its Deuteronomic characteristics and its relation to the other redactions will become clear.

The first two additions come at a juncture point in the narrative. The ark tradition found in 1 S 4-6 is broken off in the opening

---

3. Martin Noth, **Überlieferungsgeschichtliche Studien**, 3rd ed. (Tübingen: Max Niemeyer Verlag, 1967), especially pp. 61-62.

verses of chapter 7, and the compiler has joined it to a tradition describing Samuel as a judge and opposed to the monarchy.[4] The absence of Samuel in the story of the ark and his re-entry in chapter 7 for the first time since chapter 3 where he was at the shrine in Shiloh convinces critics of the presence of two originally independent traditions.

In 7:2, the writer states that the ark remained at Kiriath-jearim for "a long time." The Deuteronomists further specified "twenty years." The addition makes the preceding statement super-fluous, and it fits the chronological framework commonly attributed to the Deuteronomists.[5] Vv. 3-4 report that Samuel chastised the people for honoring the Canaanite deities. Although v. 3 states that abandoning the practice is a condition for delivery from the Philistines, the reproval is not explicitly recalled in the story that follows. This suggests that the two were not originally connected. Moreover, the viewpoint and vocabulary are Deuteronomic,[6] and the unit was easily inserted between the two traditions.[7] The only other mention of Baals and Ashtaroth in the two Books of Samuel is in 1 Sam 12 to be discussed below.[8]

The remainder of chapter 7 is a story of Samuel's battle prep-arations and his victory over the Philistines. It concludes with a statement testifying that he traveled to judge at Bethel, Gilgal and Mizpah before returning home to Ramah. The account situates Samuel within the framework of the tribal league by characterizing him as a successful military leader. The assertion of a complete and lasting victory over the Philistines (7:13) cannot be reconciled

---

4. Leonhard Rost, "Die Überlieferung von der Thronnachfolge Davids," Das kleine Credo und andere Studien zum Alten Testament (Heidelberg: Quelle & Meyer, 1965), pp. 122-159.

5. Weiser, op. cit., p. 8; Noth, op. cit., p. 22.

6. Horst Seebass, "Die Vorgeschichte der Konigserhebung Sauls," Zeitschrift fur die Alttestamentliche Wissenschaft, 89 (1967), p. 169.

7. Ibid., p. 169. The "foreign" gods (nēkor) differ from the "other" or "strange" gods used frequently by the Deuteronomists. However, this word appears in Jgs 10:16; Jos 24:12, 23; Dt 31:16; 32:12.

8. The ashtaroth appear alone in 1 Sam 31:10.

with subsequent reports of the enemy's strength and so can be credited to the theological viewpoint of its author.[9] The account does not have any clear markings of a Deuteronomic construction, and I fail to find reason to credit the redactors with its origin.[10]

The same tradition is continued in chapter 8 until it is broken off at the beginning of chapter 9. Here, the avaricious sons of Samuel are reported to have judged after their father (8:1-3). It is unlikely that two judges would have been appointed as far south as Beersheba during Samuel's time as is stated, so scholars agree that the statement is an error. The wickedness of the sons caused the people to demand the appointment of a king (8:5). Samuel was displeased by the request (8:6), but was told by Yahweh to grant their petitions (8:7, 22).

An expansion which explicates the tyrannies of a king has been used by the Deuteronomists to exaggerate Samuel's opposition to the principle of monarchy. It is found in 8:9, 11-18 and is comparable to a list found in Deut 17:14-20.[11] Because of the similarity and the hortatory tone of the insertion, there can be little doubt about its origin. The verses do not advance the narrative and can be removed with no disruption of thought and no change in Samuel's attitude toward kingship. In fact, the surgery removes some unevenness presently found in the phrasing of the chapter (vv. 10, 11, 22b). V. 5 may have been reworked as an introduction to the unit as can be seen in a comparison with Dt 17:14.[12] Both verses contain the request to "appoint a king" using the infrequent combination of *sîm* with *melek*.

---

9. Albright, **op. cit.,** p. 163 tries to circumvent the problem by asserting that Samuel's victory was a truce he negotiated.

10. Weiser, **op. cit.,** p. 8.

11. Gerhard von Rad, **Deuteronomy,** trans. Dorothea Barton (Philadelphia: Westminster Press, 1966), p. 118; Joseph Blenkinsopp, "Deuteronomy," in **The Jerome Biblical Commentary,** ed. Raymond Brown, Joseph A. Fitzmyer, Roland E. Murphy (Englewood Cliffs: Prentice-Hall, Inc., 1968), p. 112.

12. Martin Buber, "Die Erzählung von Sauls Königswahl," **Vetus Testamentum,** 6 (1956), p. 171.

In chapter 9 the compiler has drawn from a different tradition
in which Samuel plays the part of seer (*rô'êh*) and man of god
(*'iš hā'ĕlōhîm*) and is favorably disposed to a new form of government. The tradition begins in 9:1 and extends through 10:16.
These limits are so widely accepted that they hardly need comment.
Within the section the story of the rise of Saul begins to unfold.
As a son of Kish, sent to retrieve his father's lost asses, the youth
seeks the advice of Samuel. He recognizes Saul as one chosen
by Yahweh and anoints him as *nāgîd*, i.e., military leader.[13] Although there are no traces of the Deuteronomic hand in this account, several inconsistencies have led critics to suspect the presence
of two traditions now interwoven in such a way that they defy
separation.[14] The unnamed city in which Saul met Samuel seems
at once near to and far from Gibeah (compare 9:4-5 with
10:2-10); it is not clear whether Samuel resided in the city or was
visiting it (compare 9:10 with 9:12); Samuel is both an obscure
seer and a man of great renown (compare 9:18 with 9:6); there
is a distinction between the titles "seer" and "man of god" which
has been noted by an editor who added his own explanation (9:9);
and finally, Saul is sent by his father to search for the livestock
but upon returning home reports to his uncle instead (compare
9:3 with 10:14).

The next section of the narrative sheds additional light on the
fusion of the two traditions which now stand as a single seer
account. In 10:17-27, Samuel's attitude reverts to that of the
judge tradition. Critics see little problem in identifying the section
with the tradition found in chapters 7 and 8. As before, Samuel
is at Mizpah (10:17) and is opposed to the demand for a king
(10:19). He finally gives in and elects Saul by lot (10:21a).

Thus far, the critics are correct. However, in the remainder

---

13. Albright, op. cit., p. 165.
14. Hans Wilhelm Hertzberg, 1 & 2 Samuel, trans. J. S. Bowden
(Philadelphia: Westminster Press, 1964), p. 79. See also: Bruce C. Birch,
"The Development of the Tradition on the Anointing of Saul in 1 S 9:1-10:
16," Journal of Biblical Literature, 90 (1971), pp. 55-68.

of the chapter (vv. 21b-27) we find traces of a different tradition
which reflects a more favorable disposition toward Saul.[15] After
being elected by lot, Saul is reported as hiding in the midst of
baggage. He is fetched by the people, his stature receives favorable comment, and he is praised by Samuel. This change in thrust,
together with a shift from singular to plural verbs in 10:21b and
the disagreement between the Massoretic and Septuagint texts
at the precise point of transition, indicates that a second account
has been woven together with the election by lot from the judge
tradition. I suggest that the baggage scene is the election scene
from one of the two seer traditions now fused in 9:1-10:16.[16]
The reference to Saul's stature and Samuel's admiration match
the image of him in the preceding section and recall explicitly
the description of the son of Kish in that tradition (cf. 9:2).
Within the complex found in 10:17-27, only 10:25 is Deuteronomic. The verse is intrusive in its present context and the phrasing
recalls the "ways of the king" found in the Deuteronomic insertion
in chapter 8.[17]

The next Deuteronomic section is found in chapter 11, but
it will be helpful to pass over it for the time being and return to it
after treating chapter 12. Chapter 12 is a farewell address of
Samuel taken from the judge tradition seen in chapters 7 and 8.
In it, the old man defends his honesty and benevolence before the
people (vv. 2-4) and by means of an Elijah-type miracle (vv.
16-19), calls upon Yahweh to witness to the evil the people have
committed by demanding a king. The speech concludes by stipu-
lating that only continued service to the Lord will free the people
from the consequences of their sin (vv. 19-25).

There is no reason to doubt that this section is a continuation
of the judge tradition. However, a Deuteronomic unit has been

---

15. Otto Eissfeldt, **Die Komposition der Samuelisbücher** (Leipzig:
J. C. Heinrichs'sche Buchhandlung, 1931), pp. 8-9.

16. The presence of a second report of Saul's ecstasy in 1 S 19:18-24
is suggestive of the same conclusion. See Albright, op. cit., p. 156.

17. Hertzberg, op. cit., p. 90; Julius Wellhausen, **Die Composition des
Hexateuchs und der historischen Bücher des Alten Testaments** (Berlin:
Walter De Gruyter & Co., rpt. 1963), p. 243. Mišpat is used in both.

inserted into the section in vv. 6-15. The addition follows the pattern of the familiar covenant formula, a favorite form of the Deuteronomists, and like the redactions found in chapters 7 and 8, is an exhortation that does little to advance the narrative.[18] In fact, if removed, Samuel's call for witness in v. 5 would be followed smoothly by Yahweh's miraculous sign begun in v. 16. In its present location, there is some unevenness in vv. 5 and 6 which the Septuagint has attempted to correct. The insertion lists examples of Yahweh's protection which Israel has enjoyed in the past. It begins with the saving deeds in Egypt and continues to single out various judges by name to illustrate Yahweh's abiding support. Included is the proper name "Samuel" which is out of place in a speech given by the same person (v. 11). Mention is given to the Baals and Ashtaroth (v. 10) as in chapter 7, and the section concludes by citing the threat of Nahash of the Ammonites as the reason the people asked for a king (v. 12). Its author intended to illustrate that Yahweh had always provided for his people, even in the days of the judges, and that they should have had confidence in the face of Nahash as well. Shortly, we will see that Nahash is introduced in chapter 11 in a section which is also Deuteronomic.

The expansion in chapter 12 is distinctly pro-judge and, because of its form and content, should be assigned to the list of Deuteronomic redactions. The concluding verses of the chapter (vv. 19-25) also bear signs of reworking in order to weave the insertion into its present context. There, Samuel's admonitions are somewhat repetitious (e.g., vv. 20, 21), and there are minor textual difficulties that indicate redaction (e.g., v. 21).

The reference to Nahash in chapter 12 is introduced by two references to him in chapter 11. The chapter contains the colorful account of the conflict between the Ammonites and the men of Jabesh (vv. 1-11). The latter were allowed several days to muster support from the territory of Israel. When they sought his help, Saul championed their cause by cutting his oxen into pieces and

---

18. James Muilenburg, "The Form and Structure of the Covenantal Formulation," **Vetus Testamentum**, 9 (1959), pp. 360-364.

sending portions throughout the territory with a call to arms. The rally was successful, and under Saul's leadership, the Ammonites were soundly defeated. The remainder of the chapter (vv. 12-15) makes it seem that the peoples' enthusiasm for Saul and Samuel's celebration at Gilgal were the result of Saul's victory in vv. 1-11.[19] The chapter is a compilation. The reference to Samuel in v. 7 and the remark about Judah in v. 8 can be set aside as secondary.[20] The "renewing" of the kingdom in v. 14 is also secondary.[21] We may go further by noting that vv. 1-11, the Ammonite campaign, is an independent unit. It does not fit well after the reports of Saul's election in the preceding chapters, and if removed, a possible connection can be seen between the judge tradition broken off after the election by lots in chapter 10, the proclamation of the kingdom in the original portion of 11:12-15, and Samuel's final self-defense in chapter 12.

By itself, 11:1-11 stands as another explanation of Saul's election.[22] Samuel plays no part in it, and there is no anointing. Saul receives his call directly from Yahweh, and he responds in the same way as the earlier judges who took part in the intertribal war in Jgs 19-21.[23] The association between the account of the Ammonite war and the earlier tribal strife becomes even more clear when we recall that in Judges the body of a concubine was cut into pieces and distributed as a call to war (Jgs 19:29) and that Jabesh-gilead was important (Jgs 21:8-9). Saul is clearly cast in the pattern of the earlier judges.

The account in 11:1-11 has been problematic in all explanations of the compilation of the Books of Samuel.[24] I propose that the unit is a later insertion that has been added to the narrative by the Deuteronomic historians. The parallel between this descrip-

---

19. Hertzberg, op. cit., p. 94.

20. Weiser, op. cit., pp. 70-71.

21. Ibid., p. 70.

22. Hertzberg, op. cit., p. 91; Wellhausen, op. cit., p. 246.

23. John L. McKenzie, The World of the Judges (Englewood Cliffs: Prentice-Hall, 1965), p. 165; Weiser, op. cit., p. 71; Hertzberg, op. cit., p. 94.

24. Even Buber admits that it is exceptional. See Buber, op. cit., p. 165.

tion of Saul and those of the judges in the Deuteronomic Book of Judges is clear. The classic pattern which was used to portray Saul was not applied to Samuel in the earlier report of him as judge in chapters 7 and 8 because the pattern was not available when that tradition was written.[25] It was available to the Deuteronomists, and they used it in writing 11:1-11. Confirmation for this proposal is found in the fact that the section introduces another Deuteronomic addition. Thus, we have a tradition about Saul's rise which is independent of the Samuel traditions. In its original form, it was pro-Saul and pro-judge, but anti-monarchic.[26]

A preliminary conclusion can be drawn from the survey of the Deuteronomic redactions. It is that neither the anti-monarchic nor pro-monarchic attitude was the creation of the Deuteronomic historians. Instead, they amplified the theological character of the judge tradition by adding negative descriptions of the monarchy and by explaining Saul's success as a call to charismatic judgeship. Incorporating the expansions into the narrative has caused some unevenness, especially in chapter 11 where the Ammonite war interrupts the progress of the story. What is more important, however, is that the tradition of Samuel's judgeship is pre-Deuteronomic.

Once the redactions have been set aside, the reader is left with a forward moving account of the transformation from tribal league to monarchy. Chapters 7-12 provide an important link with the ark tradition (1 S 4-6) which makes clear that the amphictyonic shrine, the unifying factor in the tribal league, had been destroyed by the Philistines. It indicates that the people were forced to follow Samuel's leadership. Chapters 7 and 8 demonstrate that Samuel was the legitimate spokesman for the people and for Yahweh.[27]

---

25. Against Walter Beyerlin, "Gattung und Herkunft des Rahmens im Richterbuch," in **Tradition und Situation,** ed. Ernst Würthwein und Otto Kaiser (Göttingen: Vandenhoeck & Ruprecht, 1963), pp. 1-29. Samuel is not the type of judge found in the accounts of the classical judges. See Buber, **op. cit.,** p. 119.

26. Buber has distinguished the anti- and pro-Saul attitudes from the anti- and pro-monarchic. See **Ibid.,** pp. 164-168.

27. Hertzberg, **op. cit.,** p. 69.

His credentials as charterer of Israel's course were in order. He had been called by Yahweh while at Shiloh (1 S 3) and was still in communication with him (8:7-9, 22). He merited the support of the tribal people by his leadership against the Philistines (7:10-14). In short, he was better equipped than anyone else to serve as kingmaker.

The next section reports how Saul came to be chosen as the leader of Israel. Chapters 9-10 continue the drama begun by the peoples' request for a king. The section tells the story of Saul's rise from a youth tending his father's herds to anointed leader of Israel. Again it is Samuel who stands as Yahweh's voice in the selection (9:15-17). Saul's legitimacy is dependent upon his anointing by Samuel (10:1) and is made manifest by his ecstatic experience at Gibeah in which the spirit of Yahweh reveals itself (10:5-13). Samuel's enthusiasm for Saul as *nâgîd* is followed by a report of his reluctant acceptance of the leader as *melek* in 10:17-27. The transition is clumsy, but one must admit that the narrative advances in spite of it. Election by lot indicates a general indifference toward the outcome, but nevertheless, Saul is proclaimed king (10:24). The remainder of the narrative is devoted to the confirmation of Saul's kingship at Gilgal (11:12-15), Samuel's final admonitions about the dangers of monarchy, and his warning that fidelity to Yahweh is the only salvation for the people (chap. 12). In his closing address, Samuel reaffirms his legitimacy as an agent of Yahweh even after the foundation of the monarchy (12:16-19, 23). It is Samuel's condition for accepting the new form of government, namely, that the king remain subservient to the spirit and to Yahweh's charismatic spokesmen. The section in chapters 7-12 ends with the stage set for Saul's decline (1 S 13-14) and David's entrance into the story (1 S 16).

The section in chapters 7-12 is clearly transitional, and Samuel is its principal character. It marks him as the key figure in the establishment of the monarchy. The chapters are, however, also a step on the way to the monarchy of David, and the intent of the compiler of 1 and 2 Samuel was to demonstrate David's legitimacy.[28] Viewed in the perspective of the Davidic reign, Samuel emerges as the one who can establish and dispose of monarchs. This is an important consideration because the narrative traces the history of Israel from the time its faith centered around the amphictyonic shrine at Shiloh until it came to rest in the capital city, Jerusalem. In this expanded view, Samuel becomes the dominant figure in the books that bear his name.

If the narrative is divided according to the judge and seer traditions that have been noted above, each offers a separate view of the monarchy. The judge tradition is in chapter 7, chapter 8, part of 10:17-27, probably part of 11:12-15 and in chapter 12. It describes Samuel as opposed to kingship but eventually brought to tolerate the institution after he was confronted by the sins of his sons (8:1-3) and told to withdraw his opposition by Yahweh (8:7, 19-22). Saul was elected by casting lots (10:20-21), and some were dissatisfied with the selection (10:27; 11:12-13). The tradition concluded with Samuel's address (chap. 12). The combined seer tradition extends from 9:1 to 10:16 and through part of 10:17-27. Samuel is portrayed as favoring Saul's rise but is careful to avoid the use of the word "king." Instead, he anoints Saul *nâgîd*, the election is secret, and in at least one version, no publication is made of it.

When studied individually, neither the judge nor the seer tradition is totally opposed to the principle of monarchy, and neither is completely in favor of Saul as king. The judge tradition, commonly called anti-monarchic, portrays Samuel as eventually accepting the change once he is assured that the spirit will not be stifled. The seer account is not as clearly pro-Saul as it is pro-Davidic. The tradition is used elsewhere in 1 S (chap. 16), and it reserves the title of *melek* for David. In its author's view, David was the first king of Israel.[29]

Several other factors can be noted about the traditions. First,

---

28. See Artur Weiser, "Die Legitimation des Königs David. Zur Eigenart und Enstehung der sogen. Geschichte von Davids Aufstieg," **Vetus Testamentum**, 16 (1966), pp. 325-354.

29. McKenzie, "Four Samuels," p. 10.

there is no literary evidence which forces us to conclude that one tradition was written much later than the other. Beersheba mentioned in the judge tradition was probably important as early as the time of David; the Davidic thrust of the seer tradition would have been popular as early as his reign as well. The second observation may be stated in the form of a hypothesis: to eliminate either tradition from the original compilation of the extended narrative that legitimized David would create a theological and historical lacuna in the narrative. The removal would sacrifice more than the critic would allow. The judge tradition is necessary as a link with the history of tribal Israel and for the legitimacy of Samuel. When the amphictyony failed, Israel groped for survival and searched for an alternative to a government that had been structurally and religiously anti-monarchic. Thus, there is nothing late about this attitude, and it should be represented by anyone writing a history of the period. On the other hand, the seer tradition cannot be easily removed because it explains the anointing of Saul and of David (1 S 16). It would be hard to imagine a legitimation account in which the spirit was not conferred. This does not imply, however, that the traditions did not at one time exist separately, but rather that each is a theological explanation of the monarchy, and the theology of the Books of Samuel depends upon the presence of both views.

In spite of their discrepancies, the Samuel traditions agree that his endorsement was necessary for whomever was to be the leader of Israel. In the first Book of Samuel, he is portrayed as wearing the robes of priest and prophet as well as those of judge and seer.[30] Because of this, scholars have been challenged to search for the historical role of Samuel which would explain his importance in the history of Israel.

John L. McKenzie has argued that the real Samuel was the leader of the sons of the prophets and that all the descriptions are attempts to portray him as the hero of the circle that produced

---

30. **Ibid.**, pp. 4-11.

the individual tradition.[31] As a group, the sons of the prophets were opposed to any institution or structure that would stifle the spirit and place Israel's tradition of charismatic leadership in jeopardy.[32] They were an eccentric group, and one that must have had considerable influence in Israel. As leader of this group, Samuel's own disposition toward monarchy wavered.[33] He possessed the spirit and served as a spokesman for Yahweh. He was torn between the conservative, traditional reluctance to sacrifice charism for institutionalism and the practical need for a type of leadership less sporadic and more stable than the judges. He shared the belief that a kingless government was a theological necessity for a people who believed that Yahweh was their only king. But like others, he could see that Israel's faith was seriously threatened by the Philistines and would be annihilated if things continued as they were. The federation needed a king "like other nations," and Samuel came to accept this fact only after insuring that the charism of Yahweh would be respected in the new institution.

The wavering disposition of the historical Samuel is reflected in the arrangement of the traditions in 1 S 7-12. The ambivalence displayed in the compilation is actually historical, and the compiler has been faithful to the historical situation by including conflicting attitudes. The discussions about an earlier or later tradition may be academic because the problems of the period could not be overlooked by the compiler. He had access to traditions with different views, and he used them in an effort to be faithful to the history of the period. He explained how Israel coped with the crisis that emerged with the collapse of the tribal league. It was a crisis of faith for Israel whose faith tradition was in con-

---

31. **Ibid.**, pp. 3-18. McKenzie rejects the hypothesis that the real Samuel was a judge as many scholars maintain. I follow him in my exposition of Samuel's historical role.

32. J. Lindblom, **Prophecy in Ancient Israel** (Philadelphia: Fortress Press, 1965), pp. 83-90.

33. Albright agrees. See Albright, **op. cit.**, p. 163.

flict with practical necessity. Samuel responded to his calling and met the crisis by giving the kingless people a charismatic monarch who would remain obedient to the spirit of Yahweh. This is Samuel's lesson contained in 1 S 7-12.

14   Intercommunion in an American Perspective

SARA BUTLER

Probably the most honest way to begin a chapter on "Intercommunion in an American Perspective" is to admit that for most Christians in our land this is a non-problem. It is instructive to observe why and for whom this is the case. It is no problem for those who experience increasing difficulty with any speech about God at all and for those who find scandalously provincial the churches' attention to domestic squabbles in an age threatened by nuclear war, racial conflict, and mass starvation.[1] These persons have either lost all taste for the great Christian symbol of reconciliation or else employ it freely in gatherings of their own which they attest are the authentic heirs of the community of Jesus. For such as these the question of eucharistic sharing has already been resolved in one or the other direction. Again, provision for intercommunion is of no interest to the vast numbers still untouched by the ecumenical movement. Their complacency has not been disturbed. They are not unhappy about the "unhappy divisions" deplored by ecumenists. Their eyes do not perceive the scandal of eucharistic assemblies which proclaim Christian division more eloquently than Christian unity.

On the other hand, intercommunion is a non-problem for many—even most—sincere Protestant Americans, not because of any insensitivity to the ecumenical cause but because the practice of open communion, or general admission, is the long-standing custom in their churches. For these, the news that Roman Catho-

---

1. See the introduction to **Intercommunion Today:** The Report of the Archbishop of Canterbury's Commission on Intercommunion (London: The Church Information Office, 1968), p. xiv.

lics, Eastern Orthodox Christians, and some Lutherans would not be permitted to join in a common communion service usually comes as a surprise and cause for no little amazement.

The question of intercommunion, then, exists as a problem chiefly for professional ecumenists and pastors and laity of those Christian traditions which have a discipline regulating and/or prohibiting the admission to communion of baptized Christians outside their own particular fellowships. In practice, this affects mostly the ecumenically-aware, for example, partners in an ecumenical marriage, members of a "natural" community such as a college or seminary, and persons whose participation in some cause or common mission rooted in the Gospel brings them to the point of desiring to share in this sign of unity and reconciliation. Of course, it is not only those bound by a restrictive discipline who suffer the pain of division; their fellow Christians necessarily feel the sting of a measure introduced to exclude the heretic and protect the faithful. For all of these, then, the question of eucharistic sharing in a divided church *is* a live and often touchy issue.

To pose the problem starkly: the policy of limited admission maintained by Eastern Orthodox, Roman Catholic, Lutheran, and (at least in theory) Episcopal churches can hardly be perceived as anything but an affront by Christians of other denominations; the implied judgment revealed in refusal to partake at the communion services offered by these fellow believers compounds the insult insofar as it suggests an inadequacy of faith and ministerial authorization. Surely some revision of discipline must be made which more clearly reflects the present ecumenical situation. Eucharistic regulations formulated for the sake of publicly excluding an individual or a community which had knowingly broken the bonds of fellowship by overstepping the boundaries of orthodoxy in belief and practice do *not* suit the current state of affairs in which ecclesial divisions are, for the most part, inherited. It is widely felt that it would be more appropriate to allow for occasional controlled and authorized eucharistic sharing in an effort to embrace, reconcile, and unite Christians sincerely straining to overcome their divisions.

On the other hand, one would be hoping for too much from

such a step unless all Christian churches engaged in serious eucharistic reform and renewal. This admonition, while pertinent
for all, must be addressed most forcefully to those churches which
relegate the celebration of the Lord's Supper to the periphery
of church life. The policy of general admission (so feared as an
ecumenical shortcut by European ecumenists) has meant little
in terms of ecumenical rapprochement because of the failure of
much of American Protestantism to understand the Eucharist
as sign and source of the Church's unity. To the extent that this
sacrament is still regarded as incidental and is celebrated only
on rare occasions, the time for eucharistic sharing as a sign
of growing unity seems far off indeed.

The picture is brightened somewhat by the realization that the
liturgical renewal so vigorously promoted by certain clergy and
by church committees on worship has been, surprisingly, aug-
mented by the experience of eucharistic fellowship gained in
underground communities and other parallel structures springing
up out of a socio-political context. This *ad hoc* approach to the
Eucharist in a "worldly context" has helped bring about a new
appreciation of the relationship of Eucharist to Church and of both
to mission.[2] Given the desperate need of modern society for a sign
of reconciliation and healing, the rediscovery of eucharistic sym-
bolism in Selma, Washington, and Harrisburg can only be cause
for rejoicing.

This last observation reminds us of the recurring temptation
to consider the whole theological effort a waste of time. In a
recent *Concilium* essay entitled "Do New Problems of our Secular
World Make Ecumenism Irrelevant?" Yves Congar speaks of
"little academic groups congratulating each other"[3] in a way that
invites winces. Still, comfortingly, he goes on to insist that the
Church as institution stands in need of these little groups if it is
ever to make the transition from one stage of life to another. But

---

2. See the excellent account and analysis of this phenomenon in Lewis
S. Mudge, **The Crumbling Walls** (Philadelphia: Westminster Press, 1970).

3. **Post-Ecumenical Christianity,** ed. Hans Küng (New York: Herder
& Herder, 1970), p. 17.

progress is so slow and tedious! And one feels very much in the position of students signing the People's Peace Treaty: our declaration of a cessation of hostilities cannot take effect without action from the official negotiators in Paris. Just so, study teams, even official dialogue groups, can only recommend their conclusions to the churches for study; they cannot take the big steps.

All this is a prelude to the more optimistic section of this chapter. As an observer of the intercommunion question on the American scene for the past several years,[4] I am happy to report that the equivalent of a People's (or, at least, a theologians') Peace Treaty has all but been signed by a majority of professional ecumenical negotiators. With respect to the three main areas of discussion necessarily involved in any consideration of eucharistic sharing, the following can be confidently affirmed: First, a significant consensus on the meaning of the Eucharist has been achieved. Second, there is a rapidly growing consensus on the recognizability of ministries in the separated churches. And third, there is a growing consensus on the nature of the Church's unity. Let me devote the remainder of my time to these assertions.

First, for those who have not had the luxury of keeping up to the minute on the agencies of ecumenical discussion presently in operation, let me remind you that America can boast of the largest number of bi-lateral consultations and church union negotiations of any country in the world. Since 1957 (a landmark date because it saw the first large-scale national effort to deal with doctrinal divisions in the Faith and Order Conference held at Oberlin, Ohio) the following Christian churches have engaged in formal conversation: Lutheran/Presbyterian and Reformed Lutheran/Episcopal, Episcopal/Orthodox, Lutheran/Orthodox, Presbyterian and Reformed/Orthodox, Episcopal/Assemblies of God; and Roman Catholics with Episcopal, Lutheran, Presbyterian and Reformed, Orthodox, United Methodist, Christian Church (Dis-

---

4. An early report by the present writer, "Intercommunion: The State of the Question," appeared in **Readings in the Theology of the Church,** ed. Edward J. Dirkswager, Jr. (Englewood Cliffs, N. J.: Prentice-Hall, 1970), pp. 78-104.

ciples), and the American Baptist Convention.[5] Beyond these, the most significant effort at ecumenical communication is unquestionably the Consultation on Church Union, the negotiations directed at uniting nine major denominations in America (African Methodist Episcopal, A.M.E. Zion, Christian Methodist Episcopal, Christian Church (Disciples of Christ), Episcopal, Presbyterian Church in the U. S., United Church of Christ, United Methodist, United Presbyterian Church in the U.S.A.) into one family called the Church of Christ Uniting. The participation of nineteen other churches as observer-consultants in the hard work of formulating a Plan of Union has placed this effort at the focal point of American ecumenism.[6] Now let us turn to the evidence of the theological consensus which has emerged from many of these agencies.

Speaking to the first point, it may be noted that since 1957 some nine statements of consensus on eucharistic doctrine have been produced—six by members of bi-lateral consultations (Lutheran/Reformed, Lutheran/Roman Catholic, Anglican/Roman Catholic, Disciples/Roman Catholic, Anglican/Orthodox, and Roman Catholic/Orthodox[7])—and three in the context of inter-

---

5. Until its recent demise, the progress of these conversations was reported in capsule form in **Unity Trends**. Unfortunately, the proceedings of these meetings are not readily available to the public, with the exception of the Lutheran/Reformed, Lutheran/Roman Catholic, and Roman Catholic /Disciples materials.

6. **A Plan of Union** for the Church of Christ Uniting may be obtained from The Consultation on Church Union, Princeton, N. J. In addition to all of these, one must note the deliberations and decisions of Faith and Order studies at the national level and at the state and local level, of the National Workshops on Christian Unity sponsored by Roman Catholic ecumenists, and of such groups as the international conference of Jesuit ecumenists held here.

7. For Lutheran/Reformed, see **Marburg Revisited**, ed. Paul C. Empie and James I. McCord (Minneapolis: Augsburg, 1966), pp. 103-104. For Lutheran/Roman Catholic, see **The Eucharist as Sacrifice** (U.S.A. National Committee of the Lutheran World Federation and the Bishops' Committee for Ecumenical and Interreligious Affairs, 1967), pp. 187-97. For Anglican /Roman Catholic, see **One in Christ**, II (1966), 302-305, and IV (1968), 298-99. The Disciples/Roman Catholic statement is found in **Mid Stream**, VII, No. 2 (Winter, 1967-68), 90-91; the Anglican/Orthodox statement

confessional conversations—the Oberlin Faith and Order Conference, the Consultation on Church Union, and most recently a National Council of Churches-sponsored Faith and Order study on "The Eucharist in the Ecumenical Movement."[8] This last study, the work of eighteen theologians of some twelve churches in the U.S., has produced a doctrinal consensus which it claims is the most extensive agreement yet, representing as it does members of such diverse Christian communities as Russian Orthodox, Southern Baptist, Society of Friends, Missouri Synod Lutherans, and Roman Catholics. Inasmuch as this statement of belief was largely a drawing together, according to a principle of maximalism, of earlier agreed statements, it came as a kind of culmination of the long quest for doctrinal unanimity on this topic.

A brief summary of points commonly affirmed by these several statements would be:

(1) The Lord's Supper is at once the commemoration of a past, saving event, the present realization of communion with Christ, and the anticipation of future glory;

(2) the once-for-all sacrifice of Christ is effectively re-presented through this sacramental memorial;

(3) the whole Christ, true God and true man, is personally present in the entire eucharistic action;

(4) this presence is accomplished not through the faith of the believer but through the power of the Holy Spirit and the word of promise; and

(5) the Eucharist is the Church's central act of worship and the visible expression of its unity.

---

was found in Religious News Service reporting for April 24, 1964; and the Roman Catholic/Orthodox was published in The [Brooklyn] Tablet, December 25, 1969, p. 4.

---

8. See The Nature of the Unity We Seek, ed. Paul S. Minear (St. Louis: Bethany Press, 1958), pp. 199-205, for the Oberlin consensus. The final version of the C.O.C.U. statement is in A Plan of Union (Princeton: C.O.C.U., 1970), pp. 35-37, and "The Eucharist in the Life of the Church: An Ecumenical Consensus" may be found in The Ecumenist, VIII (September-October, 1970), 90-93.

The question of eucharistic sharing inevitably poses the question of the authorization of the minister, especially when not only simple admission to the Sacrament but *reciprocal* admission is envisioned. As I have already mentioned, ecumenical conversations regarding ministry in this country have made important strides towards overcoming the doctrinal barriers to a reconciliation of ministries.

A good deal of common ground has been marked out as the basis for future discussion, especially through the efforts of the Consultation on Church Union, the Anglican/Roman Catholic, Presbyterian and Reformed/Roman Catholic, and Lutheran/Roman Catholic consultations.[9] A general survey of the documentation reveals agreement on the following points:

(1) the ministry of Christ is the foundation and source of the Church's ministry;

(2) as exercised by the Church this ministry of reconciliation is one of witness and service in and for the world;

(3) all baptized Christians share in the general ministry as members of a priestly people;

(4) some are called by the Holy Spirit to exercise the special ministry of Word and Sacrament in service to the Christian community;

(5) the Church, acknowledging this God-given call, sets these persons aside for this purpose and authorizes them by the act of ordination, a radical empowering so decisive that it may not be repeated;

(6) in carrying out their ministry, the ordained members represent the whole community before God.

---

9. See **A Plan of Union**, pp. 38-55, for the C.O.C.U. statement on ministry. The Anglican/Roman Catholic announcement was made in **One in Christ**, IV (1968), p. 299, and the Presbyterian and Reformed/Roman Catholic statements have appeared in **Journal of Ecumenical Studies**, V (1968), 462-65, and VII (1970), 686-90. The Lutheran/Roman Catholic agreement is to be published as **Lutherans and Catholics in Dialogue: Eucharist and Ministry** (St. Louis: Concordia, 1971).

It appears that a "functional" norm may be applied to issues left unresolved (e.g., the conditions of "proper authorization" and the sacramental dimension of this ministry); that is, as in the case of eucharistic belief, where formulations fail to agree, consultation of the understandings embodied in Christian practice reveals basic unanimity and helps bridge the ecumenical gap.[10]

Finally, although this was not a question formally addressed by any group other than the Roman Catholic/Disciples conversation and C.O.C.U., a common ecclesiology seems to be emerging from American interconfessional talks. The image of the Church as fellowship of all baptized believers, on the one hand, and that of the Church as a visible, structured communion (implying a rigid pattern of doctrine and ministry), on the other, have begun to give way to a more dynamic view. This third approach considers the Church from an eschatological perspective. The Church *in via* is called to be a fellowship of baptized believers living in harmony and charity; ideally, this common life should be visibly manifest "in each place" and "in all places and ages"[11]— therefore, in some manner of structured communion.

The Church *in via* is imperfectly one, but called to be a sign of reconciliation to the world. It needs to achieve unity at the level of the local congregation, for this *is* the Church in the concrete, but it must also become visibly one as a world-church. If this visible fellowship is to speak to men of our times, its structures must serve and foster the full expression of Christian life and witness. In their search for unity, the churches seem to be approaching a consensus on the vision of this goal, seeing it more

---

10. This functional norm has been elaborated in two important articles by George Tavard, "The Function of the Minister in the Eucharistic Celebration," **Journal of Ecumenical Studies**, IV (1967), 629-49, and "Does the Protestant Ministry Have Sacramental Significance?" **Continuum**, VI (1968), 260-68.

11. In the words of the famous New Delhi statement on unity; see **The New Delhi Report**, ed. W. A. Visser t'Hooft (New York: Association Press, 1962), p. 116, for the complete formulation.

and more as a federation of local churches *in communion* with each other. The task now is to re-establish *communion*.

In the American interconfessional conversations, movement towards this vision of the Church has come chiefly from two sources. On the one hand, it has been supported by the acceptance of the episcopal principle by the member churches of C.O.C.U., especially where this represented a departure from a "free church" ideal in favor of the visible unity of a structured communion. The proposed title for the church prepared for by C.O.C.U., the Church of Christ Uniting, carries out the theme of the Church *in via*. On the other hand, this vision has gained considerable ground in the Roman Catholic Church, largely as the result of the official recognition of the ecclesial reality of other Christian bodies given by the Second Vatican Council. The implications of this modification of the traditional Roman Catholic position have been repeatedly and vigorously spelled out by the many theologians of this communion now participating in the ecumenical dialogue in this country. The understanding of the Church which results from this "new" ecclesiology involves a much greater appreciation of the primacy of the "fellowship of the baptized" aspect over the "hierarchical communion" aspect; it places structure clearly at the service of communion of faith and life.

The impetus from these two sources has gone a long way towards closing the gap between the ecclesiological positions which advocate either general admission or closed communion. The literature indicates that the Church *in via* ecclesiology has wide acceptance among American theologians now engaged in inter-confessional conversations to the extent that it has largely replaced the earlier models and can be presumed as a common ground of discussion.

This incipient ecclesiological consensus is the foundation of the by now widely accepted conclusion that the present situation of imperfect ecclesial communion does not exclude but, on the contrary, seems to demand some measure of eucharistic sharing. To prohibit this is to obscure the degree of fellowship in the one

Lord now happily experienced and to invite disregard of ecclesiastical discipline. To permit and authorize occasional sharing is to strengthen the will to unity. It is unthinkable that God would find this form of eucharistic worship less pleasing than that which canonizes our sinful divisions.

15 A Poly-Structured Church: Primitive Reality and Present Option

BERNARD P. PRUSAK

Speaking to the matter of ministerial structures in the Church can prove a very delicate task. Most Roman Catholics have experienced only one pattern of church structure in their lifetimes. The official position holds that there is an essential difference between the common priesthood of the baptized and the ordained or ministerial priesthood. The latter is said to be conferred in the sacrament of Orders which bestows specific powers or gifts of the Spirit. The ordained is thereby initiated into a definite hierarchical structure composed of bishops, priests, and deacons in descending strata of jurisdictional superiority.[1] Vatican II added that the universal episcopal college, of which the Pope is head, succeeds to the college of twelve apostles with Peter at their head.[2] Such hierarchical notions have centuries of tradition behind them. Especially since Trent, Catholic clergymen have been trained to accept and teach the present pattern of bishops, priests, and

---

1. Trent promulgated its doctrine on the Sacrament of Orders in Session 23 on July 15, 1563. Cf. H. Denzinger—A. Schönmetzer, **Enchiridion Symbolorum** (Barcelona-Freiburg: Herder, 1965), nos. 1767-1778. The position of Vatican II is contained in Chapter three of **Lumen gentium** (sections 18-29): "The Hierarchical Structure of the Church with Special Reference to the Episcopate." W. Abbott, ed., **The Documents of Vatican II** (New York: Guild Press, 1966), pp. 37-56.

2. In developing the notion of collegiality Vatican II also determined that episcopal consecration is sacramental and confers the fullness of priesthood, the apex of the ministry. At his consecration the new bishop is said to receive the **munera** of sanctifying, of teaching and of governing, which can be exercised only in hierarchical communion with the head and members of the college. **Lumen gentium**, sections 20-22; **Christus Dominus**, sections 1-6; text in Abbott, pp. 39-44; 396-399.

deacons as the only normative possibility.[3] Ordination confers power and authority in that sense.

Everything seems quite definitive but one wonders if it really is. A synod of bishops is now able to meet at Rome to discuss a theology of priesthood relevant to modern times. Ecumenical dialogue has forced some Catholic participants to ask whether we may any longer simply categorize Protestant ministers as laymen with invalid orders.[4] The holiness of their communities often belies our strictly canonical criteria for determining the presence of Christ at the communion services over which they preside. Finally, all the recent re-arrangement of ecclesial structures by the Catholic hierarchy has not yet overcome a sense of frustration shared by many at the local level.

Our present attempt to conceptualize and theologize upon ministerial structures in the Church is undertaken with an awareness of two possible oversimplifications. One is the temptation to isolate and absolutize our present experience of the Church's form and then project such a time-conditioned image back into the period of Christian origins. The result could be a static and incomplete understanding of a dynamic community with a life history of constantly developing order. The other oversimplification involves the total rejection of all the present forms of Church structure as if they were only a corruption of the ideal, which is

---

3. As to whether Trent intended its list of orders to be taxative, cf. A. Duval, "The Council of Trent and Holy Orders," in **The Sacrament of Holy Orders** (Collegeville, Minn.: The Liturgical Press, 1962), pp. 242-245. Section 20 of **Lumen gentium** says that bishops have succeeded to the place of the Apostles **by divine institution**. Karl Rahner interprets this as definitive institutional permanence. At the same time he notes that monoepiscopacy gradually developed: "Article 20," **Commentary on the Documents of Vatican II**, Vol. I, ed. H. Vorgrimler (New York: Herder & Herder, 1967), pp. 190-192.

4. Harry J. McSorley, "The Roman Catholic Doctrine of the Competent Minister of the Eucharist in Ecumenical Perspective," **One in Christ**, 5 (1969), pp. 405-422; "Trent and the Question: Can Protestant Ministers Consecrate the Eucharist," **Worship**, 43 (1969), 574-589. Daniel O'Hanlon, "A New Approach to the Validity of Church Orders," **Worship**, 41 (1967), 406-421.

to be discovered and revived from a primitive pure state of Christianity. Such an approach would be guilty of archaism.

Our return to the sources is not a hunt for usable antiques. We do not wish simply to restore what once was. Rather this essay is an attempt to historically validate and presently facilitate an attitude of openness to new structures. We advocate a principle of operation which, in its concern for genuine unity among all who live the "Way," might again accept and allow the development of a diversity of structures and forms so long as they serve unity and charity. This study intends to raise the question of why new church orders might not be allowed to develop from the grass roots alongside those that currently exist, not to supplant them, but to complement their ministry. Such structures need not be the exclusive creations of the present curial agencies, nor even require hierarchical approbation for their birth. Our position maintains that the total community and not simply the hierarchy can be the validating agent of a newly developing church order.[5] New ministerial configurations should demonstrate their right to exist inasmuch as the total community recognizes their service to Christian unity and charity. It is in the doing that ministry demonstrates that it is from the Spirit and is authenticated.

This position of openness proceeds from the growing awareness among ecclesiologists of the post-Vatican II era that the New Testament and other early Christian sources reveal a complex structural pluralism within the primitive *Ekklesia*. Only gradually did new exigencies cause one pattern to prevail and eventually to obliterate the others. That this one institutionalized pattern might again be complemented by new creative ministries is the question at hand.

---

5. This position is strengthened by observing how ministries of truly Christian service developed and were recognized in Protestant communities. J. Edgar Bruns, "The Unity of the Church and its Ministry," **The Ecumenist,** 3 (1965), 21-23; Hans Küng, "What is the Essence of Apostolic Succession?" in **Apostolic Succession,** also edited by Küng, **Concilium,** Vol. 34 (Glen Rock: Paulist Press, 1965), p. 28; Harry McSorley, "Protestant Eucharistic Reality and Lack of Orders," **The Ecumenist,** 5 (1967), 68-75.

The polemical approach of the post-Reformation period previously overshadowed the apparent co-existence of diverse structures developed in mutual service to the needs of the early communities.[6] Catholics, anxious to vindicate their conception of the Church, found in the Scriptures a visible perfect society, united primarily by the authority of an external and well defined hierarchy in permanent succession. The adversaries were "liberal Protestants" who maintained, from the same sources, that the first Christians were united exclusively by the invisible bond of the Spirit, nurtured by a purely charismatic leadership from which permanent functions only later evolved.

Structural Pluralism in the New Testament

As a matter of fact the New Testament presents no uniform plan or terminology when it speaks of the structure of Christian communities.[7] The Church is said to be built upon the foundation of the Apostles (Rev 21:14 and Eph 2:20) but in Scripture and in tradition many different senses of the word "apostle" can be found.[8] Luke stresses the *Twelve* as witnesses and guarantors of

---

6. The works of Kurtscheid and Zapelena especially validate this paragraph. B. Kurtscheid is constantly refuting Sabatier: **Historia Iuris Canonici: Historia Institutorum ab Ecclesiae Fundatione usque ad Gratianum** (Rome: Catholic Book Agency, 1951 reprint), pp. 12-14. T. Zapelena constructs an entire ecclesiology around adversaries: **De Ecclesia Christi**, 2 Vols. (Rome: Univ. Gregoriana, 1955 & 1954).

7. Cf. B. Dupuy, "Is there a Dogmatic Distinction between the Function of Priests and the Function of Bishops?" in **Apostolic Succession,** p. 80; H. Küng, **The Church** (New York: Sheed & Ward, 1968), pp. 3-24, 428; R. Schnackenburg, **The Church in the New Testament** (New York: Herder & Herder, 1966), pp. 22-35, esp. p. 30; J. D. Quinn, "Ministry in the New Testament," in **Lutherans and Catholics in Dialogue IV: Eucharist and Ministry** (Washington, D. C.: U. S. Catholic Conference—New York: U.S.A. National Committee of the Lutheran World Fed., 1970), pp. 69-100.

8. J. D. Quinn, "Ministry in the N.T.", pp. 70-84; E. Schlink, **The Coming Christ and the Coming Church** (Philadelphia: Fortress Press, 1968), p. 218; R. Schnackenburg, "L'apostolicite: état de la recherche," in **Istina,** Vol. 14 (1969), pp. 5-32; "Study Document on Catholicity and Apostolicity,"

the tradition concerning both Jesus' earthly ministry and his resurrection. Paul has a wider concept which accentuates the missionary dimension of an apostle who responds to a call by the risen Christ. It is not within the scope of this chapter to enter the debate as to whether a group of twelve were actually associated with the historical Jesus or were the creation of the first or second generation Church.[9] We will simply note that there is no consistent concept of Apostle in the New Testament.

There is also no absolute evidence as to whether and how the "Twelve" appointed successors. The Apostles are said to have founded communities of believers, or Churches, but that they appointed individual men to succeed them with specified prerogatives is left unsaid except for the rather late allusions of the Pastoral Epistles.[10] There we find a defensive concern for the continuity of the Churches which were now threatened by enemies of sound teaching.[11] Designation or appointment were added

---

prepared by Joint Theological Commission of the Joint Working Group between the R. C. Church and the W.C.C., **The Ecumenical Review,** Vol. 23, No. 1 (January, 1971), 51-69; H. von Campenhausen, **Ecclesiastical Authority and Spiritual Power in the Church of the First Three Centuries** (Stanford: Stanford University Press, 1969), p. 14.

9. For various opinions and a bibliography cf.: J. Giblet, "The Twelve, History and Theology," in the collection edited by him, **The Birth of the Church** (New York: Alba House, 1968), pp. 66-81; J. F. McCue, "Apostles and Apostolic Succession in the Patristic Era," **Lutherans and Catholics in Dialogue IV** (see note 7), pp. 139-149; J. D. Quinn, "Ministry in the N.T.," pp. 74-76; K. H. Rengstorf, "Apostolos" and "Dodeka" in **Theological Dictionary of the New Testament,** edited by G. Kittel and G. Friedrich, English edition by G. W. Bromiley (Grand Rapids: Eerdmans, 1964-1968), Vol. 1: 407-445; Vol. 2: 321-328; von Campenhausen, **Ecclesiastical Authority,** p. 14; R. Zehnle, **The Making of the Christian Church** (Notre Dame, Fides, 1969), pp. 28-35.

10. Cf. Tit 1:5-7; 2 Tm 1:6. We shall discuss Acts 14:23 and 1 Tm 1:18 and 4:14 below.

11. E. Käsemann, "Ministry and Community in the New Testament," **Essays on New Testament Themes** (London: SCM Press, 1964), pp. 85-86. Acts' (20:17-38) account of Paul's address to the Ephesian **presbyteroi-episkopoi** also reveals such a defensive concern.

defensive measures to guarantee a continuity of faithful witness.

Another group whose description in Acts makes them seem almost a parallel structure to the Twelve are the *Seven*.[12] Although we tend to automatically apply the title *deacon* to the Seven, just as we apply apostles to the Twelve, there is no such designation in Acts. When the Greek-speaking Jewish Christians of the Jerusalem community complained that the widows of their minority group were being neglected in the daily distributions, the Apostles laid hands upon seven men chosen by the community and entrusted them with the service or *diakonia* of waiting at table.[13] This was meant to allow the Twelve to completely dedicate themselves to prayer and the ministry of the word. It is therefore surprising that the Seven are never presented as waiting at table. Rather they carry out the same functions as the Twelve, preaching the gospel, the *diakonia* of the word.[14]

The preaching of the Hellenist Seven, and specifically of Stephen, sparked a reaction among the Jews. Stephen's martyrdom signaled the beginning of violent persecution for the church in Jerusalem. "All *except the apostles* were scattered over the country districts of Judaea and Samaria."[15] The Hellenists who had been scattered went through the countryside preaching the Word. Philip evangelized Samaria, baptized the eunuch on the road to Gaza, appeared at Azotus, toured the country, and preached in all the towns until he reaches Caesarea where he settled.[16]

Apparently the Twelve did not have to flee Jerusalem at this point since they still appeared Jewish enough to satisfy their

---

12. Acts 6:1-6.

13. E. Haenchen, "The Book of Acts as Source Material for the History of Early Christianity," **Studies in Luke-Acts,** edited by L. Keck and J. Martyn (New York: Abingdon, 1966), p. 264; R.P.C. Hanson, **The Acts** (Oxford: Clarendon Press, 1967), p. 90; E. Schweizer, **Church Order in the New Testament** (Naperville, Illinois: Allenson, 1961), p. 49.

14. Acts 2:4; 6:8-8:1; 8:4-40; 21:8.

15. Acts 8:1. Translation from **The New English Bible** (Oxford and Cambridge: University Presses, 1970). Hereafter cited as **NEB.**

16. Acts 8:5, 26, 40 and also 21:8.

fellow Jews.[17] They are presented as following up the work of Philip in Samaria in the persons of Peter and John.[18] Peter initiates his own general tour in the course of which he first confronts the question of gentile converts.[19]

The immunity of the Twelve from persecution was not long lived. King Herod soon beheaded James, the brother of John, and arrested Peter.[20] Peter miraculously escaped and warned James and the other members of the Jerusalem church.[21] Another event seems to indicate that the other Apostles took his warning and left Jerusalem. No mention is made of the Twelve when Barnabas and Paul arrive with the funds from a collection taken in Antioch for the relief of the famine-stricken Christians in Judaea.[22] Their contribution is received by another group, the elders or *presbyteroi,* who now appear to have taken over this administrative function from the Twelve.

Acts applies the plural term "presbyters" to locally resident leadership groups both within Judaism and Christianity.[23] Apparently the Sect of the Nazarenes in Jerusalem copied the prototype of Judaism and its synagogue. In Acts 11:30 and 21:18 the elders are mentioned with no reference to the apostles. In Acts 15 Luke joins the elders and apostles in his version of the "apostolic council" of Jerusalem. Besides an administrative function they are also pictured as sharing the authority of the apostles in teaching and decision making. Unlike Paul's version of the Antiochene-

---

17. E. Haenchen, "The Book of Acts," pp. 262-264; E. Schweizer, **Church Order,** p. 42.

18. Acts 8:14-17.

19. Acts 9:31-10:48 and 11:1-18.

20. Acts 12:1-5.

21. Acts 12:17.

22. Acts 11:27-30.

23. References to Jewish elders are found in Acts 4:5, 8, 23. Cf. P. Benoit, "Les origines apostoliques de l'Episcopat selon le N.T.," in L'Eveque dans m'eglise du Christ, edited by H. Bouësse and A. Mandouze (Paris: Desclee de Brouwer, 1963), pp. 19-25. H. von Campenhausen stresses that the functions of Jewish and Christian elders differed: **Ecclesiastical Authority,** p. 78.

Judaic law controversy in Galatians, Luke maintains that Paul
and Barnabas were dispatched to Jerusalem to consult both the
apostles and elders.[24] Paul says that he, Barnabas, and Titus
consulted with the *Pillars* of the Jerusalem church who are James,
Cephas, and John. He does not mention any letter or the elders.
Probably Luke has joined two sources into one narrative: the
"apostolic council" and the later meeting which composed a
circular letter.[25] We shall simply conclude that the authority
of the presbyters does not seem to threaten the role of the apostles.
On the local level, apostles, *pillars,* and presbyters manage to
co-exist and share overlapping roles. There is no clear liturgical
function except for the anointing of the sick by the elders
mentioned in James 5:14.

One of the *pillars* who definitely is connected with the elders
is James, the brother of the Lord.[26] Jean Colson speculates that
James assumed a special position since his relationship to Jesus
reminded the community of the Master.[27] He is able to survive
in Jerusalem even after the dispersion of the apostles, probably
because the Jews were able to tolerate his very Jewish style of
Christianity.[28] His stature grew and is revealed by the fact that
Peter sends word to him of his escape from prison.[29] When Paul
comes to Jerusalem to first make Peter's acquaintance he also

---

24. Compare Acts 15:2 & 22 and Gal 2:1 & 9.

25. Cf. R.P.C. Hanson, **The Acts,** pp. 153-159 (His discussion of date
and authorship is also valuable: pp. 1-28); H. Lietzmann, **A History of the
Early Church** (New York: World Publishing Co.—Meridian Books, 1963)
Vol. 1, p. 107ff.; also Acts 21:25.

26. Gal 1:19 and Acts 15 and 21:18.

27. **L'Eveque dans les communautes primitives** (Paris: du Cerf—Unam
Sanctam, 21, 1951), pp. 23-24. Other references to the relatives of Jesus
and their apparent status in the Jerusalem Church are found in Acts 1:14
and perhaps Acts 12:17. Mk 6:3 and Mt 13:55 provide the names of James,
Joseph, Simon, and Jude. J. D. Quinn ("Ministry in N.T.", p. 88) speculates
that the leadership of the Jerusalem community was in the hands of the
family of Jesus.

28. Acts 21:18-26 and Gal 2:12ff.

29. Acts 12:17.

visits James.[30] James' role in the "apostolic council" is unquestionable in all sources.

James appears as the sedentary head of a local community. He resembles what we would today call a bishop, but it would be an anachronism to simply designate James' function by that term.[31] He appears as the bond of unity among the elders who are gathered about him. At the same time he acts as the representative, the resume, or the incarnation of the Jewish Jerusalem Church. He does not venture forth to found new churches as the apostles do. He remains within the community in which he presides and serves. His ministry seems directed to the Jews among whom he makes many converts. His fear of alienating the Jews and risking the reversal of his success leads James and his followers into conflict with Paul's attitudes on the Law as applied to gentile christians.[32]

There is only one place where another category, the *prophets,* is explicitly mentioned in regard to the Jerusalem community. In Acts we read that Judas Barsabbas and Silas, leading men (*andras hāgoumenous*) in the community and prophets, were delegated to carry the letter of the "apostles and elders" to Antioch.[33] Whether these men were presbyters is problematic. That possibility would have interesting implications for understanding the relationship between charism and order or office in the primitive community.

Until now we have limited our discussion to the structures of the Jewish Jerusalem church. Now we turn to Antioch. Hellenist exiles from Jerusalem during the persecution which arose over Stephen's preaching first brought the gospel message to Antioch but limited their preaching to the Jewish community.[34] An important change occurred when natives of Cyprus and Cyrene arrived

---

30. Gal 1:18-19. We have already mentioned the visit in Acts 21:18.
31. Colson, L'Eveque, pp. 22-24.
32. Gal 2:12ff. and Acts 15:1-5; 21:21ff.
33. Acts 15: 22, 27 and 30-34.
34. Cf. Acts 11:19-26 for this entire paragraph.

and began to evangelize the gentiles. A great many became believers and, as in the case of Samaria, Jerusalem sent an emissary in the person of Barnabas who brought along Saul from Tarsus. "For a whole year the two of them lived in fellowship with the congregation there, and gave instructions to large numbers."[35]

The role of Barnabas and Paul is uncertain. It seems Barnabas verified the genuinity of the community and was a bond between it and the original community at Jerusalem. In stressing any internal role, one must remember that both were only temporary representatives of the Jerusalem church. They later used Antioch as a center from which they went out to evangelize and establish other churches. They were sent on these missions by the Spirit and commissioned by the "prophets and teachers" of the Antioch church in whose list they are also named.[36]

The "prophets and teachers" mentioned in connection with Antioch are a puzzle. It seems that as individuals they were primarily missionaries who may also have served as local leaders during their visits to the city. After prayer and fasting they laid hands upon Barnabas and Saul and sent them on their first missionary journey.[37] There is no mention of strictly resident elders or presbyters at this stage of development in Antioch. The functions of missionary and local elder may have possibly been united in the same persons. Acts 14:21-26 indicates that Paul and Barnabas, with prayer and fasting, appointed elders in Lystra, Iconium, and Pisidian Antioch before returning to Syrian Antioch. Since Luke wrote after 70 he may have projected the structure of that period back into Paul's activity.

It is difficult to specify exactly the structure of the Pauline

---

35. Acts 11:26; **NEB**.

36. Acts 13:1-3. Cf. Colson, **L'Eveque**, pp. 30-35; Kurtscheid, **Historia Institutorum**, pp. 17-18; I. A. Zeigler, **Historia Iuris Canonici**, Vol. 2: **De Historia Institutorum Canonicorum** (Rome: Univ. Gregoriana, 1940), p. 31ff.

37. The context is that of worship since Acts 13:2-3 begins with the word "leitourgoun."

churches except for the leadership of Paul.[38] At best one can say that there was leadership in Paul's communities but its structural implementation differed from church to church.[39] These local variations were further complicated by a temporal progression or development. In his earliest epistle Paul simply urges the Thessalonians . . . "to respect those who labor among you and are over you in the Lord and admonish you, and to esteem them very highly in love because of their work." [40] In coping with the problems of the Corinthian church, Paul makes no explicit mention of presbyters. He recognizes a multiplicity of gifts and ministries.[41] Order and organization are demanded in that each was to use his gift in the Spirit and then step back to allow another to exercise that same gift or another which he lacked.[42] The charismatic non-presbyteral ministry was validated by its very operation in a community of faith where the totality of gifts acted as a check upon an individual gift.[43]

This is reflected in Paul's discussion of gifts in 1 Corinthians 12. In the summary at the end of that chapter Paul emphasizes that "God has appointed in the Church first apostles, second

---

38. Cf. M. Bourke, "Reflections on Church Order in the New Testament," **Catholic Biblical Quarterly**, Vol. 30 (1968), pp. 493-511.

39. G. D'Ercole, **Vescovi, Presbyteri, Laici nella Chiesa delle Origini** (Rome: Laterano, 1963), p. 46ff.

40. I Thessalonians 5:12-13; cited from **The Oxford Annotated Bible, Revised Standard Version,** edited by H. B. May and B. M. Metzger (New York: Oxford University Press, 1965). Hereafter referred to as **RSV.** The concept of **co-workers** in the ministry is found in 1 Thess 3:2. They are named in 1 Thess 1:1; 3:6 and 2 Thess. 1:1; also 1 Cor 1:1 and 2 Cor 1:1 & 19; 8:16-19, 22-23.

41. Cf. 1 Cor 12 and Rom 12.

42. 1 Cor 14: 29-30 and 1 Cor 7:7: Each has his own charism. Cf. E. Käsemann, "Ministry and Community in the N.T.," p. 76; also his "Paul and Early Catholicism," in **New Testament Questions of Today** (Philadelphia: Fortress Press, 1969), p. 246; K. McDonnell, "Ways of Validating Ministry," **Journal of Ecumenical Studies**, Vol. 7, No. 2 (Spring, 1970), pp. 244-250.

43. Cf. 1 Cor 12: 10-11. K. McDonnell, "Ways of Validating Ministry," pp. 229, 250-251.

prophets, third teachers, then workers of miracles, then healers, helpers, administrators, speakers in various kinds of tongues." He asks, "Are all apostles? Are all prophets? Are all teachers?"[44]

The non-presbyteral prophetic ministry reflected in the Letter to the Corinthians cannot be universally extended to all of Paul's churches. The letter addressed to the gentile "saints" does tell them that they are "built upon the foundation of the apostles and prophets, Christ Jesus himself being the cornerstone."[45] However, the letter to the Philippians is addressed: "To all the saints in Christ Jesus who are at Philippi, with the *episkopoi* (overseers-guardians-"bishops") and *diakonoi* (deacons)."[46] The later Pastoral Epistles, whose authorship is debated, are addressed to Paul's co-workers and reveal yet another stage of church order.[47] They enumerate the criteria for choosing an *episkopos* (use of the singular is explained by the context) and again refer to deacons.[48] For the first time, in a letter connected with Paul, we also find mention of *presbyteroi*.[49] Here, as in Acts 20:17 and 28, we find that the terms *episkopoi* and *presbyteroi* are used interchangeably. Probably, in both instances we have an inter-

---

44. 1 Cor 12: 28-29; **RSV**.

45. Ephesians 2:20; **RSV**. Both **RSV** and the **Jerusalem Bible**, edited by A. Jones (New York: Doubleday, 1966), omit any mention of "who are at Ephesus" in 1:1 and note that the phrase was a later addition. Some, citing Col 4:16, feel it was originally sent to Laodicea. Others believe it was a circular letter with a blank address. Cf. **Jerusalem Bible,** p. 261 and the note for Eph 1:1 on p. 331.

46. Phil 1:1; **RSV**.

47. The two strongest opinions regarding authorship are the "secretary theory" and the "fragment theory." The former usually attributes the work to Luke who is thought to have re-edited it about 80-85. The latter would attribute the Pastorals to a pseudonymous author between 90-120. In footnote 81 we spell out some important conclusions which may be drawn from the "fragment theory."

48. 1 Tm 3:2; Tit 1:7 and 1 Tm 3:8, 12. J. Colson discusses the role of Titus and Timothy in **Les fonctions ecclesiales aux deux premier siecles** (Paris: Desclee de Brouwer, 1956), pp. 145-162.

49. 1 Tm 5:1, 17, 19; Tit 1:5.

mingling of two sources, the earlier of which reflects the originally
Pauline system of *episkopoi*.

Allowing for all the previous development and continued local
variations it seems that two general church orders co-existed at
one point.[50] The Pauline or western system was typified by those
urban centers where a college of *episkopoi* (overseers or guardians),
assisted by deacons, presided over the Christian community with
no single individual acting as resident rector or head. Paul's
churches had assigned that role to their dynamic founder even
though he was an itinerant apostle constantly founding new
churches. Paul's solicitude and concern for all his churches is
apparent from his epistles. When a letter proved insufficient
he would visit an errant community.[51]

The other pattern is the eastern or Jewish system of *presbyters*
and individual head. It is sometimes called the Johannine structure
from the passages in Revelation (1:4 and 2:1ff.) where letters are
addressed to the "angels" of the seven churches in the province
of Asia. Authors speculate that these *angels* are local rectors,
resident in each community after the model of James in Jerusalem.
As was the case with James they were probably surrounded by a
college of presbyters.

After Paul's death his role was gradually assumed by a resident
head in the manner of the Jerusalem and eastern communities.
The result was a fusion of two different systems of local organization. The interchangeability of the terms *episkopoi* and *presbyteroi*
in Acts and the Pastorals, as noted above, is a sign of the interaction of the two patterns of church order. The First Epistle of
Peter is another instance of Paul's charismatic and Spirit oriented
order blending with stronger presbyteral and episcopal structures.
After a brief discussion of gifts, Peter addresses the presbyters as
a fellow-presbyter.[52] He admonishes them to feed the flock of God

---

50. Colson, L'Eveque, pp. 81-87; von Campenhausen, **Ecclesiastical Authority**, pp. 76-77.

51. Cf. 1 Cor 11:34 and 2 Cor 11:20 and 13:1-2.

52. 1 Pet 4:9-11 and 5:1-4. There is a strong possibility that Silvanus,
or Silas, the prophet and companion of Paul, was the "ghost writer" for

watching (*episkopountes*) over it not as tyrants but by being examples. The chief Shepherd is Christ.

This growing concern for official designation, or the evolution of office, should not be considered a simply human creation in opposition to the charism of the Spirit. The Pastoral Epistles reflect a time which felt the need for guarding the tradition and protecting the faithful. The Pauline college of *episkopoi,* as overseers or guardians, filled the need of the time. That such a ministry developed is as much the work of the Spirit as the earlier, and still undisplaced, prophetic ministry.[53]

From the references to an imposition of hands in the Pastoral Epistles we may conclude that this had become a means of appointment to leadership.[54] At the same time, however, the prophetic element is equally stressed. Since official designation was a way of guaranteeing the continuity of faithful witness in a time of false teachers, it was fitting that Timothy's charism or gift be given him through (*dia*) prophetic utterances together with (*meta*) a laying on of hands by the college of elders.[55]

The many structures coexisting in the New Testament communities were united by their mutual service for unity. The first

---

1 Pt. This would explain the evidence of Paul's theology. Cf. 1 Pt 5:12; 1 Thess 1:1; 2 Thess 1:1; 2 Cor 1:19 and Acts 15: 22 & 27; L. F. Hartmann, "Peter, Epistles" in his **Encyclopedic Dictionary of the Bible** (New York: McGraw Hill, 1963), col. 1819.

---

53. Cf. R.P.C. Hanson, "Institutions in the Early Church," **Institutionalism and Church Unity**, ed N. Ehrenstrom and W. G. Muelder (New York: Association Press, 1963), p. 95; K. McDonnell, "Ways of Validating Ministry," p. 259; Schlink, **Coming Christ**, p. 201; Schnackenburg, **Church in N.T.**, p. 35; von Campenhausen, **Ecclesiastical Authority**, pp. 80-81.

54. 1 Tm 4:14; 2 Tim 1:6; 1 Tm 5:22 may be open to other interpretations regarding the reason for that imposition. Acts 14:23 alludes to an appointment by hand: **cheirotonesantes**.

55. 1 Tm 4:14 together with 1:18. **RSV, NEB**, and **Jerusalem Bible** render these passages with rather substantial variations. For that reason we have provided our own version. Also refer to 2 Tim 1:13-14 and 2:2.

unity they effected was that of common faith in Jesus the Christ. This basic unity of the baptized was externalized and strengthened at the eucharistic assemblies where the Christians became aware of themselves as a concrete community or *Ekklesia*. The writers of the New Testament did not concentrate on the "organ" or personal cause of unity as much as on the concrete realization of the unity. As is the case with Paul, they were more interested in building up the Body of Christ.[56] For this reason the New Testament does not bother to explicitly name those who presided the Eucharist.[57]

Other Early Christian Sources

The pattern of church order which is so familiar in our time began to solidify in the post-apostolic period. But even then we are still in a time of continuing transition. The unsigned *First Epistle of Clement* was written in Rome shortly before the end of the first century in reaction to a rebellion against the presbyters of Corinth.[58] It speaks of *presbyteroi-episkopoi* and deacons.[59] Besides continuing the apostolic tradition and ministry as successors appointed with the consent of the whole Church, the *episkopoi-presbyteroi* also seem to have had a special service or liturgy of offering gifts, which some interpret as presiding the Eucharist.[60] This Pauline church seems to have retained a collegial structure for there is still no reference to any monarchical figure at this point.

The important new element is that Clement exhorts the Corinthian Christians not to disturb the existing order, but to fit into

---

56. Acts 2:41-47; 1 Cor 10:16-17; 12:12-31 and Rm 12.

57. Except for Jesus at the Last Supper no other person is explicitly mentioned. There are allusions to Paul in Acts 20:7 & 11 and 1 Cor 10:16 and perhaps to the apostles in Acts 2:42.

58. I Clement 47:6 and 57:1.

59. I Clement 1:3; 21:6; 42:4; 44; 47:6; 54:2; 57:1. The terminology of this epistle shows a relationship to 1 Pet. It likewise reflects Pauline theology. E. J. Goodspeed and R. M. Grant, **A History of Early Christian Literature** (Chicago: Univ. of Chicago Press—Phoenix Book, 1966), p. 9.

60. I Clement 44:4 and 40.

the pattern by patience and docility. Order and obedience are extolled throughout the letter. The system of elders is presented as an apostolic creation for order. Structure is given a sort of sacral and immutable character and for the first time seems included in the category of doctrine.[61]

The *Didache* or *Teaching of the Twelve Apostles* was probably written in Syria or Alexandria and has been dated anywhere between 70 and 180. Possibly it should be dated around 90 A.D.[62] Chapter 15 speaks of *episkopoi* and deacons whom it presents as resident in each church. They are distinguished from apostles and prophets who appear as itinerant missionaries.[63] It is disputed whether the document refers to the eucharist and furthermore whether wandering charismatic prophets were allowed to preside it.[64] Chapter 15 seems to indicate that a transition from prophets and teachers to *episkopoi* and deacons was now in process and was not without some tension. Criteria for determining false prophets are provided in Chapter 11. The faithful are also reminded not to despise the *episkopoi* and deacons whom they have appointed for themselves, for they perform for them the service of the prophets and teachers. Both groups are recognized as leaders.[65]

The tension between prophetic and appointed structures also permeates the *Shepherd* of Hermas. This document was written at Rome, probably in various stages with the possibility of a different author in some places. Although the reference in the *Muratorian Fragment* would date it about the middle of the second century, the rather undeveloped concept of church order points to a date between 90 and 100.[66]

---

61. von Campenhausen, **Ecclesiastical Authority**, pp. 87-88 and 91-92.

62. Goodspeed-Grant, p. 13; F. L. Cross, **The Early Christian Fathers** (London: Duckworth, 1960), pp. 10-11.

63. Chapters 11 and 13.

64. Chapters 9 and 10.

65. Chapter 15.

66. J. B. Lightfoot—J. R. Harmer, **The Apostolic Fathers**, 1891 edition (Grand Rapids: Baker Book House, 1970 reprint), pp. 161-162; also Cross, pp. 23-24; and Goodspeed-Grant, pp. 31-32.

Hermas appears as a respected prophet who is given authority to teach the "saints" by virtue of his visions.[67] He refers to apostles, *episkopoi*, teachers, and deacons as a unity in one passage, but elders are also discussed elsewhere.[68] The apostles and teachers appear to have a universal ministry.[69] The leaders are pictured as shepherds after the manner of I Peter.[70]

What is unique about Hermas is the fact that he must call the leaders of the Church, who sit in the front seats, to repentance because they are now overly concerned with precedence and foment rivalry in their ranks.[71] Deacons are embezzling the funds for widows and orphans, and false prophets are demanding money while vying for the chief seat.[72] The first apostles and teachers were not guilty of such greed.[73] Neither is a good *episkopos* who, according to Hermas, is a man of hospitality toward the poor.[74]

This is definitely a time of tension for teachers in the Church.[75] Hermas himself apparently experienced difficulty in gaining public recognition. Such recognition was connected with sitting in the *cathedra* or teacher's chair and certain front seats.[76] This accounts for the deplorable rivalry over precedence among leaders and prophets. What we have is a sad development. Appointment or

---

67. **Vision** III, 1-2; III, 4; III, 8, 9-11.

68. **Vision** III, 5, 1; elders: **Vision** II, 4, 3; III, 1, 8. von Campenhausen maintains that the concept of **elders** was an umbrella term which embraced prophets, teachers, old and proven pastors and counsellors, and later confessors and ascetics. He distinguishes the "appointed" (1 **Clement** 54:2) or "leading elders" (Hermas, **Vision** II, 4, 3) who in his opinion were the **episkopoi: Ecclesiastical Authority**, pp. 84-85.

69. **Sim.** IX, 25.

70. **Sim.** IX, 31, 5ff.

71. **Vision** II, 6, 1; III, 9, 7 & 10.

72. **Sim.** IX, 26, 2; **Mand.** XI, 1 & 12.

73. **Sim.** IX, 25, 2.

74. **Sim.** IX, 27.

75. **Vision** III, 1-2; also III, 4. L. W. Barnard, **Studies in the Apostolic Fathers and their Background** (New York: Schocken Books, 1966), pp. 153-156.

76. **Vision** III, 1-2; **Mand.** XI. In **Vision** I, 2, 2 the ancient lady, who is the Church, sits on a **cathedra**. Also see **Vision** III, 10.

designation have been co-opted as a symbol of prestige by unworthy officials. Office, which began as a guarantee for continuity in the charism of service and teaching, is now, in some cases, an end in itself, divorced from any concern for charism.

With the seven letters of Ignatius of Antioch, written early in the second century, we find indications that the monarchical eastern pattern has definitely extended its influence. Ignatius speaks of a monarchical *episkopos* (or bishop) presiding the individual churches or eucharistic assemblies as if this were normative.[77] The one *episkopos* is advised and assisted by a college of presbyters.[78] The deacons are now said to be subject to the presbytery whereas formerly they were mentioned only in relationship to *episkopoi*.[79]

Ignatius maintains that no church can be recognized if it does not have a bishop, presbytery, and deacons.[80] However, we cannot apply Ignatius' letters as definite evidence for the universality of the monarchical episcopate even at this time.[81] The very fact that he places so much emphasis on a monarchical bishop indicates a certain defensiveness which should make us cautious. Furthermore, when he writes to the Romans he mentions no individual leader.

---

77. *Smyrnaeans* 8:1-2. This text indicates that the **episkopos** could appoint another to preside an individual Eucharist. J. McCue interprets this to mean that permanent ordination was not necessary; "Bishops, Presbyters, and Priests in Ignatius of Antioch," **Theological Studies**, Vol. 28, No. 4 (1967), pp. 828-834.

78. **Philadelphians** 4.

79. **Magnesians** 2:1.

80. **Trallians** 3:1.

81. From the pauline **Letter to the Philippians** (1:1) it would appear that Philippi definitely had a college of **episkopoi** assisted by deacons. Polycarp, writing after Ignatius, mentions only presbyters and deacons in his letter to that church (**Phil.** 5:1). In the hypothesis that Polycarp's mono-episcopal vision had **de facto** reserved the title of **episkopos** for the strictly monarchical situation, his substitution of **presbyteroi** would actually indicate that collegial leadership still survived in Philippi. Furthermore, if one should join such an observation to the opinion that the Pastoral Epistles were written between 90 and 120, there would be evidence

Only at the end of the second century is the monarchical episcopate definitely universalized. The fact and the reason are indicated in the lists which Hegesippus and Irenaeus composed for the principal churches of their time.[82] They were intended to counter gnostic teachers by proving that orthodox leaders succeeded to the genuine apostolic teaching.

Other changes were still to come. With imperial recognition and new material wealth the Church of the fourth century would see its bishops become administrators and even civil court judges.[83] The presbyterium then dissolved as the elders became liturgical leaders of the subdivisions made from overlarge episcopal assemblies. They assumed the new title of priest (*hierus*).[84] At this point we shall halt our study of developing church order.

Conclusions

Having drawn a broad outline of the early Church this essay suggests that structural pluralism was a natural concomitant of the original Christian readiness to see the Spirit acting in every structure that genuinely served the living of the "Way." We conclude that such structural pluralism might again be a desirable and viable option for today's Church.

There is thus an alternative beyond reforming the presently

---

against any extensive monarchical episcopacy at the beginning of the second century. Instead it would appear a limited reality having a growth potential commensurate with the stature and enthusiasm of its articulate proponents.

82. Cf. **Adversus Haereses** III, 3, 2-3 and Eusebius, **Eccles. Hist.** IV, 22.

83. J. Gaudemet, **L'Eglise dans l'Empire Romain (IVe-Ve siecles)**, Tome 3 in **Histoire du Droit et des Institutions de l'Eglise en occident**, directed by G. Le Bras (Paris: Sirey, 1958), pp. 230-240. P. de Labriolle, **et al.**, **De la mort de Theodose a l'election de Gregoire le Grand**, Vol. 4 in **Histoire de l'Eglise**, directed by A. Fliche and V. Martin (Paris: Bloud & Gay, 1948), p. 539.

84. J. Gaudemet, p. 101. Also refer to P. M. Gy, "Notes on the Early Terminology of Christian Priesthood," and B. Botte, "Collegiate Character of the Presbyterate and Episcopate," in **The Sacrament of Holy Orders** (see note 3), pp. 98-115 and 75-97.

absolutized and canonically protected structures simply through the hierarchically controlled processes of reshuffling and collegial injection. Taking our cue from the example of the earliest tradition, we might step back and recognize totally new patterns, allowing them to again grow and survive from the grass roots since they serve the manifold needs experienced by contemporary Christians. We are open to the fact that these new ministerial structures might be developed by those who stand both within and without the present hierarchical pattern. This fact requires a new consciousness on the part of many who compose the present hierarchical structure or accept its leadership. They must be assured that a sharing of functions with new groups or styles of ministry need not dissolve or compromise the ministry of present groups. In Luke's mind the position of the Twelve and Peter was not hurt by the rather radical Seven, or by presbyters, or by the somewhat conservative James, or by the liberal Paul.

The wisdom of the rabbi, Gamaliel, as recorded in Acts (5:38-39), saved the early Christian Church from extinction: "I tell you; leave them alone. For if this idea of theirs or its execution is of human origin, it will collapse; but if it is from God, you will never be able to put them down, and you risk finding yourselves at war with God."[85] The Sanhedrin took Gamaliel's advice. Perhaps a similar openness toward ministries and church orders, which they have not decreed, is required on the part of the present crucial agencies. They must judge any new pattern hesitantly, in close relationship with the total believing Church. Only in that way will their own human prejudices of established and comfortable routine and vested interest be overcome. If the new structures are from the Spirit they will find acceptance among believing Christians. With regard to pluralism we might recall that Vatican II recognized unity in diversity as a value.

---

85. **NEB.**

16 Gandhi's Ahimsa: The Transformation of an Ethical Value

WILLIAM CENKNER

Ahimsa is a unique ethical value in the Indian experience. Although translated literally as nonkilling, it is used generally for noninjury, harmlessness, and in the case of Mohandas Gandhi, nonviolence. *Ahimsa paramo dharma* (Noninjury is the highest law) is an axiom emerging from ancient Indian folklore and entering into the highest ethical formulations of Hinduism, Jainism, and Buddhism. Better than any other concept in the Indian experience, it is an example of an ethical norm which received clearer definition and precision in the development of the ethical consciousness of the people. To grasp the significance of Mohandas Gandhi's reconceptualization of this term as an ethical value and his use of it in the social order, it must be seen in the attitudes which framed it.

Although the *ahimsa* (noninjury) doctrine was posited within the most ancient traditions of Hinduism, its origin remains nebulous and its content somewhat imprecise.[1] Vedic society required the killing of animals for various purposes; in fact, animal sacrifice, and occasionally human sacrifice, were an integral part of Vedic ritual in order to obtain from the gods such favors as

---

1. For a consideration of ahimsa in the Indian tradition see: W. Norman Brown, **Man in the Universe, Some Cultural Continuities in India** (Berkeley: The University of California Press, 1966); for a modern Indian's conception of ahimsa see Agehananda Bharati, "A Contemporary Interpretation of Ahimsa," in **Gandhi: His Relevance For Our Times**, ed. G. Ramachandran and T. K. Mahadevan (Bombay: Bharatiya Vidya Bhavan, 1967); the most thorough treatment is James Weldon Plaugher, **The Religious Aspects of Gandhi's Ahimsa** (Stanford University, Ph.D. unpub. diss., 1965).

success in war, increase in produce and offspring, and longevity. In the later Vedic period meditation and asceticism were substituted for ritual sacrifice whereby the power of the sacrifice (*Brahman*) was encountered in the spiritual sacrifice of the inner man.

The first occurrence of the word *ahimsa* (noninjury) in Sanskrit literature can be traced to the *Chandogya Upanishad* where it is mentioned inconspicuously among a list of five virtues: namely, austerity, almsgiving, uprightness, *ahimsa* (noninjury), and truthfulness.[2] In the same *Upanishad* killing is forbidden "except on a sacred spot," that is to say, in ritual sacrifice.[3] It may have been the intent of this injunction to limit killing to the nonhuman order. The word appears more frequently in the epical literature of India. King Yudhisthira in the *Mahabharata* elevates *ahimsa* (noninjury) to the highest order when he is pressed to give the moral law. He clearly draws upon the axiom *Ahimsa paramo dharma* (Noninjury is the highest law).[4] Moreover, in this same epic, it is given a four-fold dimension: "A person should neither commit *himsa* (killing) mentally, vocally, or by action; nor should he eat meat."[5] It followed then that not only the physical aspect of violence to man or to animals was inferred, but also the more subtle aspects, such as anger, revenge, and violent speech, were to be avoided.[6] The *Bhagavad Gita,* a part of the *Mahabharata,* mentions the doctrine of *ahimsa* (noninjury) in four passages. It is among a list of virtues, a list of knowledge, and also enumerated among the five austerities of the body.[7] Although there is no intimation of the content of the doctrine, its applicability becomes increasingly more comprehensive.

Finally, the *ahimsa* (noninjury) norm is found in the law texts

---

2. Chandogya Upanishad, 3.17.4.

3. Chandogya Upanishad, 7.15.

4. Mahabharata, 1.11.13.

5. Mahabharata, XIII.114.4-9.

6. Dhairyabala P. Vora, Evolution of Morals in the Epics (Bombay: Popular Book Depot, 1959), p. 222.

7. Bhagavad Gita, 10.4-5; 16.1-3; 13.7-11; 17.14.

ascribed to Manu.[8] Great ambivalence appears in the applicability of the norm for in some passages meat eating is condemned and in other passages it is permitted. Obviously, the ethical consciousness of India did not easily evolve an absolute norm of practice.

Nonetheless, in the traditional religious literature of Hinduism, ethical concepts are gradually sharpened. For example, in the earliest texts, *himsa* (killing) was forbidden due to its consequent effect upon man. It was listed among virtues, which implied that the practice of virtue brought one closer to liberation (*moksha*) and offered an escape from the world of suffering (*samsara*). Meat was forbidden in the diet because he who eats the meat of an animal will be eaten in the next world by that same animal.[9] Consequently, ethical value was drawn from the effect of the act alone. In the *Bhagavad Gita,* however, ethical precepts received value not from the effect of the activity but from its motive. In fact, value was drawn solely from the motive of the activity. If a person dedicated all his activity to *Brahman* (The Supreme) and performed his duties without attachment to the fruits of the activity, his actions would not cleave to him and would not keep him within the world of suffering.[10] The importance in the *Bhagavad Gita* on individual motive and character rather than the action itself indicated a great stride in the development of ethical concepts in India.[11] This aspect was absent in the earlier literature.

Within Hinduism the *ahimsa* (noninjury) norm was a result of the doctrine concerning the unity of all life. *Ahimsa* (noninjury) became a prime ethical value within India and within Hinduism, specifically, because it was derived from the Indian conception

---

8. The Laws of Manu, 2.177; 10.63; 11.159; 5.55; 5.11ff.

9. The Laws of Manu, 5.55. Manu's laws are somewhat ambivalent for he also prescribes the eating of consecrated flesh (5.36-38) because it brings good to both the consumer and the animal (5.39-42) but if he does not eat consecrated flesh he will be reborn as a beast for twenty-one lives (5.35).

10. Surendranath Dasgupta, A History of Indian Philosophy (Cambridge: The University Press, 1932), Vol. I, pp. 513-514.

11. Dhairyabala P. Vora, Evolution of Morals in the Epics, op. cit., pp. 196-197.

of the unity of all living things. This belief inevitably led to the conviction that wherever life existed, it was inviolable.[12] Such Hindu customs as vegetarianism and reverence for the cow may have been further consequences of the *ahimsa* (noninjury) doctrine which rested upon the inviolability of life. The *ahimsa* (noninjury) norm, posited in Hinduism, offered a practical expression of a deep sensitivity for life. The intimate union of all living beings, which regulated all Hindu ethics, received perfect enunciation in the precept of *ahimsa* (noninjury).

Jainism is one of the most severe ascetical traditions in the religious history of man. For the Jains the doctrine of rebirth and transmigration led to the idea that all living things possessed souls. This belief led further to a horror of taking life in any form. Jain ethics placed great stress upon the virtues of noninjury (*ahimsa*), truthfulness (*satya*), nonstealing (*asteya*), and celibacy (*brahmacharya*). But the root of all virtue and the norm of all activity was in accordance with nonkilling.[13] Morality for the Jains was a means of liberating man from all suffering; severe asceticism became the way to avoid injury to living beings. *Ahimsa* (noninjury) was the supreme ascetical path of undefilement. Thus, Jain monks breathe through a piece of cloth placed over the face in order to avoid swallowing creatures of the air; in darkness the Jain burns no light lest moths and insects are burned; the Jain monk cautiously steps forward in order to avoid trampling creeping things; Jains abandoned agriculture because they could not cultivate land without damaging life. No Indian sect has carried the precept of nonkilling to such an extreme because the Jains alone detected the boundless nature of this ethical norm.

Among the great Jain vows (*Mahavrata*), nonkilling is the primary vow, extends to all forms of life, and it is intimately connected with the observance of the other vows. Truthfulness (*satya*) prevents verbal violence by forbidding idle gossip, vulgar, frivolous or malicious talk; nonstealing (*asteya*) forbids taking

---

12. W. Norman Brown, Man in the Universe, op. cit., p. 44.
13. Surendranath Dasgupta, A History of Indian Philosophy, op. cit., Vol. I, p. 200.

a man's property for it would be injurious to him; celibacy (*brahmacarya*) forbids all sensual indulgence which would violate another; nonownership of property (*aparigraha*) avoids violence to society. In the Jain ethic nonkilling is an attempt to rise above the mundane in order not to be polluted by it. A medieval king, a convert to Jainism, is reported to have been a savage advocate of *ahimsa* (noninjury) by inflicting the death penalty upon a merchant who was found in possession of meat near a temple in his capital city.[14] Yet the same King, Kumarapala of the 12th century, commissioned the poet Hemacandra to pen the praises of nonkilling in these sensitive verses:

Ahimsa is like a loving mother of all beings.
Ahimsa is like a stream of nectar in the desert of Samsara.
Ahimsa is a course of rain-clouds to the forest-fire of suffering.
The best herb of healing for the beings that are tormented by the disease. Called the perpetual return of existence is *Ahimsa*.[15]

It would seem that nonkilling among the Jains belonged originally to an ethic of personal perfection and not to an ethic of action. For self-perfection violence appeared to the Jains as that which universally must be avoided. The Jains were the first to express the fact that ethics knows no bounds.[16] *Ahimsa* (noninjury) indicated a sensitivity for life and for living beings that was boundless, and it expressed the boundlessness of both ethical value and practice.

Although *ahimsa* (noninjury) is a single ethical norm, one among many, in Hinduism, and an exclusive norm of conduct in Jainism, it is integrated into the whole complex of religious life only in Buddhism. For this reason noninjury neither appears frequently nor explicitly in the Buddhists' texts; yet, it is implied

---

14. W. Norman Brown, **Man in the Universe**, op. cit., p. 57.
15. Quoted in Albert Schweitzer, **Indian Thought and Its Development** (Boston: The Beacon Press, 1936), p. 82.
16. **Ibid.**, p. 80, 83.

and serves as the ethical foundation of the higher spiritual life of Buddhism. Five prohibitions form the basic suppositions of the spiritual life of Buddhism: killing (*himsa*), stealing, impurity, lying, and intoxication.[17] Consequently, a type of nonviolence is the ethical basis for the high spiritual teaching of which Buddhism is primarily concerned.

In the Buddhist tradition *ahimsa* (noninjury) soon develops into loving-kindness, an attractive virtue reflecting the intimate and deeply affectionate character of Buddhist man.[18] *The Discourse on Loving-Kindness,* appearing early in Buddhist literature, indicates how within a nonviolent context a loving-concern for others grows:

> May every creature abound in well-being and in peace.
> May every living being, seen or unseen
> Those dwelling far-off, those near-by
> Those already born, those waiting to be born
> May all attain inward peace.
> Let no one deceive another
> Let no one despise another in any situation
> Let no one from antipathy or hatred
> Wish evil to anyone at all.
> Just as a mother with her own life
> Protects her son, her only son, from hurt,
> So within your own self foster
> A limitless concern for every living creature.
> Display a heart of boundless love

---

17. Thomas Berry, **Buddhism** (New York: Hawthorne Books, 1967), p. 42.

18. Loving-kindness is distinguished into **maitri** (a passive type of friendliness) and **dana** (an active type of friendship) of which the latter should find expression in some extrinsic way. Loving-kindness is generically known as **metta** and is an object of meditation. See H. Saddhatissa, **Buddhist Ethics, Essence of Buddhism** (New York: George Braziller, 1970), pp. 89-93. This exceptional text offers a fine introduction to the ethics of the Theravada school of Buddhism.

For all the world in all its height and depth and broad extent
Love unrestrained, without hate or enmity.[19]

A deep concern for others became the object of special training among Buddhist monks, and a thorough study was undertaken in extending loving-kindness to greater areas of life.[20]

Ahimsa (noninjury), as an integrative virtue, formed the basis for the preliminary steps of the famous Buddhist Eightfold Path. Virtuous conduct, the formative aspect of the Eightfold Path, included right speech, right action, and right livelihood: namely, speech, action, and occupation which fostered life and not death. For the lay folk who would not enter into the meditational stages of the Eightfold Path, *ahimsa* (noninjury) became a practical ethical precept. Among the virtues recommended to the laity, the sense of noninjury to others, whether in thought, word, deed, or emotion, dominated each virtue.[21]

Although Buddhist ethical life is situated within a context of *ahimsa* (noninjury) and grows into loving-kindness, it reaches full development in compassion. Compassion is a going-forth from the confinement of one's own spiritual life to a sharing in the lives of others. It is based on a strong love relationship which must include all living beings.[22] It is unrestricted and unlimited in quality or comprehensiveness. For the early Buddhists a self-orientated life was the rule; but in later Buddhism man entered into and shared in the life and suffering of the whole society. The suffering savior passages of Isaiah and its theme in Christianity find a parallel in Mahayana Buddhism's doctrine of suffering. It is clearly evident in passages of Santi Deva's *Compendium of Doctrine*:

19. **Sutta Nipata,** 146-151. Eng. tr. **Buddha's Teachings,** in **HOS,** Vol. 37 (Cambridge, Mass.: Harvard University Press, 1932).
20. Thomas Berry, **Buddhism, op. cit.,** p. 41.
21. **Majjhima Nikaya,** i.287.
22. Thomas Berry, **Buddhism, op. cit.,** pp. 101-102.

I must save all beings from the torrent of rebirth with the raft of my omniscient mind. I must pull them back from the great precipice. I must free them from all misfortune, ferry them over the stream of rebirth.

For I have taken upon myself, by my own will, the whole of the pain of all things living. . . . I shall give myself into bondage, to redeem all the world from the forest of purgatory, from rebirth as beasts, from the realm of death. I shall bear all grief and pain in my own body, for the good of all things living. . . . I must be their charioteer, I must be their leader, I must be their torchbearer, I must be their guide to safety.[23]

This sublime teaching took many centuries to develop in the Buddhist tradition. Yet, the emperor Ashoka, a convert to Buddhism in the 3rd century B.C., adhered strictly to the practical application of *ahimsa* (noninjury) by abolishing the royal hunt and meat at meals. He enforced noninjury in a set of rules recorded in the Pillar Edict and attempted to enforce it through further moral legislation.[24] Nonetheless, the great contribution of Buddhism was the coupling of *ahimsa* (noninjury) with the virtue of compassion. Noninjury and compassion became formative of the religious sensitivities of Asian man. Wherever Buddhism spread in the Asian world, *ahimsa* (noninjury) and compassion entered into the moral and ethical texture of Asian life.

Thus, Hinduism, Jainism, and Buddhism have contributed to the meaning and universality of this ethical value. *Ahimsa paramo dharma* (Ahimsa is the highest law) was accepted in various ways by these traditions. In India the *paramo dharma* (highest law) was not exclusive since other ethical norms, truth for example, received the same formulation. It was indicative, however, that the *paramo dharma* (highest law) was inclusive,

---

23. Shantiveda, **Siksasamuccaya,** ed. Cecil Bendall (St. Petersburg: Imperial Academy of Sciences, 1902), pp. 278-283. Quoted from **The Buddhist Tradition in India, China, and Japan,** ed. Wm. Theodore De Bary (New York: The Modern Library, 1969), p. 85.

24. W. Norman Brown, **Man in the Universe, op. cit.,** pp. 56-57.

integrative, and reflected a more basic value. It included within itself other ethical qualities and was closely integrated with a range of ethical values. *Ahimsa* (noninjury) spoke to a more basic truth and, in this case, rested upon a sensitivity for the unity of all life.

The concept of the unity of all life is acknowledged in the Indian tradition; it is present in India when the *ahimsa* (noninjury) norm is being formulated. *Ahimsa* (noninjury) as norm and value spoke to the ethical order while the concept of the unity of all life spoke to the metaphysical order. In Indian philosophy, more particularly in Hinduism, the metaphysical and ethical orders are one.[25] There is no clear distinction between the order of being and the order of acting; ontological and existential reality are one. Consequently, *ahimsa* (noninjury), an existential and ethical value, is in fact the practical meaning of the unity of all living beings, the ontological and metaphysical reality.

Although *ahimsa* (noninjury) appeared consistently in a negative form, it is limited to neither negative meaning nor understanding. A negative prefix is a common device in Sanskrit literature which indicates the different levels of meaning intended.[26] For example, *ahimsa* (noninjury) is logically and intellectually opposed to killing, violence, and chaos; it is linked to friendliness, kindness, and compassion on an affective level of meaning; finally, it is opposed to anger, lying, presumption, and rancor on an emotional level. Moreover, it is not limited to a negative precept or law. In India *ahimsa* (noninjury) was that value which raised the quality of life to a high level of meaning and reverence. It gave to Indian man a sensitivity for *all* life. It became both a religious virtue and a goal in the great religions. As a virtue it was recommended to both the ascetic and the layman; it prob-

25. See I. C. Sharma, **Ethical Philosophies of India** (London: George Allen & Unwin Ltd, 1965) wherein this principle is enunciated throughout and becomes the central theme of the study.

26. Jan Gonda, "Why Ahimsa and Similar Concepts Often Expressed in a Negative Form," **Four Studies in the Language of the Veda** ('s-Gravenhage: Mouton & Co., 1959), p. 102.

ably had more significance for the laity in its practical and concrete form since the householder found himself in more circumstances where it could be exercised. In short, noninjury may well be the prime ethical value which has changed the quality of life in the history of religious man in India.

Mohandas Gandhi emerged as a political and spiritual leader of his people at the climax of the Indian renaissance which had begun a century earlier. Contemporary Hinduism had already experienced the encounter of East and West, and in particular the encounter with Christianity. It must also be recalled that Gandhi went to London as a youth in 1888 for three years, and except for a brief return to India he lived in South Africa for the following twenty years. During this time he read seriously the religious scriptures of the world and the contemporary social theorists for the first time. His initial reading of the *Bhagavad Gita* was in 1889 in an English translation. During this formative period of his life, he read the New Testament, Leo Tolstoy's *The Kingdom of God Is Within You,* John Ruskin's *Unto This Last,* Thoreau's *Civil Disobedience,* and the essays of Emerson. Although Tolstoy seemed to be the key western ideological influence upon Gandhi, it was left to John Ruskin to move him in the existential order to total dedication in public life.

At the same time Gandhi instinctively drew upon his own heritage, especially upon Jainism which was prevalent in his native state of Gujarat. The intensity with which *ahimsa* (noninjury) is understood in Jainism was reflected in the centrality Gandhi gave to *ahimsa* (noninjury) in his own life. Although he relied heavily upon the Indian traditions, his encounter with western scriptures, and the social theorists, he said in 1916:

> ... though my views on ahimsa are a result of my study of most of the faiths of the world, they are now no longer dependent upon the authority of these works. They are a part of my life, and if I suddenly discovered that the religious books read by me bore a different interpretation from the one

I had learned to give them, I should still hold to the view of ahimsa.[27]

Gandhi steered a middle course between the rigorism of the Jain condemnation of all killing and the liberal *Code of Manu* which permitted killing for ritual sacrifice. More precisely, he used *ahimsa* (noninjury) to formulate an ethic that would be rooted in the spiritual life of India and, at the same time, would be able to cope with the socio-political problems of contemporary India. Gandhi's ethic was a bridge between tradition and modernity. His concept of *ahimsa* (noninjury) retained deep continuity with Indian spirituality and, at the same time, introduced change within the tradition. This was not conceived once and for all in any ideological way, but it was the direct result of his experimentation in the pragmatic order with the demands of daily living. In his autobiography he viewed life as a series of experiments with truth and concluded that "life consists in nothing but those experiments."[28] Within this context he developed the meaning and content of *ahimsa* (noninjury).

For Gandhi *ahimsa* (noninjury) retained the spiritual significance which India had given to it: namely, a sensitivity for living beings, a reverence for all life, a pervasive tolerance. It became, however, in his ethic a more dynamic and comprehensive value than ever before in the Indian experience. Gandhi's *ahimsa* (noninjury) was equivalent to love, and in its purest form it was redemptive suffering. Neither in Hinduism, Jainism or Buddhism, nor in the writings of the Indian sages does *ahimsa* (noninjury) become synonymous with love. Although traditional India looked upon *ahimsa* (noninjury) in a positive manner as compassion and reverence for mankind, love was not integral to the concept

---

27. M. K. Gandhi, **Modern Review**, October 1916, quoted in **Speeches and writings of Mahatma Gandhi** (Madras: Natesan, n.d., 4th ed.), p. 345.

28. M. K. Gandhi, An Autobiography, **The Story of My Experiments with Truth** (Boston: Beacon Press, 1957, 2nd ed.), p. xii.

itself. Gandhi was able to detect similarities between the *Bhagavad Gita* and the Sermon on the Mount because love was both implicit and integral to his concept of *ahimsa* (noninjury). This became the basis for his reconceptualization.

He looked upon *ahimsa* (noninjury) as the extension of family love. Some have spoken of Gandhi's mandala in which *ahimsa* (noninjury) reaches out in concentric circles of friendship where the intimate relationships of family life are extended to neighbors, the citizens of the state, and finally to all mankind. He wrote:

> In concrete terms it covers family relations, relations with constituted authority, internal disorders and external aggression. Put in another way it covers all human relations.[29]

Gandhi frequently compared *ahimsa* (noninjury) to Pauline charity:

> Ahimsa means love in the Pauline sense and yet something more than love defined by St. Paul, although I know St. Paul's beautiful definition is good enough for all practical purposes.[30]

Further precision in his concept of *ahimsa* (noninjury) developed its active and creative dimensions. For Gandhi "suffering injury in one's person . . . is of the essence of nonviolence and is the chosen substitute for violence to others."[31] He could say that "if love is not the law of our being then my whole argument falls down."[32] Consequently, *ahimsa* (noninjury) or love, in its

---

29. M. K. Gandhi, **Non-Violence in Peace and War**, ed. Bharatan Kumarappa (Ahmedabad: Navajivan Press, 1942 & 1949), Vol. I, p. 340.

30. M. K. Gandhi, **Harijan**, March 14, 1936.

31. M. K. Gandhi, quoted in Joan V. Bondurant, **Conquest of Violence, The Gandhian Philosophy of Conflict** (Berkeley: The University of California, 1965), p. 27.

32. M. K. Gandhi, **Non-Violence in Peace and War**, op. cit., Vol. I, p. 131.

most perfect and highest expression is self-sacrifice, self-suffering, redemptive love.

In his reconceptualization of this ethical value, Gandhi raised it to a high spiritual order, and it is this factor that gave him continuity with the spiritual heritage of India. Although the concept had been reconceived in terms of meaning and comprehensiveness, it remained in the spiritual order. He was, however, an innovator. He brought change to the tradition by placing *ahimsa* (noninjury) into socio-political life. His full reconceptualization was in terms of the ethical demands facing Indian man: namely, a society and a political order in need of change.

Since Gandhi's theory of nonviolence emerged from his personal experience and experimentation in private and public life, his dedication to the social welfare of India was a gradual commitment which ultimately developed into a religion of service. He was not a revolutionary personality by birth. Although he possessed an ambivalence in the definitions of his role, he could say:

Men say I am a saint losing myself in politics. The fact is I am a politician trying my hardest to be a saint.[33]

Nonetheless, Gandhi's strength as an Indian leader and the key to his compelling personality lay precisely in his saintliness. The mass of Indians, the peasant society, looked upon him as a holy man in the old tradition; at the same time, he was creating a pattern for the socio-political personality who could respond effectively to the problems of modern man. In this context Gandhi placed *ahimsa* (noninjury) into the ethic of socio-political man.

Ahimsa (noninjury), according to Gandhi, qualified one for

---

33. M. K. Gandhi, quoted in Louis Fischer, **Gandhi, His Life and Message for the World** (New York: Mentor Books, 1954), p. 35. At the same time Gandhi could say: "The politician in me never dominated a single decision of mine." See M. K. Gandhi, **Satyagraha, Non-Violent Resistance**, ed. Bharatan Kumarappa (Ahmedabad: Navajivan Press, 1951), p. 109.

selfless service and made possible the renunciation of self and the total dedication to social concerns.[34] As an ethical value of social man, nonviolence must be realized interiorly before it can become a norm for service or placed in the social arena. Nonviolence becomes an effective norm of service when it is transformed by love. Gandhi wrote:

> Service of love was the highest service one could render to another. It asked for no consideration or return. Love becomes a sordid bargain when it asks for return or compensation; it degrades, spontaneous service of love pacifies and elevates.[35]

Ahimsa (noninjury) specifies one's motivation for public service; if it is completely selfless, it humanizes and spiritualizes the activity.[36] The efficacy, however, of nonviolence is reached when it becomes sacrificial. A readiness to suffer in the service of love frees the individual from the bondage of himself and social consequences. Thus, Gandhi had forged a social norm of high altruistic dimensions.

Nonviolence is most often understood in the framework of social change and the revolutionary movement in both India and the West. It is exercised in man's relational life within the dialectic of social and political change. Love for an adversary is the core of Gandhian nonviolent protest. The protestor desires the well-being of the adversary but seeks to change his pattern of life and thought. It is a "heart-conversion" that is sought.[37] Radical change in the opponent means a change of heart brought about by the love and suffering of the protestor himself. This orientation was followed consistently by Gandhi for he often spoke of *ahimsa*

---

34. M. K. Gandhi, **Non-Violence in Peace and War,** op. cit., Vol. I, p. 319.

35. **Ibid.,** Vol. 2, p. 97.

36. M. K. Gandhi, **Hindu Dharma,** ed. Bharatan Kumarappa (Ahmedabad: Navajivan Press, 1950), p. 176.

37. M. K. Gandhi, **Non-Violence in Peace and War,** op. cit., Vol. 2, p. 201.

(noninjury) "melting the stoniest of hearts."[38] According to Gandhi:

> The principal implication of ahimsa is that the ahimsa in us ought to soften and not to stiffen our opponent's attitude to us; it ought to melt him; it ought to strike a responsive chord in his heart.[39]

In conflict situations arising in the social and political order, some form of violence is the usual quality exchanged in the relationship between opponents. There is no possibility to change the relationship, in such a conflict, because the same quality is exerted by both parties. The balance of the relationship is altered by the quantity of pressure or force; yet, the relationship remains the same with the resolution of the conflict. Force is confronted and replaced with more force. For a radical change of relationship, a quality other than violence has to be placed in the relationship between the protestor and his adversary. This is the function of *ahimsa* (noninjury). This new quality is the spiritual force of ethical persuasion; it is directed to change the attitudes, convictions, and life-patterns of the adversary. *Ahimsa* (noninjury) is intended to elicit humane response from an individual who has been radically transformed.

Throughout his life Gandhi distinguished between nonviolence of the weak and nonviolence of the brave. The former is, in fact, passive resistance which uses methods of persuasion, propaganda, moral force, and non-cooperation.[40] It is a weak expression of nonviolence because it attains only the lower levels of *ahimsa* (noninjury). To reach the heights of *ahimsa* (noninjury), which Gandhi thought to be infallible and invincible, nonviolence of the brave must be a complete pattern of life. Total commitment and

38. **Ibid.**, Vol. 2, p. 104.

39. M. K. Gandhi, **The Mind of Mahatma Gandhi**, ed. R. K. Prabhu and U. R. Rao (Ahmedabad: Navajivan Press, 1945), p. 124.

40. M. K. Gandhi, **Non-Violence in Peace and War, op. cit.**, Vol. 2, pp. 271, 312-315.

the seeking of self-suffering constitute *ahimsa* (noninjury) formally and make possible nonviolence of the brave.[41] This form of nonviolence gathers up the entire force of sacrificial love and pits it against an opponent. The distinction between nonviolence of the weak and nonviolence of the brave is the difference between *ahimsa* (noninjury) as a technique for socio-political change and *ahimsa* (noninjury) as a complete pattern of life for social man. In short, Gandhian nonviolence was a reconceptualization of a traditional ethical value raised to a high spiritual and social plane whereby the quality of life could be enhanced.

Gandhi's *ahimsa* (noninjury) is a new emergent in the history of ethical thought. From the primordial sensitivity of the Indian traditions, he was able to place nonviolence firmly in the spiritual order. He went far beyond traditional reverence for life. The unique quality Gandhi brought to *ahimsa* (noninjury), in its spiritual dimension, was to place it *in* history. The ethical demand of *ahimsa* (noninjury) required that man be a love-creature *in* history. A historical consciousness has increased steadily among the majority of contemporary Hindu philosophers and religious figures, which has given a new orientation to Indian man. From the western nonviolent tradition, especially Tolstoy and the Sermon on the Mount, Gandhi was able to place *ahimsa* (noninjury) into the social order. The unique quality he brought to its social dimension was to offer man a social ethic whereby he could transform society. *Ahimsa* (noninjury) was an ethical demand calling man to restructure society through reconstruction of social relationships. Consequently, if this value is a new emergent in ethical thought, it cannot be reduced or explained by reference solely to precursors of the nonviolent tradition. The meaning Gandhi gave to nonviolence was not present before him. His conception is a new one which reflects synthesis and originality.

He arrived at this synthesis because he saw himself as one who had to bridge tradition and modernity. There are lines of

---

41. **Ibid.**, Vol. 2, pp. 127, 140, 258-259.

continuity and change operating throughout his life and thought.[42]
The ethic which Gandhi formulated, however, revolved around
the real, historical transformation of man in society. He believed
that a love ethic could transform man and society if it became
the entire frame of reference in personal life. The redemptive
aspect of *ahimsa* (noninjury) was primarily self-redemptive since
it meant that man must change himself before he sought change
in society. Only if an individual has the capacity to transform
himself can he anticipate a transformation of the social and
political order. *Ahimsa* (noninjury) is directed, nonetheless, to the
transformation of the social order through a change in human
relationships and not through a change of social structures or
institutions. In this respect Gandhi's *ahimsa* (noninjury) is a
dialectic whereby man's relational life is changed.

The key to Gandhi's social thought is characterized in one
word: *sarvodaya*. It literally means the uplift of all. The goal is
to lift man both spiritually and socially to new levels of life and
experience. Gandhi saw the rise of man and society as parallel
and concomitant processes in the evolution of man and society.
This is the vision which his reconceptualization offered to Indian
man. He gave to India a means to enter history seriously and
effectively. There is the sound of the prophet in Gandhi's teaching
because he focused upon a decisive issue. Namely, can man truly
change? Gandhi's *ahimsa* (noninjury) reflects a faith in man
and the divine. Consequently, to judge nonviolence from the
point of view of success or failure may be a superfluous question
for it would deny its spiritual basis. The question may be whether
modern man has the depth of faith to dare this option in either
private or public life.

---

42. I have traced these lines of Gandhi's thought in my article "Gandhi
and Creative Conflict," **Thought,** Vol. XLV, No. 178, Autumn 1970.

V

RELIGIOUS STUDIES:
TOWARD NEW QUALITY & VITALITY

17 Religious Studies as Academic Festivity

GEORGE H. FREIN

All topics legitimately listed in the academic catalogue can appropriately be thought of as festivals or celebrations. History, for example, celebrates the past; biology celebrates the living organism; poetry is a festival of language. The festive character of the academic life is hardly exhausted by convocations and commencements. To be sure these events are celebrations of a kind, but the activities of the academic life proper—reading, writing and research—are themselves the essential festivals of that life.

In such a scheme of the curriculum, with festivity functioning as the middle term, religious studies would seem to be a celebration of the power manifested in the forces of nature and history. Other academic fields, too, celebrate the forces of nature and history and religion itself exalts in these powers. Religion proper celebrates the power that seems to set itself off from the profane and is thus apprehended as sacred. Religious studies as properly academic affairs celebrate the intelligibility of the sacred. The area or field of celebration is what distinguishes religious studies from other fields and disciplines. Though not a sacred festival, religious studies is a festival of the sacred. It is an academic festival—a celebration of the intelligibility of the human experience of the sacred. Theology—at least to the extent that it is a part of a phenomenology of religion—would also seem to be an academic festival in which the religious experience of a people seeks an understanding that, in itself and in its source in God, is shaped by the structure of festivity.

Religious studies departments and departments of theology have worked hard to be taken seriously by the academic community (a very necessary task, still not finished) but in the process they may have mistakenly copied from other disciplines and fields of study an overly serious self-concept. By accepting the prevailing work ethic uncritically, theologians and religion scholars may have failed to make a uniquely appropriate criticism of the arts and sciences curriculum.

Both the curriculum and the society it serves are in need of criticism on this point. Elementary and secondary education are shot through with the work ethic and, though the longer children stay in school the less work they frequently do, the language of work increases constantly. There is "homework," "seatwork," "busywork," "workbooks," "work study," "extra work," "work contracts," not to mention "get-busy-and-do-your-work-work." Higher education is hardly less work-oriented. Not only is a college education offered as a necessary preparation for a good job but it frequently copies the language, liturgy and ethos of business and industry. Professors as well as students are busy, hard-working laborers in the knowledge industry. Historians work at the past, scientists work on their research projects and religion scholars are out to demonstrate that their new science is as arduous as any on campus. In this climate it is little wonder that many students find their week-end jobs as waitresses and bus boys a welcome break from the week-day grind of study. Even Harvey Cox, in his description of *homo festivus,* seems to put thinking on the work side of the ledger when he writes that "Man is by his very nature a creature who not only works and thinks but who sings, dances, prays, tells stories, and celebrates."[1]

Cox is right, however, when he argues that Western man has paid a frightful price for his present opulence: human life has been profoundly impoverished by the loss of the sense of festivity. "Man is essentially festive and fanciful."[2] Our personal and social lives have been greatly diminished by the loss of this essential component. Even our physical survival has been made doubtful by a radically unfestive manipulation of nature, creating the specter of cosmic death through the destruction of the ecology.

Contemporary efforts at being festive are only a little helpful. Robert Neale writes about "funsters" who "seek diversion from

1. **Feast of Fools** (Cambridge: Harvard University Press, 1969), p. 10.
2. **Ibid.**, p. 12.

work, but the result is only diversion from life."[3] Fun for many
people is escape from work or preparation for work so that even
fun turns out to be work. Gordon Dahl says modern technology
has filled our leisure time with so many consumer items that we
work harder being good consumers than we do on the job.[4] He
suggests that "The leisure that people need today is not free time
but a free spirit; not more hobbies or amusements but a sense
of grace and peace which will lift us beyond our busy schedules."[5]
With Hugo Rahner he recommends the Greek virtue of *eutrapelia,*
"that nimbleness of mind and spirit which makes it possible for
man to play even when he is in earnest."[6]

Academic life is precisely that "nimbleness of mind and
spirit." Hugo Rahner's description of *eutrapelia* would seem to
sketch the academic life as it ought to be—"a kind of mobility
of soul, by which a truly cultured person turns to lovely, bright
and relaxing things, without losing himself in them—a spiritual
elegance of movement in which his seriousness and moral character can be perceived."[7] Academia should be more a place of
leisure than of labor. Johan Huizinga would seem to suggest that
school is a place for play with its roots in those archaic festivals
at which riddles were asked and a competition set up for their
solution. A sacred thing, full of secret power, the riddle is a form
of play that frequently had life and death consequences. It is
also, he suggests, the ludic source of the philosophical and theological interrogative.[8] Probably, even more basic than play in the
eventual formation of schools and scholars is the sense of wonder.
The kind of wonder, for example, that Loren Eisley experienced
in his boyhood in Nebraska and that still pervades his science
would seem to be not only the child's source of knowledge but a

---

3. **In Praise of Play** (New York: Harper & Row, 1969), p. 173.
4. "Time, Work and Leisure Today," in **The Christian Century** 88:6
(Feb. 10, 1971), pp. 185-189.
5. **Ibid.,** p. 188.
6. **Ibid.**
7. **Man at Play** (New York: Herder & Herder, 1967), pp. 94-95.
8. **Homo Ludens** (London: Routledge, Kegan and Paul Ltd., 1949),
p. 112.

present necessity for all authentic academic life. Sam Keen, who has issued a "Manifesto for a Dionysian Theology," indicates that wonder is basically a Dionysian attitude. Though in *Apology for Wonder* he argues that the authentic life emerges from the Apollonian-Dionysian dialectic, he acknowledges the "tyranny of Apollo" in our intellectual institutions.[9]

Wonder, curiosity, play and festivity seem to be the perpetual sources of study. Childhood's wonder and awe at the world and the philosopher's wonder that there is a world at all give rise to questions (particularly fanciful questions that begin "What if ...) and produce tentative, hence playful, answers. Work would seem to deal with the world less in terms of wonder and more in terms of practical necessity for food, clothing and shelter.

Academic life, even when relevant to social and political problems (as I would argue it ought to be), is fundamentally festive. Harvey Cox, using the work of Johan Huizinga, Roger Caillois and Josef Pieper, lists three ingredients of festivity: (1) conscious excess, (2) celebrative affirmation and (3) juxtaposition to everyday life.[10] All three are characteristics of the life of scholarship, though Cox does not draw out this conclusion. First, reading, writing and research is an excess. Not only do book-lovers, authors and researchers tend to "overdo it" but they amplify, by their scholarship, the mere presence of what they find and study. They celebrate the appearance of the phenomena and in the process rejoice in it. Even though not everything that scholars study is pretty the study of it is an affirmation of life, the second of Cox's ingredients. Racism is an ugly thing, as history, sociology and Black studies indicate, but its study also reveals the beauty of the black bondsman and even the possibility for white redemption. Scholarship itself is a celebration that negates ultimate absurdity and permanent skepticism. Finally, academic life itself, and not just occasional college festivals, stands in juxtaposition to every-

---

9. **Apology for Wonder** (New York: Harper & Row, 1969), pp. 151-199 and "Manifesto for a Dionysian Theology," in **New Theology No. 7** (New York: Macmillan, 1970), pp. 79-103.

10. **Feast of Fools**, pp. 21-24.

day life. It is an exception to the everyday because it is done for its own sake and not for an immediately practical reason that is rewarding not so much in itself as in what it effects in the practical order.

This last element may be the one that keeps us (and particularly our students) from experiencing the academic life as a form of festivity: we hold the festival five days a week! I would think, however, that though what Cox calls juxtaposition is necessary to set the festive off from the work-a-day world, it is not inherently impossible for the festival to be continual as for example in the heavenly feast envisioned in Christian eschatology. Studying need not cease being a delight that exalts in what it reads about, writes of and researches simply because it is a daily activity. But being a way of earning our daily bread it can (and all too frequently has) become a matter of work done in a spirit that finds its joy elsewhere. This is especially likely in a society where the work ethic so widely prevails that even dancers are said to "work out." Research, however, is not a form of the daily or predictable. It is more like poetry in which hypothesis begins in fantasy. "What if physical reality is not brick-like as it daily appears but more like a microcosmic solar system...?" The result of such toying with the world is surprise. Reading and writing, far from being the everyday tasks of the schoolboy who is concerned merely with the mechanical skills of decoding words and penmanship, are for real students a form of sharing in the surprise of another's discovery.

Scholarship is not less festive than any other feast that can be thought of simply because it is academic. There may not be a lot of shouting, dancing and drinking but there is conscious excess, celebrative affirmation and juxtaposition to the everyday.

In the case of religious studies there are special reasons that make it particularly appropriate to emphasize that these studies are a form of academic festivity. Religious phenomena include in a very fundamental way a variety of responses to the sacred that are festive: myth, ritual, sacred song, dance, ecstasy. The intelligibility of these phenomena that religious studies seeks is a constant celebration of the festive. Religious studies are not sacred festivals but are academic activities that are in constant contact with the Dionysian dimension of human behavior. The study of pre-literate religions and much Oriental religious behavior as well is especially a search for the intelligibility of the bodily and sensuous, components that are vital for celebration. Further, religious studies conducted with existential awareness are as relevant to students as feasts are for those who take part in them, not only to let off steam, but chiefly to enter more and more deeply into their being in the cosmos. As the religious researcher describes man's search for and response to the sacred, both in its healthy and pathological forms, he exalts for students this form of being in the world and at the same time raises questions for them about the meaning of their being. Religious studies are thus characterized by two significant festive forms: (1) the conscious awareness of the human body and (2) an awareness of the role of the body in the search for authentic being in the world.

Again it is important to keep in mind that religious studies are *academic* festivity and so they celebrate not only the sacred but also the powers of the mind that examine human behavior as it focuses on the sacred. Here Harvey Cox's description of what festivity is not is helpful. Festivity, he says, is not superficiality and it is not frivolity.[11] Religious studies that are conducted as academic festivals need not be superficial or frivolous. In fact, to the extent that the study of religious phenomena is a real celebration it raises existential questions, faces the reality of evil and the presence of tragedy. Religious studies conducted under the rules of academic scholarship are not superficial because every religious tradition and phenomenon has the right to be studied and every study can draw the student into an examination of his assumptions about the constitution of the universe and his place in it. For this reason too, religious studies that first of all attempt not to glorify one religious truth claim but to glory in the description of the whole range of man's religious behavior are not frivolous even though they are a sort of festive excess. Not only in the crises of life, but also—and perhaps primarily—in the

---

11. **Ibid.**, pp. 24-26.

excesses of life, do the questions of being and life's meaning arise. "To find our life," are the words with which the Huicholes Indians of Mexico undertake the Peyote hunt and its ensuing ecstasy.

Religious studies professors are particularly sensitive to the necessity to be thorough and serious in their studies. They should also know that the festive, like the play and games of children, has a demanding kind of seriousness of its own. The very excess and life affirmative qualities of the festival insist upon a recognition of all the dimensions of life. Nothing need be excluded from the festival. There is a place for tragedy, evil, guilt and death. While the worker who merely manipulates the raw material of his environment can never come to grips with these elements of life the celebrant, especially the scholar, can—if not overcome them—at least contemplate them, toy with them. I would argue that the *academic* festival may more fully deal with such things than any existing religious feast because it can bring together all particular feasts and fasts into one exaltation of the human spirit. The student of religion can bring together Holi, Ramadan and Eucharist in a way not possible to the religious celebrant.

That the festival of religious studies is rational or intellectual does not militate against its being truly festive. Many students today would argue the point and much of the recent literature on the subject would seem to support their contention but the mind can feast as well as the body. Reasoning is not confined to the Apollonian culture dominated by the work ethic. The activity of scholarship, and I think especially religion scholarship, is continuous with the existential implications of festive dance, song and excess. Love of learning and books is itself part of the love of life. The rules of evidence and rational discourse that the modern university imposes on its members do not prohibit religion scholarship nor demand that it be fundamentally discontinuous with the spirit of dance, play and festivity that seem to lie at the roots of religious sentiment. The *spirit* of the modern university may not always be festive but here religious studies true to their sources may be able to make a contribution to the university.

Finally, perhaps this argument can be concluded with some suggestions for an answer to the question, "How can the religious studies professor or theologian be festive without ceasing to be scholarly?" In his delightful little book, *Man at Play*, Hugo Rahner wrote about the playing of God, the playing of man and the playing of the Church. Theologians and religion scholars need to follow Rahner's lead and write a chapter titled "The Playing of the Teacher." Some items for such a chapter might be:

—The misleading language of "going to work" overlays the life of scholarship. Reading, writing and research acquire their seriousness from the radically expansive and excessive character of being and not from the prevailing work ethic.

—To be truly academic the religion scholar need not demand a great deal of work from his students so much as insist that students follow their curiosity and sense of wonder into all religious traditions and not just their own. Rules of contemporary scholarship require that seriousness arise not out of intensity of commitment but out of a willingness to look at all phenomena and every form.

—Religious studies can become more fun without becoming less academic if religious behavior is studied and students are not limited to the study of studies. While there is a place for the analytic, even in the festive, it must come only after much basic description has been done. The religious studies professor must be a good storyteller.

—Theologians must take up with their accustomed gravity the themes of a Dionysian theology. As Sam Keen suggests they must educate for serendipity, for the contemplation of a dancing God— a God even for Nietszche who said, "I could believe only in a God who could dance."[12]

—Teaching methodology is important. I would argue that teaching which lectures students is a work ethic methodology. I would suggest that a methodology appropriate to academic festivity should be "improvisational." The scholar should be able to join the conversation his students are having about religion and cosmic reality and improvise on the themes of their conversation as he

---

12. Sam Keen, **To a Dancing God** (New York: Harper & Row, 1970), pp. 38ff.

introduces them to other themes in the field of religion scholarship. I take improvisation to be a higher form of play than the laborious reading of notes.

To be festive without ceasing to be academic is a challenge and an opportunity for religious studies in the academic setting. This challenge is not met by offering students good ecclesiastical liturgy, though that may be something they need as churchmen. As students they need to discover that the life of learning—that reading, writing and research—is a circus, a festival that encircles life. As students of religion they need to know that the study of religious behavior, far from being an arid labor, has all the excitement and seriousness of the search for the intelligibility of the power manifest in nature and history.

18   College Theology Teachers: Status of The Profession

MATTHEW C. KOHMESCHER

Early in 1970 the College Theology Society appointed a committee to study the current Status of the Profession of college theology teachers and to report back to the board of directors. This committee met and drafted a 5-page questionnaire which it sent to the Presidents, Vice-Presidents, and Theology Department Chairmen of 214 Catholic institutions. A second questionnaire of one page was sent to one bishop in each of 150 dioceses in the United States. We received replies from 48 Presidents (22.4%), 75 Vice-Presidents or Deans (35%), 95 Chairmen (44.3%) and 44 Bishops (29.3%). A preliminary report of 42 pages contains the statistics and detailed comments. Following are highlights, general trends and some possible conclusions to be drawn from this study. Let us preface the report, though, with a few general comments.

First, it is difficult to read the bare statistics and come up with an accurate interpretation. A few respondents replied to none of the questions. Others skipped answers to certain questions. Many, though they checked off the points dealing with current actual conditions, said nothing about their desired or proposed conditions. Does this mean they wished to maintain the same actual conditions or were they in doubt about what should exist? In any case the returns for the "proposed" conditions must be interpreted very cautiously. A few repondents misread certain questions and their answers indicated this. E.g., the committee had hoped that all would recognize what "arbitrary" meant and would answer accordingly. Such was not the case. Further, in some instances the chairmen checked off "entire department" but did not check themselves off separately, though the question required them to do so.

Either they possessed no administrative authority or they considered it sufficient to count themselves as part of the Department. We are judging it to be the latter. Finally, the respondents often checked off more than one answer so that accurate "totals" are hard to come by.

Second, I think it important to recognize the breakdown of the institutions responding. Here, and throughout this paper, I am basing myself on the report of the departmental chairmen.

41 of the schools had a full-time undergraduate enrollment of less than 1,000. 43 were between 1,000 and 5,000. Only 7 were over 5,000. 18 of the schools had less than 200 students enrolled in theology classes last fall. 34 had between 200 and 500. 15 were between 500 and 1,000. 13 were over 1,000. 56 of the schools had between 1 and 5 full-time faculty in the department. One had none. 25 had between 6 and 10. 12 had over 10.

Third, many of the chairmen were fairly new to the job. 64 had been on the job between 1 and 4 years. 15 between 5 and 8 years; 9 over 8 years. This probably explains why in general the Departmental chairmen always were less well acquainted with university procedures (e.g., what appeals machinery to follow when departmental recommendations were vetoed), and why they were unaware that the AAUP procedures (which they said they followed) recommended consultation of appropriate members of the department when there was a question of retention, non-reappointment, dismissal, etc. But again, in small departments, what should be done?

Fourth, with a few exceptions there was not a significant difference between the reports of the Presidents, Vice-Presidents or Deans, and those of the Chairmen. All seem to agree upon what were the facts.

Fifth, in the Administration of the Department the Chairmen usually had the power and the responsibility. At times it does seem that the President is in on too many departmental matters but in a small school this is more likely to happen than in a large university. At least I hope that is the explanation. I did not run any statistical studies to establish this point.

Sixth, the "Status" of the theology teacher in general seems to be good—comparable especially to that of other instructors in the Humanities.

Seventh, by and large students participate very little in the affairs of the department and are rarely consulted on matters of hiring, retaining, promoting an instructor. Actual consultation with them ran from 5% to 10%, but the proposed conditions at times did go up to 25%. This was surprising!

In regard to the specific items on the questionnaires the following comments can be made. I am presuming that most of you who are administrators might recall the actual questionnaire and that the rest of you will be able to follow along with a minimum of difficulty.

HIRING

This was the first part of the questionnaire. The chairman is involved (but not necessarily other faculty) and is almost always responsible for initiating the process. Departmental recommendations cannot usually be vetoed for arbitrary reasons. There were five exceptions with these reasons given: former priest or religious (2); whim, sex, background; power structure at work; health, personal appearance, orthodoxy. There was no difficulty in hiring laymen, lay women, priests, religious; and only a certain amount with non-Catholics (89% could) and former religious (80% could). But only 58% could hire laicized priests and the same percentage for divorced persons. 79% of those who answered said they should be able to hire former priests and 65%, divorced persons. The Bishops in answering a similar question had 48% against hiring a former priest, 23% against former religious, 27% against divorced persons (plus 15% more if the divorced person had remarried). In giving preferential treatment 22 chairmen said they did give such to members of the religious community running the school, 8 to priests or religious because of the contributed services factor, 3 to Roman Catholics, 2 to lay men or women, and 1 to qualified blacks. Almost all the listed restrictions in hiring a theology instructor were of a professional /academic nature (degree, experience, competence), but the following were also noted: former priest/religious (2); commitment to Catholic values; good Catholic; broad outlook, not narrowly confessional. The Bishops in discussing what criteria should be used in hiring/retaining/promoting, etc., were much more vocal in asserting the "Catholic" factor: 14 (35%) mentioned orthodoxy, 10 (25%) fidelity to the Magisterium and 11 (28%) a living faith (or good Catholic). It should be noted at the same time that the bishops were almost unanimous in expressing the need for academic competency.

RETENTION

93% of the chairmen follow AAUP recommended policies/procedures, and 3.5% follow their own handbook. One school has all priests and/or religious and seemingly different policies are followed in their regard. One respondent voiced a strong opposition to the requirement of giving a year's notice to one who had been on the staff for several years. The chairmen were always involved in the decision but a departmental committee (selected faculty, etc.) was not always consulted even though the AAUP recommends this. No one could veto for arbitrary reasons. The reasons given for not retaining were mainly professional: lack of professional growth (91%), poor rapport with students (92%), poor class preparation (95%) were most frequently mentioned. 7% did indicate pressure from within the University and 7% position on controversial issues as a reason. 3.5% checked pressure from without the University, and 3.5% involvement in controversy. In addition the following reasons were listed: laicization (1), marriage of a cleric without permission (1), unsound doctrine or methods (1), exercise of undesirable influence on students (1), involvement in controversy if disruptive of functioning of the institution.

PROMOTIONS

100% of the chairmen indicated the department was governed by the same policies that governed the rest of the Humanities. The Chairman was always involved but this was not always true for a departmental committee (selected faculty, etc.). Ordinarily, no arbitrary veto was possible. Reasons given for non-promotion were basically of a professional/academic nature but the following two occurred once each: unorthodoxy, whimsical fancy. Some preferential treatment was noted: "poor teaching is tolerated longer for priests and nuns," "preference for men at present," "Catholics" (3). One surprising statistic is that 7 chairmen said no one outside the department made the *final* decision and 11 proposed this!

TENURE

90% of the Chairmen indicated they followed the AAUP policies. The 8 who did not gave these reasons: no policy as yet (2), college does not have tenure (2), does not apply to religious (1), under study (1). 10% said there was a distinction in treatment based on clerical/religious status. Such were not granted tenure. 60% indicated that the granting of tenure was associated with academic rank. Only 11% said there was a limit to the number of tenured positions in the department and 17% proposed this. With the questioning of tenure today, and with a seemingly evident need not to be tied down with an all tenured-faculty, this point does need some rethinking. (The Presidents and Vice-Presidents had a similar percentage on the actual conditions but they showed a greater concern for the future with percentages of 32 and 26 respectively.) There were a few instances (4%) of special reasons for not granting tenure to a member of the department: teaching dubious doctrine (2), position in method and conduct unacceptable to the Catholic theological community at large, laicization (2), fear that the priest or religious will be laicized and demand full salary.

DISMISSAL

93% follow AAUP recommended procedures. Of the 6 who said no, one has its own; one has none (but no known offenses) and a third said "if leave priesthood without formal laicization, marriage of priest without church permission." As usual the Chairman is involved but not necessarily a departmental committee (or selected faculty) even though the AAUP recommends this. In 9% of the responses no one outside the department made the final decision. And, if I read the explanations correctly, it is again true that no arbitrary vetos are possible, though there may be differences of opinion. There may be one exception: "Personal. Religious. They can retain people the department would dismiss. Could not dismiss if department wanted retained." Only 5% indicated some distinction in treatment based on clerical/religious status: "Religious status could secure retention." "Poor teaching is tolerated longer for priests and nuns." "Clergy must be in good standing." No distinction was noted regarding sex, religion, race, etc.

SALARY-BENEFITS

92% said theology salaries compare favorably with humanities faculty. The reasons given for the other 8% usually concern a lower salary for clergy/religious but almost all seem to be working to equalize this and to have one scale for all. One Vice-President had this surprising comment: "If anything, better." 90% said the department compared favorably with other departments in offices, furnishings, telephones, secretarial help, etc. Only two valid criticisms were lodged here: secretarial help (1), office space (1). On sabbaticals the department compared favorably 94% of the time and this might be higher since most of the comments dealt with the fact that the school did not have a sabbatical program or that the department was young and needed time to establish itself. Only 2 comments could be construed as actual negative votes.

ACADEMIC FREEDOM

In reporting on this section I would like to give the questions the committee asked with the tabulated results. I find it difficult to summarize most of them.

1. Are there any special limitations in the contract and/or letter of appointment which apply in a particular way to members of the

department? 4% of the Chairmen (and 4% of the Presidents) said yes. The Presidents made these remarks: "Proper regard for the magisterium." "Probably should have explicit clause on religious and priests who act so as to incur excommunication or the like." "They are not to label as 'Catholic doctrine' something which is not. But they certainly are free to lecture as they will." One chairman said that "one may be summarily dismissed for denying Catholic doctrine or morality in his teaching duties." Another comment was unexpected: "Since members of the department are screened by the Chancery this is not necessary." But should they be so screened?

2. Are the university goals fairly well delineated and understood? 82% of the chairmen said yes, but the comments indicate that it was easier to say yes to "delineated" than to "understood." The same is true for the answers to question:

3. which dealt with departmental goals. 84% of the chairmen said yes to this. A few indicated that current study was going on.

4. Does the individual instructor have freedom in regard to the following: choice of texts, revision of syllabus, initiative in proposing a new course, innovation in methodology, etc.? All the chairmen gave an affirmative reply.

5. Does the individual have any choice in the way his teaching is evaluated? 34.5% said no. The various comments here indicate the problem that seems to exist everywhere—just what is good teaching and how do you evaluate it? Various attempts are being made but no magic formula has yet been discovered. Some schools have no evaluation at all. I suggest that this is an area to which we can give greater attention. It does seem that many of the problems that existed in the past are disappearing and that we can focus our attention and our energies on more constructive items in the future.

6. Can a member of the department function as a critic of society (church, nation, etc.) without undue pressure being brought to bear upon him from sources outside the department? 91% said yes, with a little emphasis on "prudence." In the event of such pressure (7) 82% indicated that means of defense were available to him. In this regard we can also point out that the Bishops,

on a parallel question dealing with the handling of grievances and complaints from clergy, parents, alumni, etc., almost unanimously suggested "due process" within the university.

MAGISTERIUM

Three simple questions were asked here but the answers showed that this is a very complex issue, or at least one which lacks a uniform understanding on the part of college and university people. Is there a relationship to the teaching office of the Church? To the pastoral ministry of the Church? To the Bishop?

49% of the Presidents said there was a relationship to the teaching office, 71% of the Vice-Presidents or Deans and 59% of the Chairmen. On a similar question all but one bishop saw such a relationship. The various comments on this, and the following questions, show that there is a lot of work to be done here. It would seem to be to the advantage of all concerned that these points be more universally agreed upon—at least among those on the same campus! One department (Gannon College of Erie, Pa.) has spelled out in print exactly how they see themselves in this regard. In general all the respondents indicated a respect for the magisterium, acknowledged their professional obligations when presenting the teaching of the magisterium and emphasized the academic character of theology as a discipline. The Bishops for the most part agreed that theology was an academic discipline but focused strongly on the teaching of "Catholic" doctrine to "Catholic" students at our "Catholic" universities.

On the second question (relationship to the pastoral ministry of the church) 44% of the Presidents said there was; 26% of the Vice-Presidents or Deans and 42% of the Chairmen. When it came to specifying the nature of this relationship too many referred to the fact that the priest members of the department also functioned as priests. This is not the answer. Perhaps this comment from one chairman indicates a better direction to take: "Our department is academically oriented in its teaching but insofar as knowledge is a determinant of how one lives his life, it is also pastoral."

On a parallel question, all the bishops save one saw a relationship and usually in a deeper and better way than a number of college administrators. On the third question (relationship to the bishop) 46% of the Presidents said there was; 24% of the Vice-Presidents or Deans, and 33% of the Chairmen.

GENERAL

The final two sections dealt with general questions regarding the department and the chairmen. Some of the statistics we listed in the first part of this paper. Here are the highlights of the others.

44% of the Chairmen indicated that theology was required of all students, Catholic and non-Catholic. And 69% of those who responded proposed this as a desired requirement. Six, nine and twelve were the number of hours most frequently required. Twelve hours was the most common full-time teaching load in the department, with 100-120 students being the number of students taught. 16% of the Chairmen said this differed from the teaching load in other humanities departments: five saying it was lighter, and three, heavier. The average class size for theology classes that fall was roughly 30.

72% of the departments were engaged in interdisciplinary courses or programs but there were no restrictions on further development of such endeavors. Only 67% participated in adult education programs of the community. With 97% of the Bishops looking to the Catholic colleges to be of service in this area, it seems that all the departments should give serious thought to contributing in a fuller and more organized manner to the continuing education of the laity (and clergy) of their communities! 95% of the departments are participating in some way (e.g., speakers) in the affairs of the church or civic community.

As to the office of chairmen, 63% said their term of office was limited, with 3 years being the most commonly mentioned number. 98% could be reappointed. In the appointment of the chairmen, the faculty are decisively involved 70% of the time; students only 14%. 38% said the department faculty elected the chairman.

Conclusions and Suggestions

1. Departmental chairmen need to be better prepared for the job. Although no questions dealt directly with this, a number of answers given and comments made indicated that most chairmen were learning on the job.

2. Although it is not recommended that we proliferate committees, it does seem that greater attention needs to be given in order to assure that the chairmen do consult appropriate members of the faculty on all questions regarding the hiring, retention, promotion, etc., of the faculty.

3. There should be greater student involvement in the work of the department.

4. Those schools which follow two sets of policies—one for the lay faculty and one for the clerical/religious faculty—should give serious thought to having just one uniform policy for all, and in all matters.

5. The relationship of the school and the department of theology to the magisterium needs further study and clarification.

6. The *College Theology Society,* in the future, should give priority to the topic of improving college teaching.

7. Since most schools follow AAUP policies, there seems to be little need for the CTS to get involved in most due process cases. However, it might be of value for the CTS to establish a bureau which could supply a committee of "peers" which schools or departments may wish to call upon in the handling of some complaints.

8. Lastly the CTS should consider setting up in this or another bureau a supply of "evaluators" who may be called upon to visit and to evaluate local theology departments and programs. Quite probably those schools which appoint their chairmen to a limited term of office may wish to have qualified outside personnel give their evaluation of what is going on. This could contribute to the continuing development and improvement of what we are all doing.

PETER H. BEISHEIM teaches religion at Stonehill College.

SARA BUTLER, M.S.B.T., is Director of Adult Religious Education for the Mobile Deanery, Diocese of Mobile, Alabama.

DANIEL CALLAHAN has published extensively of late regarding moral concerns and the quality of life.

WILLIAM CENKNER, O.P., is on the religion faculty of the Catholic University of America.

CHARLES E. CURRAN, another Catholic University theologian, has recently been at Georgetown University's Kennedy Center for Bio-Ethics.

A. JOSEPH EVERSON teaches religion at Luther College (Decorah).

ROBERT L. FARICY, S.J. is a professor of theology at the Gregorian University in Rome.

JAMES W. FLANAGAN teaches Scripture at Loras College.

GEORGE H. FREIN is on the faculty at the University of North Dakota.

STANLEY HAUERWAS teaches at the University of Notre Dame.

NATHAN R. KOLLAR, O.Carm., is a member of the faculty in the Washington Theological Coalition.

MATTHEW C. KOHMESCHER, S.M. chairs the department of theological studies at the University of Dayton.

MERLE LONGWOOD is on the staff of Concordia College (Moorhead).

JOHN J. MAWHINNEY, s.j., *is in the Religious Studies Department of Gonzaga University, Spokane, Washington.*

HUGH McELWAIN, o.s.m. *is a member of the Catholic Theological Union.*

WILLIAM E. MURNION *is Chairman of the Department of Religion at Newton College of the Sacred Heart (Massachusetts).*

BRENDAN ROSENDALL, o.f.m. Conv., *is on the faculty of the College of St. Thomas.*

BERNARD P. PRUSAK *teaches in the religious studies department of Villanova University.*

GEORGE DEVINE (EDITOR), *is Chairman and Associate Professor in the Department of Religious Studies at Seton Hall University.*